THE
SECOND GREAT AWAKENING
IN CONNECTICUT

BY

CHARLES ROY KELLER

ARCHON BOOKS
1968

LIBRARY OF CONGRESS CATALOG CARD NUMBER: 68-26923
PRINTED IN THE UNITED STATES OF AMERICA

TO

H. R. K. AND A. K.

PREFACE

AS the title of a recently published book Professor James Bissett Pratt uses the question which he addresses to his present-day readers, *Can We Keep the Faith?* He has the impression, he writes, "that the young people of our day feel much less interest in 'God, freedom, and immortality;' in the incarnation, the relation of God to man, and most of the fundamentals of the Christian faith . . . than has any generation of young people since the Protestant Reformation."

The same problem was propounded in the closing years of the eighteenth century when many people in the new United States felt that Christianity was facing a serious crisis. Attracted by the alluring philosophies and the less-demanding variations of religion which had been brought across the Atlantic from Europe, and distraught by a quarter-century of conflict with the French, the English, and the Indians, followed by a decade of independence which afforded no respite from pressing political, economic, and social problems, many Americans seemed to be turning away from the faith of their fathers. Whether Christianity could survive was questioned by some; others believed that it would be so changed as to be ineffective in checking the dangerous moral deterioration which in their opinion had already progressed too far.

"Can we keep the faith?" Only the future holds the answer to Professor Pratt's question; but the people of more than a century ago replied with a resounding affirmative. The triumph of infidelity did not materialize. Indeed, the first half of the nineteenth century was an age of faith, a period when most people lived their lives without questioning the existence and power of God, His close relationship to man, and the basic tenets of Christianity. Supernatural religion was in the ascendancy. Alexis de Tocqueville, who visited the United States in 1831, wrote, "There is no country in the world where the Christian religion retains a greater influence over the souls of men than in America."

How is this significant development in American intellectual and religious history to be explained? The triumph of fidelity occurred because the champions of orthodoxy everywhere rose up against the foe and by valiant and vigorous efforts succeeded in routing him in what is here termed the Second Great Awakening, second in time to the Great Awakening of Jonathan Edwards and George Whitefield but not in importance in American history. In this study attention is centered on Connecticut, but the Awakening in that state was paralleled by more or less similar developments throughout the country.

Prepared originally as a doctoral dissertation at Yale University, this work, in somewhat different form, was awarded the John Addison Porter Prize in June, 1934. To Professor Ralph H. Gabriel, under whose direction the doctoral dissertation was written and who made many valuable suggestions while this book was being prepared for publication, a deep debt of gratitude is hereby gladly acknowledged. Dr. Sherrod Soule, now superintendent-emeritus of the Connecticut State Conference of the Congregational Church, and Miss Elsie F. Deming, assistant treasurer of the Missionary Society of Connecticut, have been most helpful and encouraging. The author is also indebted to the late George S. Godard and the staff of the Connecticut State Library; to Mr. Albert C. Bates, librarian-emeritus of the Connecticut Historical Society, and to Mr. Thompson R. Harlow, the present librarian; to Dr. Elbert E. Gates, secretary-emeritus of the Connecticut Baptist Convention; to Miss Anne S. Pratt, Miss Emily H. Hall, and several other members of the Yale University Library staff; and to the staff of the Williams College Library. Special recognition goes to Professor

Leonard W. Labaree whose efficient editorship has added much to this publication, and to my wife, Helen Ramsayer Keller. My thanks are also extended to the President and Trustees of Williams College for grants from the Class of 1900 Fund.

C. R. K.

Williamstown, Massachusetts,
  October 11, 1941

CONTENTS

THE SECOND GREAT AWAKENING
IN CONNECTICUT

I

THE LAND OF STEADY HABITS

THE world [is] coming either to Christianity or
infidelity."[1] A young diarist, obviously disturbed,
completed his notation for May 3, 1797, and laid
down his pen. He was Thomas Robbins, a recent graduate
of both Williams College and Yale College[2] and the son of
the Reverend Ammi Robbins, who had already served his
Norfolk, Connecticut, church for thirty-six years.

Young Robbins expressed sentiments which were circulating extensively among friends of orthodox religion in
the United States. The alarm caused by the prevalence of
heterodox doctrines, religious deadness, and what seemed
to many a serious corruption of morals, was widespread.
Meeting in Philadelphia in May, 1798, the General Assembly of the Presbyterian Church issued a pastoral letter
which read in part:

When formidable innovations in Europe threatened destruction to morals and religion; when scenes of devastation and
bloodshed, unexampled in the history of modern nations, have
convulsed the world, and when our country is threatened
with similar calamities, insensibility in us would be stupidity;
silence would be criminal. . . . We perceive, with pain and
fearful apprehension, a general dereliction of religious prin-

1. *Diary of Thomas Robbins,* I, 33.
2. After studying at Yale for three years, Robbins moved to Williams
for his senior year when his father became a trustee of the Massachusetts college. Each college recognized the work done at the other, with
the result that in September, 1796, Robbins attended two Commence-
ments and received two degrees.

ciple and practice among our fellow-citizens, . . . a visible
and prevailing impiety and contempt for the laws and institutions of religion, and an abounding infidelity which in many
instances tends to Atheism itself. . . . The profligacy and
corruption of the public morals have advanced with a progress proportioned to our declension in religion.[3]

Massachusetts ministers preached sermons on the seriousness of the situation. One lamented not only the prevailing infidelity and skepticism which threatened to destroy
religion and virtue but also the introduction of every spe-
cies of vice and corruption. Another asserted that never
before had America seen a time when licentiousness, infidelity, and open opposition to Christianity so signally tri-
umphed.[4] A distinguished church historian has called the
two decades following the close of the American Revolution "the period of the lowest ebb-tide of vitality in the
history of American Christianity."[5] So serious was the
general situation that in setting a national fast for April
25, 1799, President John Adams said in his proclamation,
"The most precious interests of the people of the United
States are still held in jeopardy by the hostile designs and
insidious acts of a foreign nation, as well as by the dissemination among them of those principles, subversive of
the foundation of all religious, moral, and social obligations, that have produced incalculable mischief and misery
in other countries."[6]

The advance of irreligion and indifference must be
checked, the champions of orthodoxy chorused. The forces
of religion met the challenge, with the result that from one
end of the new United States to the other, in all denominations, evangelical Protestantism appeared during the clos-

3. *Minutes of the General Assembly of the Presbyterian Church, 1789–
1820* (Philadelphia, [1847]), pp. 152–153.
4. Anson E. Morse, *The Federalist Party in Massachusetts to the Year
1800,* pp. 103–107.
5. Leonard W. Bacon, *History of American Christianity,* p. 219.
6. James D. Richardson, ed., *A Compilation of the Messages and
Papers of the Presidents, 1789–1897* ([Washington], 1905), I, 285.

ing years of the eighteenth and the early years of the nineteenth century in what may be called the Second Great Awakening. It followed a general pattern. First, there were revivals and missionary activities, and then came Bible, tract, and education societies, Sunday schools, attempts at moral reform, and humanitarian endeavors.

Quite naturally the Awakening was not exactly the same in all sections of the country. It varied in intensity and in kind in different social, economic, and religious environments.[7] One of its most important centers, indeed one of the areas where it originated, was Connecticut, the so-called "land of steady habits." Here, where scattered revivals and some attention to home missions marked the early 1790's, a general religious awakening began in 1797. Widespread and powerful revivals helped to stimulate similar phenomena throughout the country. The Missionary Society of Connecticut, established in 1798, became one of the most effective of the numerous home-missionary societies during the ensuing quarter of a century. In the first Protestant foreign-missionary body, the American Board of Commissioners for Foreign Missions, Connecticut men and women were prominent, as they were, too, in the country-wide Bible-society, tract-society, education-society, and Sunday-school movements. They were leaders in the temperance crusade, and the first deaf and dumb asylum in the United States was opened in Hartford in 1817. In other matters citizens of the state coöperated but did not pioneer.

Correct as it may be to view New England as a special section of the United States, it is a mistake to consider all

7. For books that deal with certain aspects of the Awakening in different parts of the country, see Catherine C. Cleveland, *The Great Revival in the West, 1797–1805;* Oliver W. Elsbree, *The Rise of the Missionary Spirit in America, 1790–1815;* Gustav A. Koch, *Republican Religion,* last chapter entitled "The Triumph of Fidelity"; David M. Ludlum, *Social Ferment in Vermont, 1791–1850;* A. E. Morse, *The Federalist Party in Massachusetts to the Year 1800;* James K. Morse, *Jedidiah Morse, A Champion of New England Orthodoxy;* Niels H. Sonne, *Liberal Kentucky, 1780–1828.*

of New England as a unit. Connecticut differed in many ways from Massachusetts, especially eastern Massachusetts, while both these states presented marked contrasts with their southern neighbor, Rhode Island, and with the northern tier of states, Vermont, New Hampshire, and Maine, the latter a part of Massachusetts until 1820. Connecticut was one of the oldest settled areas in the country, towns having been established on the Connecticut River and Long Island Sound during the 1630's. It had a long history during the course of which much tradition had been built up. Relatively easy was the shift from colony status to statehood during the American Revolution, a development attributable to the fact that under the charter of 1662 Connecticut was one of the two most completely self-governing colonies. Not until 1818 did the state replace its colonial charter by a constitution. As a result of the Revolution the Massachusetts colonial governor was expelled from the country, but the Connecticut governor, Jonathan Trumbull, won distinction as an outstanding patriot leader. There were a few Tories in the state, but they were not prominent. The Revolution caused less change in the ruling class, less political and social upheaval, than was the case elsewhere in the erstwhile British colonies. This was important for the post-Revolution period.

During the late eighteenth and early nineteenth century the wealth of Connecticut increased greatly as did that of the entire country. Most people depended on agriculture for their living, agriculture which, as the result of improvements in farming, "was emerging from its self-sufficiency and [was] developing a commercial status."[8] A smaller though sizable group engaged in commerce, but relatively few people were connected with manufacturing. Although commerce attracted considerable labor and capital, and although a number of banks were established after the turn of the century and capital was diverted to manu-

8. Albert L. Olson, *Agricultural Economy and the Population in Eighteenth-Century Connecticut*, p. 30.

factures when the Embargo and the War of 1812 interfered with shipping, nevertheless, throughout the period under consideration, 1795 to 1826, Connecticut's civilization was essentially agricultural. It has been estimated that in 1820 the state's manufactures amounted to only two million dollars.[9] Even in 1850 nearly a hundred out of one hundred forty-eight towns were almost wholly agricultural in their interests, and as late as 1845 the value of the year's hay crop, $4,212,725, surpassed that of woolen and cotton goods by a million dollars, while the value of the corn crop equalled that of the output of the paper mills. J. M. Morse is quite correct in saying that one should not be misled by the large number of "factories" mentioned in statistics published in 1819.[10] These "factories" were small, and many workers turned to the mills for employment only during slack time on the farms.

The people of Connecticut were a homogeneous group who for the most part lived simple, isolated lives on farms and in farming villages. In 1790 the Reverend Timothy Dwight's rural Greenfield Hill parish in the town of Fairfield was a large one and was reported to be paying its minister the highest salary in the state.[11] Thirty years later only New Haven, Hartford, and Middletown had more than five thousand inhabitants,[12] and these small towns were far from being the urban centers that Boston, New York, Philadelphia, and Charleston were. Timothy Dwight could write proudly in 1811, "The city of New-Haven contains probably as many good kitchen gardens as any

9. Grace P. Fuller, *An Introduction to the History of Connecticut as a Manufacturing State*, p. 24.

10. Jarvis M. Morse, *A Neglected Period of Connecticut's History, 1818–1850*, pp. 14, 283. Purcell overemphasizes the importance of manufactures in his section entitled "Manufactures." Richard J. Purcell, *Connecticut in Transition, 1775–1818*, pp. 119–138.

11. Timothy Dwight, "Commemorative Address of the Life and Character of the Rev. Dr. Timothy Dwight," *Transactions of the One Hundred Fiftieth Anniversary of the Greenfield, Ct., Congregational Church*, p. 50.

12. *Census for 1820* (Washington, 1821). The population of New Haven, the largest of these three towns, was only 8,327, consisting of 7,147 in the city and 1,180 outside.

town in the state: and all, or nearly all the objects of horticulture, within the state, may be found here."[13] Diversions were few, and forms of entertainment limited. There was an almost complete lack of cosmopolitanism and very little contact with Europeans.

Practically no immigrants entered Connecticut from either Europe or other parts of the United States; on the other hand the number of emigrants to the frontier was large. "Within the last thirty years," Pease and Niles wrote in 1819, "the current of emigration from this state has swelled to a torrent."[14] These pioneers moved first to Vermont, eastern New York, and northeastern Pennsylvania, later into western New York and especially into what was known as the Western Reserve in northeastern Ohio. Alexis de Tocqueville's reference to Connecticut is familiar. In 1830, he was assured, this small state furnished one-eighth of the members of Congress although its population constituted only one forty-third of the country's total. "The State of Connecticut of itself," Tocqueville wrote, "sends only five delegates to Congress; and the thirty-one others sit for the new Western States."[15]

The chief reason for this heavy migration was undoubtedly the unsatisfactory nature of much of the state's available soil and its consequent unattractiveness in the face of more alluring lands to the west. Furthermore, large families were the rule, here as elsewhere, and younger sons who felt crowded and cramped in the old quarters were anxious to strike out for themselves. This younger group, naturally aggressive, may also have been irked by a political setup in which the elder statesmen monopolized offices and may have hoped to gain eminence in politics more rapidly in the new settlements. Finally, the existence of the West-

13. Timothy Dwight, *A Statistical Account of the City of New-Haven* (1811), p. 21.

14. John C. Pease and John M. Niles, *A Gazetteer of the States of Connecticut and Rhode Island*, p. 11.

15. Alexis de Tocqueville, *Democracy in America* (2 vols., New York, 1898), I, 375–376.

ern Reserve was an added attraction, for there lives similar to those in the home state might be lived. The population of Connecticut, 237,655 in 1790, had increased only to 297,675 in 1830.[16]

As a result of its agricultural civilization Connecticut was conservative but not backward. It constituted a long-settled area with traditions. Hartford, one of the state's two capitals, and the headquarters for most of the organizations established during the Second Great Awakening, was a thriving town. In the rather remote northwest portion of the state was another culture center, Litchfield. Here, Tapping Reeve and James Gould directed what was for half a century after 1775 the country's foremost law school, to which came not only many New Englanders but also, among others, Aaron Burr of New York and John C. Calhoun of South Carolina. Here, also, Miss Sally Pierce conducted a flourishing school for girls; here, Lyman Beecher preached from 1810 until 1826 and reared his remarkable family.

New Haven, the second of the state's capitals, was not only a prosperous commercial port but was also the site of Yale College. With its one hundred ten students, its three buildings and a kitchen, its three tutors and a professor, Yale was not much of a college when Timothy Dwight succeeded Ezra Stiles as president in 1795. An outworn curriculum and archaic methods of instruction were ill-suited to prepare young men for the strenuous life of the post-Revolutionary period. In 1817 the Reverend Gardiner Spring commented on the Yale of 1795 in the following manner: "It is a fact not to be denied, that at the time Dr. Dwight entered upon this official charge, the College was in a state of lamentable declension. Its funds

16. *A Century of Population Growth in the United States, 1790–1900* (Washington, 1909), p. 57. The population of Massachusetts during the same period increased from 378,556 to 610,408, of Vermont from 85,341 to 280,652, of New Hampshire from 141,899 to 269,328, of Maine from 96,643 to 399,455. Even Rhode Island's rate of growth exceeded Connecticut's.

were low, its policy not the most happy, its numbers small, and its morals corrupt."[17]

Under its new president Yale prospered. The student body increased in numbers, the faculty both in size and in quality. Dwight commissioned Benjamin Silliman to inaugurate the teaching of chemistry and natural science at Yale, and during his administration the medical school was established. He also sponsored greater democracy at the college by abolishing pecuniary fines as a method of punishment, by seeing to it that the freshmen did less fagging for the upperclassmen, and by doing away with the venerable regulation that no freshman might wear a hat on the campus within ten rods of the president, eight rods of a professor, or six rods of a tutor.[18]

Upon his death in 1817 Dwight was succeeded by Jeremiah Day who remained in office until 1846. Under these two presidents Yale championed religious orthodoxy much more vigorously than did Harvard during the same period. Indeed, the election of Henry Ware to the Hollis Professorship of Divinity in 1805 symbolized the capture of Harvard by the Unitarians, whereas Yale remained staunchly Congregationalist. Yale's strength throughout the first half of the nineteenth century lay in science and religion, a phenomenon worthy of special note since it shows that at this time harmony between religion and science was possible. The leaders in religion were Dwight and Nathaniel W. Taylor; the leader in science was Silliman, an orthodox Congregationalist and a persistent supporter of evangelical Protestantism.

Religiously, Connecticut differed from the rest of the New England states in some respects and from other sections of the country more completely. The Puritan tradition remained strong. Church and state were linked until

17. Gardiner Spring, *An Oration . . . in Commemoration . . . of Timothy Dwight* (1817), p. 23.

18. Franklin B. Dexter, *Sketch of the History of Yale University*, pp. 48–49, 51; F. B. Dexter, *Student Life at Yale College under the First President Dwight (1795–1817)*, pp. 18–19.

1818, and Congregationalism with over two hundred church societies and nearly that many ministers was the dominant denomination.[19] The laws compelled every person to contribute to the support of religion, but Episcopalians, Baptists, Quakers, and Methodists could "certificate off" and pay their money to their own churches. Those who had no church membership could be taxed by the Congregationalists, but it should be noted that a number of churches had invested funds and that the support of religion by the sale of pews and by voluntary subscriptions and contributions was much more common than Connecticut historians have realized.[20] Disestablishment came in 1818, the story of the struggle which preceded this change having been told by Richard J. Purcell in his *Connecticut in Transition, 1775–1818.*

Connecticut was not alone in having a religious establishment, for a similar situation existed in New Hampshire until 1817 and in Massachusetts until 1833. The state's uniqueness lay in the nature of its Congregational leadership, a subject which will be discussed in subsequent chapters, and in the organization of that church. There had been no change since the adoption in 1708 of the Saybrook

19. So dominant were they that the story of the Second Great Awakening in Connecticut may be told largely in Congregational terms. See chapter VIII for the activities of the Episcopalians, Baptists, and Methodists.

20. See among others Frances M. Caulkins, *History of New London . . . 1612 to 1852,* p. 605; F. M. Caulkins, *History of Norwich . . . 1660 to 1845,* p. 558; David D. Field, *A Statistical Account of the County of Middlesex* (1819), pp. 23–24; May H. James, *The Educational History of Old Lyme, . . . 1635–1935* (New Haven, 1939), p. 114; Ellen D. Larned, *History of Windham County,* II, 315, 319, 352; Oscar E. Maurer, *A Puritan Church and Its Relations to Community, State, and Nation,* pp. 85–86; Edward C. Starr, *A History of Cornwall,* p. 90; George L. Walker, "The Historical Address," *Commemorative Exercises of the First Church of Christ in Hartford . . . 1883,* p. 88; Richard A. Wheeler, *History of the First Congregational Church, Stonington . . . 1674–1874* (Norwich, 1875), p. 77. Christ Church, Episcopalian, in Hartford avoided taxation of members by the sale of pews, subscriptions, and contributions. The first tax after the formation of the church in 1801 came in 1809 when $400 was raised. *Contributions to the History of Christ Church, Hartford* (Hartford, 1895), I, 57–58 and *passim.*

Platform which provided for county associations and consociations and for a General Association.[21] The county (or
half-county) associations with a strictly ministerial membership held frequent meetings at which the clergymen
discussed the duties of their offices and matters of common
interest to the churches and at which they licensed young
ministers. The consociations, composed of both ministers
and laymen, were instituted to deal with ecclesiastical difficulties of all sorts whenever they should arise. To the annual meetings of the General Association, which exercised
a general advisory superintendency over ministers and
churches, came delegates from the county associations.
Connecticut had a unique presbyterianized Congregationalism. Meeting more frequently than in other New England states, in closer affiliation, possessing greater security
in office, and backed by more than a century and a half of
tradition, the Congregational clergy of Connecticut had
potentially more influence than was the case elsewhere.
Furthermore, the hold of religion was stronger because
the consociations linked prominent laymen with the ministers. The form and spirit of Connecticut Congregationalism were unaffected by the removal of the Saybrook Platform from the state laws in 1784.

That the Congregationalists were dominant in the state
during the Second Great Awakening is unquestioned.
What was the strength and what the status of the other
denominations? There were practically no Catholics in
Connecticut prior to 1830, and among the Protestants
only Episcopalians, Baptists, and Methodists need to be
considered. Significant indeed was the absence of Unitarianism; the contrast with Massachusetts where Unitarian-

21. Williston Walker, *The Creeds and Platforms of Congregationalism*,
pp. 499–516. The Saybrook Platform represented a form of organization
for Congregationalism which the Massachusetts assembly rejected three
years prior to its acceptance in Connecticut. Massachusetts' rather ineffective Ministerial Convention was not supplemented by a General Association until 1803, and even then it was vigorously opposed by the same
type of religious leaders who were strong supporters of associationalism
in Connecticut.

ism began and flourished during the period under consideration was marked. Only one Congregational church, that of Samuel J. May in Brooklyn, became Unitarian. The state's conservative tradition and closely knit Congregationalism had much to do with this, as did the developments which constituted the Second Great Awakening.

When the Awakening began, the Episcopalians and Baptists had long been active in Connecticut, but the Methodists were struggling newcomers. The Baptists had set up their first society in Groton in 1705, the Episcopalians theirs in Stratford in 1707. Strengthened as a result of the Separatist movement which the Great Awakening of the 1740's produced among the Congregationalists, and then weakened, as were all denominations, by the harrowing experiences of the American Revolution, the Connecticut Baptists in 1795 reported sixty churches, forty ministers, and about 3,500 members.[22] The Revolution was particularly hard on the Anglicans, who lost the support of the English Society for the Propagation of the Gospel and who were viewed with suspicion by the patriots. By 1793, however, the Episcopal Church in Connecticut had its own bishop, Samuel Seabury, who had secured consecration from non-juring bishops in Scotland, and was showing signs of recovery with twenty ministers in perhaps twice that number of churches.[23] Not until 1789 did the Methodists enter the state, the pioneer Jesse Lee preaching in the town of Norwalk in June and later in the year establishing the first Methodist society, consisting of only three women, in Stratford. There were about 1,200 Methodists in the state in 1796 and very few ministers.[24] During the Awakening all the Protestant denominations made significant gains; in spite of disestablishment the Congre-

22. Henry S. Burrage, *A History of the Baptists in New England,* p. 102.
23. Eben E. Beardsley, *The History of the Episcopal Church in Connecticut,* I, 420.
24. James Mudge, *History of the New England Conference of the Methodist Episcopal Church, 1796–1910,* p. 50.

gationalists still considerably outnumbered the other three groups taken together in 1830.

Connecticut was a Federalist stronghold until 1816. In this conservative state where the ruling class of colonial days had carried over into the post-Revolutionary period opposition to Jeffersonian democracy naturally appeared. For this, religion was in part responsible, since adherents of Congregationalism, "not only a religious creed and a theology, . . . [but] also a program for society,"[25] abhorred the ungodliness which they associated with Jeffersonian democracy. The Federalists in Connecticut survived the defeats on the national scene until 1816 when they suffered their first setback in the state. In that year they re-elected Governor John Cotton Smith, but the opposition, the Toleration Party composed largely of Episcopalians, Baptists, Methodists, and those who had no church affiliation, won the lieutenant governorship. In 1817 Smith was defeated by the Tolerationists' candidate, Oliver Wolcott. Shrewd political strategy had led to the nomination of the conservative Wolcott, a Federalist who had served in John Adams' cabinet but who had broken with his party over their conduct during the War of 1812. Although a constitution was adopted in 1818 and the Federalist party soon disappeared, Wolcott's election precipitated no break in the even tenor of Connecticut's ways.[26]

In Connecticut, then, a peculiar combination of economic, political, social, and religious conditions existed which help to explain why this small, conservative, Congregationalist-dominated New England state became a leader in the Second Great Awakening.

25. Perry Miller, "Jonathan Edwards to Emerson," *New England Quarterly*, XIII (1940), 599.
26. Morse, *A Neglected Period of Connecticut's History*, pp. 84–87.

II

THE CHALLENGE TO ORTHODOXY

DESPITE the strong religious tradition in Connecticut, the conservative nature of the people, and the closely knit organization of Congregationalism, the leaders of the dominant sect were far from pleased with the outlook for religion in the closing years of the eighteenth century. Particularly disturbing was the prevalence of what they called infidelity. Under this term they grouped all the ramifications of rationalism which had originated in Europe's Age of Reason and had spread across the Atlantic. Deism and other features of the Enlightenment had been brought to America in the writings of Lord Herbert of Cherbury, Bolingbroke, Shaftesbury, Hume, Voltaire, and the Encyclopedists.[1] Americans had also gained a wider acquaintance with these new ideas, both Ezra Stiles and Timothy Dwight asserted, as a result of contacts with European soldiers during the French and Indian War and the Revolution.[2] Not until after the Revolution did rationalism spread widely. Then, according to the Reverend Luther Hart, infidelity "showed herself in the work-shop, the counting room, and the parlor, in colleges and in halls of legislation, and sent out its insidious poison from the press."[3]

In 1784 Ethan Allen published his crude but significant *Reason The Only Oracle of Man*. Although not widely

1. Vernon Stauffer, *New England and the Bavarian Illuminati*, p. 70. See also many sermons preached in the last decade of the eighteenth and the first decade of the nineteenth century, especially those by Timothy Dwight.

2. T. Dwight, *A Discourse on Some Events of the Last Century* (1801), pp. 18–19; quotation from Stiles in I. Woodbridge Riley, *American Thought from Puritanism to Pragmatism*, pp. 63–64.

3. Luther Hart, "A View of the Religious Declension in New England, and of its Causes, during the Latter Half of the Eighteenth Century," *Quarterly Christian Spectator*, V (1833), 236.

circulated, this deistic publication by the hero of Ticon-
deroga attracted some attention. Ezra Stiles and the Reverend Nathan Perkins of West Hartford denounced Allen;
Timothy Dwight termed his arguments "flimsy, and un-
meaning."[4] Allen's skepticism has been summed up by
Bernard Faÿ in the following manner: "He denied the
divinity of Christ, the veracity of Scriptures, the miracles
and revelation. He demanded a traditional cult, and practical morality. His style, simple and even dull, and his direct arguments, rendered the work even more effective and
shocking."[5] Was it not also serious that Thomas Jefferson
was known throughout the country as a deist or at best a
freethinker on religious matters? When Joseph Priestley
came to the United States in 1794, he drew attention to
the deistic beliefs and materialistic philosophy which had
occasioned his retreat from England. Of him Dwight wrote
in 1799: "All the efforts of Doctor Priestley are considered
by himself as favourable to Xy; nay, as the efforts of a
Champion in her cause. I however, believe that he has done
Xy more harm than Hume himself."[6]

Of great importance in spreading what has been called
"republican religion" was Tom Paine. In his *The Age of
Reason*, published in 1794, he assailed traditional and
widely held Christian truths. He attacked the conception
of a God who, according to the tenets of orthodox Christians, played such a dominant rôle in the lives of men. He
lashed at the Old Testament.

Take away from Genesis the belief that Moses was the author, on which only the strange belief that it is the word of
God has stood, and there remains nothing of Genesis but an
anonymous book of stories, fables, and traditionary or in-

4. *The Literary Diary of Ezra Stiles,* III, 345; Nathan Perkins, *A Narrative of a Tour Through the State of Vermont,* pp. 14, 24; T. Dwight, *Travels; in New-England and New-York,* II, 406–407.
5. Bernard Faÿ, *The Revolutionary Spirit in France and America,* p. 221.
6. T. Dwight to J. Morse, Dec. 30, 1799, Morse Papers, Yale University Library.

vented absurdities, or of downright lies. The story of Eve and the serpent, and of Noah and his ark, drops to a level with the Arabian Tales, without the merit of being entertaining; and the account of men living to eight and nine hundred years becomes as fabulous as the immortality of the giants of Mythology.[7]

He ridiculed many stories in the New Testament, inquiring, for instance, how it happened that when the devil showed Christ all the kingdoms of the world "he did not discover America," and asking, "or is it only with *kingdoms* that his sooty highness has any interest?" After referring to "the fable of Jesus Christ," he called the story of the virgin birth "blasphemously obscene."[8] It was a serious matter when a Revolutionary hero stood on the side of the devil, and the horrified champions of orthodoxy denounced Paine. Charles A. Goodrich, a contemporary, observed in his *History of the United States*, "The perspicuous and simple style of Paine, his keen powers of ridicule, directed against the Bible, and above all, the gratitude which multitudes felt for the aid his pen had given our revolution, contributed to give him a peculiarly powerful influence."[9]

For the defenders of the faith France of the 1790's vividly illustrated the fate of a country which embraced infidelity. France was, Timothy Dwight proclaimed, "a kind of suburb to the world of perdition. . . . The touch of France is pollution. Her embrace is death."[10] The United States, it was feared, might travel a similar path, and the enthusiasm for France which many Americans displayed was viewed as dangerous. "When the National Assembly of France, the elected rulers of a great nation," wrote John Trumbull, the American artist, "formed a procession to the metropolitan church of Nôtre Dame, which had been

7. Thomas Paine, *The Age of Reason,* part II, p. 14.
8. Quoted in Moncure D. Conway, *The Life of Thomas Paine,* II, 187.
9. Quoted in *Connecticut Mirror,* Dec. 30, 1822.
10. Quoted in Mark A. de W. Howe, *Classic Shades,* p. 127.

consecrated during long ages to the worship of God, and there in mock solemnity bowed their knees before a common courtezan, basely worshiping her as the goddess of reason, still there were those, and not a few in America, who threw up their caps, and cried, 'glorious, glorious, sister republic!' "[11]

The champions of orthodoxy in Connecticut felt that they had ample grounds for viewing the spread of infidelity as a plague and as a disaster for society. The deistic conception of God as a Creator who let His creatures move and have their being in accordance with natural law was offensive to their belief that God was judge and father, a Supreme Being who was always close to His creatures. Renunciation of the complete sovereignty of God was heretical, as was the implied or direct denial of the divinity of Jesus and of the Bible as the inspired word of God. Doubt and suspicion in regard to revealed religion were abhorred. Deism, it was felt, led too easily to atheism, and the inevitable concomitant of infidelity was believed to be looseness of morals. To men like Timothy Dwight and his colleagues the attacks on truths which they considered essential to the maintenance of moral living were deplorable, and the perpetrators of these outrages were the veritable agents of the devil.

This attitude toward the Age of Reason was evidenced in many sermons. The Reverend Elijah Waterman of Windham in 1801 called the period "the age of Infidelity," and said that "pernicious characters . . . have now, like the locusts gone forth in bands to devour, and by their corruption to generate a pestilence in the morals and habits of social life, and to introduce distrust, jealousy and misery into all its intimate and remote relations, to poison the fountains, and impregnate the streams with convulsions and death." Benjamin Trumbull in his Century Sermon referred to the "growth of error, infidelity, atheism, the most filthy and abominable doctrines." James

11. John Trumbull, *Autobiography, Reminiscences and Letters of John Trumbull, from 1756 to 1841* (New Haven, 1841), p. 169.

Dana called infidelity a "destructive system, replete with the *depths of Satan*," and declared that "this is also an age in which infidels and scoffers triumph, beyond any former example."[12] "There are dark and ominous appearances," the Reverend Nathan Strong warned in 1798. "I do not mean the wrath and threatening of any foreign nations whatever, for if we please God and procure him on our side, we may bless his providence, and hear human threatenings without emotion. But the dark omens are to be found at home. In our hearts, in our homes, in our practice, and in a licentious spirit disposed to break down civil and religious order. In affecting to depend on reason in the things of religion, more than the word of God; so as to reject all evangelical holiness, faith in Jesus Christ, the Son of God, and the ministrations of the spirit in the heart."[13]

Infidelity's most persistent assailant was Timothy Dwight. When he became president of Yale in 1795, the students, like their contemporaries at Harvard, Princeton, and other colleges, displayed much familiarity with the current rationalism, the infidelity which the Connecticut ministers found so objectionable.[14] Lyman Beecher, who entered Yale in 1793, called it "the day of the infidelity of the Tom Paine School," and wrote, a half-century later to be sure, that his college mates addressed one another as d'Alembert, Rousseau, and Voltaire. Another student of the time, Matthew Dutton, recorded that "an aspiring, ambitious youth, hardly dared avow his belief in the Christian religion."[15] President Stiles had led no determined as-

12. Elijah Waterman, *A Century Sermon* (1801), p. 36; Benjamin Trumbull, *A Century Sermon* (1801), p. 8; James Dana, *On the Completion of the Eighteenth Century* (1801), pp. 33, 54.

13. Quoted in Stauffer, *New England and the Bavarian Illuminati*, pp. 97–98.

14. Charles D. Hazen, *Contemporary American Opinion of the French Revolution*, pp. 295–296 note; Varnum L. Collins, *Princeton* (New York, 1914), p. 215.

15. Lyman Beecher, *Autobiography, Correspondence, etc.*, I, 43; Matthew Dutton, "Reflections on the Life & Character of Doct. Dwight," MS. essay in Yale University Library.

sault on the invading philosophies. As a matter of fact, he had preached but infrequently in the college pulpit. Furthermore, the Reverend Samuel Wales, professor of divinity and college pastor from 1782 to 1793, during his later years had been prevented from assuming evangelical leadership by epileptic fits which seized him even when he was leading divine service or administering the Lord's Supper in the chapel. Little wonder that under such circumstances the college church had but two or three members, and that but a mere handful of the student body attended the college communion services! Timothy Dwight has been described as seeming "to a later generation . . . little more than a walking repository of the venerable Connecticut *status quo*,"[16] but when he moved from his Greenfield Hill parish in 1795 to become president of Yale, he was determined not to perpetuate any "venerable Connecticut *status quo*," but rather to rouse the college—and the state—from the religious torpor which enveloped them.

Dwight began immediately to argue the cause of revealed religion. When on one occasion he selected for discussion with the students the question, "Is the Bible the word of God?" his action was considered spectacular. In the disputation which followed and in his forceful sermons and addresses, the Yale president called attention to the serious challenge to orthodoxy.[17] At the college Commencement in September, 1797, he preached two memorable sermons on *The Nature and Danger of Infidel Philosophy*. He first analyzed the arguments of Lord Herbert of Cherbury, Shaftesbury, Tindal, Hume, Bolingbroke, and others, exhibiting, as he said at the end of the first discourse, "the nature, and the actual state, of this Philosophy." Then he explained the dangers of these doctrines to his young listeners. "As mere Infidelity," he declared, "it teaches nothing but to contest all principles, and to adopt none. As Scepticism, it is an ocean of doubt and agitation, in which there are no soundings, and to which there is no

16. Vernon L. Parrington, *Main Currents in American Thought*, I, 361.
17. Beecher, *Autobiography*, I, 43.

shore. As Animalism and Atheism it completes the ravage
and ruin of man, which, in its preceding forms, it had so
successfully begun. It now holds out the rank Circaean
draught, and sends the deluded wretches, who are allured
to taste, to bristle and wallow with the swine, to play tricks
with the monkey, to rage and rend with the tiger, and to
putrify [sic] into nothing with the herd of kindred
brutes."[18]

In May, 1798, the Reverend Jedidiah Morse of Charles-
town, Massachusetts, who had been reading John Robison,
*Proofs of a Conspiracy against all the Religions and Gov-
ernments of Europe,* announced to New England the news
of this secret plan to destroy religion and liberty.[19] According to Robison, there had been organized in Germany
in 1776 a society called the Illuminati which aimed to
abolish Christianity and to overturn all civil governments.
That it had been successful during the two succeeding
decades was evidenced by the fact that civil and ecclesiastical institutions had been shaken in many countries.
Morse declared that the Illuminati had formed branches
in the United States.

Timothy Dwight continued the discussion of Illuminism
in his Fourth of July address for 1798. After making it
clear that he held the Illuminati responsible for the political and spiritual ills of the world, he urged the people of
Connecticut to be on their guard. His language, although
extravagant, reveals what many felt about the incursions
of infidelity.

The sins of these enemies of Christ, and Christians, are of
numbers and degrees which mock account and description.
All that the malice and atheism of the Dragon, the cruelty
and rapacity of the Beast, and the fraud and deceit of the
false Prophet, can generate or accomplish, swell the list. No
personal or national interest of man has been uninvaded; no
impious sentiment, or action, against God has been spared;

18. T. Dwight, *The Nature, and Danger, of Infidel Philosophy* (1797),
pp. 47, 86.
19. Stauffer, *New England and the Bavarian Illuminati,* p. 229.

no malignant hostility against Christ, and his religion, has
been unattempted. Justice, truth, kindness, piety, and moral
obligation universally have been, not merely trodden under
foot, . . . but ridiculed, spurned, and insulted, as the childish bugbears of drivelling idiocy. Chastity and decency have
been alike turned out of doors; and shame and pollution
called out of their dens to the hall of distinction and the
chair of state. . . . For what end shall we be connected with
men of whom this is the character and conduct? Is it that we
may assume the same character, and pursue the same conduct? Is it that our churches may become temples of reason,
our Sabbath a decade, and our psalms of praise Marsellois
[sic] hymns? . . . Is it that we may see the Bible cast into a
bonfire, the vessels of the sacramental supper borne by an ass
in public procession, and our children, either wheedled or ter-
rified, uniting in the mob, chanting mockeries against God,
and hailing in the sounds of Ca ira the ruin of their religion,
and the loss of their souls? . . . Shall we, my brethren, become partakers of these sins? Shall we introduce them into
our government, our schools, our families? Shall our sons become the disciples of Voltaire, and the dragoons of Marat;
or our daughters the concubines of the Illuminati?[20]

Excitement over the Illuminati soon subsided in the absence of more substantial proofs of their activities than
Robison's volume, but the clergy were discussing infidelity
in their assemblies. In 1794 the General Association recommended that "considering the importance of Christianity to mankind" and "the danger to which youth are at
the present time exposed," serious endeavors should be
made to promote the influence of religion. Resolutions
were accordingly passed, calling for meetings of young
people for religious instruction, meetings for prayer and
conference, and the establishment of libraries "to consist

20. Quoted in *ibid.,* pp. 250–251. Dwight's sermon was entitled *The
Duty of Americans, at the Present Crisis* (1798). His alarm was increased because, in addition to Robison, he had been reading Abbé Barruel, *Memoirs, Illustrating the History of Jacobinism,* the first part of
which bore the heading, "The Antichristian Conspiracy."

especially of the most important books relating to the de-istical controversy."[21] "What shall be done to put a Stop to the Growth of Infidelity?" was the question on which the Fairfield County East Association deliberated in October, 1794,[22] while the Hartford County North Association minutes for the following year contained a statement on the subject.

This Association having made enquiry concerning the spread of infidelity, deeply regret the prevalence of Deism, and other errors, and a spirit of irreligion: And in particular, learn with grief, that sceptical writings are industriously circulated. We therefore conceive ourselves called upon, in the present state of religion, in our country, to oppose the spread of infidelity in all prudent ways, and especially by studying more diligently and exhibiting more frequently the great evidences of the christian religion: and to endeavour that Students in Theology, who may be under the care of any of us be directed to study more largely the deistical controversy; and that we assist each other in procuring the most approved authors on the subject.[23]

More respectable forms of heterodoxy likewise disturbed the orthodox. Universalism was attracting some attention among those who objected to the narrowness of the gate to heaven designed by the Calvinists. When a Universalist publication, *Calvinism Improved*, written by the Reverend Joseph Huntington of Coventry, appeared posthumously in 1796, the orthodox answer was soon forthcoming, a treatise by the Reverend Nathan Strong entitled *The Doctrine of Eternal Misery Consistent with the Infinite Benevolence of God*.[24] Moreover, there was opposition in

21. *The Records of the General Association of Connecticut, 1738–1799*, pp. 156–157.
22. Records of the Fairfield County East Association, Connecticut Congregational House, Hartford.
23. Records of the Hartford County North Association, Congregational House.
24. Robbins, *Diary*, I, 49 note. Jonathan Edwards the younger preached a sermon against Universalism; in 1793 the General Association dis-

Connecticut to the Unitarian movement which had started in Boston in 1787.[25]

Not only the rise of infidelity and of the more polite forms of heterodoxy, but also an all too prevalent indifference to religion alarmed the Congregational leaders.[*] "For several years past," the Reverend Nathan Perkins declared in 1800, "contempt of the holy sabbath—desertion of public worship—omission of family-religion—and disregard of divine ordinances have spread, in a degree, which calls for tears of grief; threatening, in their progress, to lay waste all the most valuable interests of society."[26] Timothy Dwight called attention to "a cold, contemptuous indifference toward every moral and religious subject" which was common after the Revolution.[27] In November, 1795, he preached a sermon to the Yale students on the subject of indifference to religion which, according to Benjamin Silliman, he considered worse than direct opposition.[28] At Lebanon it was reported that "family religion was very unfashionable. The house of God was much forsaken on the Sabbath, and when a lecture was preached on another day, the preacher saw little else than empty pews." At the

cussed the matter and voted an affirmative answer to the question, "Whether a professed belief of the final salvation of all men be a censurable heresy?" A Universalist society was organized in Southington about 1792. Norris G. Osborn, ed., *History of Connecticut*, III, 385.

25. See, for example, *Extracts from the Minutes of the General Association of Connecticut, 1806*, p. 7.

26. Nathan Perkins, *Two Discourses on the Grounds of the Christian's Hope* (1800), pp. 38–39.

27. Dwight, *A Discourse on Some Events of the Last Century* (1801), p. 19.

28. Silliman's MS. diary is in the Yale University Library.

* EDITOR'S NOTE. Beginning at this point and running through the next few pages a number of passages, both of text and of quotation, occur which also appear in William W. Sweet's *Religion on the American Frontier*, vol. III, *The Congregationalists* (Chicago, 1939), pp. 6–7. As editor of the Yale Historical Publications, I have investigated this parallelism and am entirely satisfied that the passages in question occurred originally in Mr. Keller's typescript doctoral dissertation deposited in the Yale University Library in June, 1934, of which the present volume is a revision. This note is added after consultation with Professor Sweet and with his courteous approval. L.W.L.

1788 meeting of the General Association, in response to a request from the Hartford County North Association which reported a general and increasing neglect in attending public worship, a committee was appointed to draw up an exhortation on the subject to be read in the churches throughout the state. The Reverend Luther Hart wrote that the churches were composed almost entirely of people considerably advanced in life and that they held practically no meetings except on the Sabbath; while the Reverend Joel Hawes described this period as one in which the Holy Spirit appeared "to have withdrawn his gracious presence from the churches; ministers and people were extensively 'settled on their lees,' and a moral dearth, of the most portentous character, had overspread the land."[29]

A lamentable decline in morals, the Connecticut ministers were convinced, had also appeared, in large part as a result of the spread of infidelity and indifference to religion. Laws on the statute books revealed the ascetic code of those who viewed the moral situation with alarm. A lengthy act for the observance of the Sabbath admonished all persons to apply themselves "to duties of Religion and Piety, publicly and privately," set a fine of fifty cents for each failure to attend public worship, and prohibited all travelling and secular business on the Lord's Day.[30] There was legislation, too, against swearing, blasphemy, atheism and deism, gaming and drunkenness,[31] and by still another statute, significantly entitled "An Act for the more effective putting in Execution the Laws against Vice, Immorality and Profaneness, and for promoting Christian

29. George L. Clark, *A History of Connecticut*, p. 368; *Records of the General Association, 1738–1799*, p. 127; L. Hart, "A View of the Religious Declension in New England," *Quarterly Christian Spectator*, V (1833), 212, 217; Joel Hawes, *Historical Sketches of the First Church in Hartford*, p. 18.

30. *Acts and Laws of the State of Connecticut, Revision of 1796*, pp. 368–371. The paragraph prescribing a fine for failure to attend public worship was repealed in 1816. *The Public Statute Laws of the State of Connecticut, 1808–1820*, p. 261.

31. *Acts and Laws, Revision of 1796*, pp. 148, 182–183, 219, 407–408.

Knowledge," the selectmen of the several towns were instructed to see that each householder possessed at least one
Bible.[32]

Apparently the laws were not being enforced. The Reverend Jonathan Edwards declared in 1792 that "never at
least in this country was it so necessary as at the present
time, that ministers be well skilled in the whole system of
Christian theology," one reason being that "irreligion and
profaneness never prevailed in it to so great a degree."[33]
A scene where "piety seemed to be flying away from our
land—Religion declined—morality languished—vice grew
bold—profaneness, revelling, dishonesty, and sinful amusements increased," was described by the Reverend Nathan
Perkins.[34] In Lebanon, "youth spent much time at balls,
which were encouraged by many of the old."[35] James Morris noted in his *Memoirs* that at Litchfield "the Church
. . . was made up of numbers of ignorant, unprincipled
and unexemplary men. . . . Profane swearing and open
Sabbath-breaking and drunkenness were not uncommon
among professors of religion. The young people were
clownish, ignorant and uncivil in their amusements."[36]
Appealing to his congregation in 1798 the Reverend John
Ely suggested, "In this day of so general declension, when
vice and irreligion abound, it becometh all classes of people
to examine into their hearts and lives, and see whether they
do not contribute something to the general corruption and
irregularity."[37]

To Timothy Dwight the situation was alarming because
"the profanation of the Sabbath, before unusual, profaneness of language, drunkenness, gambling, and lewdness,

32. *Ibid.*, pp. 429–430. "Theatrical Shows and Exhibitions" were proscribed by law in 1800. *Acts and Laws of the State of Connecticut, 1805
Edition*, pp. 521–522.

33. Jonathan Edwards, *Sermon Preached at the Ordination of the
Rev. Dan Bradley* (1792), p. 35.

34. Perkins, *Two Discourses* (1800), p. 39.

35. Clark, *History of Connecticut*, p. 368.

36. *Memoirs of James Morris*, p. 46.

37. John Ely, *A Sermon delivered in the First [Congregational]
Church in Danbury, Nov. 25, 1798*, p. 5.

were exceedingly increased."[38] Yale when Dwight became
president was described by one contemporary observer as
being "in a dreadful state of disorder, impiety & wickedness."[39] Lyman Beecher recalled that "wine and liquors
were kept in many rooms; intemperance, profanity, gambling, and licentiousness were common."[40] A letter penned
shortly after Dwight assumed office throws light on conditions at Yale in 1795. It read in part:

It is surprising to see what a difference there is in the behaviour of the students since last year; at present there is no
card playing, at least but a very little of it, no night revel-
lings, breaking tutors windows, breaking glass bottles &c, but
all is order and quietness, more as I believe than was ever
known for any length of time in this college.[41]

Under such conditions the rise of Republicanism was
likewise considered dangerous, for in all sincerity Congregational ministers and many Congregational laymen believed that the spread of Republicanism with its democratic
spirit and its sympathetic attitude toward France was in
part responsible for the current prevalence of irreligion
and immorality. Outside Connecticut in the 1790's the Republicans made notable progress under Jefferson's leadership, and although no formal organization existed within
the state during this period, a few men with Republican
leanings gained seats in the legislature. The Republican
vote in Connecticut in 1800, somewhat over three thousand,
was well behind the Federalist total but was large enough
to cause alarm.

Religion was a strong factor in Congregational opposition to Republicanism. When Jefferson was elected to the
vice-presidency in 1796, the Reverend Judah Champion

38. Dwight, *A Discourse on Some Events of the Last Century* (1801),
p. 19.
39. M. Dutton, "Reflections on the Life & Character of Doct. Dwight."
40. Beecher, *Autobiography*, I, 43.
41. T. Bishop to T. Robbins, Jan. 11, 1796, Robbins Papers, Connecticut Historical Society.

of Litchfield prayed, "O Lord, wilt Thou bestow upon the
Vice-President a double portion of Thy grace, for Thou
knowest he needs it."[42] A minister in Branford called Jefferson "a debauchee, an infidel, and a liar." Thomas Robbins, who abhorred the very thought of Jefferson, recorded
that "infidels in religion are apt to be Democrats." When
Jefferson's victory in 1800 seemed possible, Robbins rejoiced that such matters were in the hands of God and
wrote, "I do not believe that the Most High will permit a
howling atheist to sit at the head of this nation!" His attitude is further revealed by the entry in his *Diary* for
July 4, 1800, "In the morning we had news of the death
of Mr. Jefferson. It is to be hoped that it is true." When
he learned of Jefferson's election, he wrote, "Our only consolation is that the Lord reigns."[43] Samuel G. Goodrich,
who published his *Recollections of a Lifetime* in 1856,
warned the people of that time that they could hardly
comprehend the odium which had once been attached to
democracy. "They [the people of the late eighteenth cen-
tury] not only regarded it as hostile to good government,"
he wrote, "but as associated with infidelity in religion, radi-
calism in government, and licentiousness in society. It was
considered a sort of monster, born of Tom Paine, the
French Revolution, foreign renegados, and the great
Father of Evil."[44]

That many people in Connecticut were disturbed during the closing years of the eighteenth century by the
spread of infidelity, by indifference to religion, and by

42. Osborn, ed., *History of Connecticut*, III, 350.
43. Robbins, *Diary*, I, 84, 114, 118, 127–128.
44. Samuel G. Goodrich, *Recollections of a Lifetime*, I, 117–118. See
William A. Robinson, "A Misused Quotation," *American Historical Review*, XXXIII (1927), 81–83, for a discussion of the familiar quotation
frequently misused to discredit the Congregational-Federalists of Connecticut. It was not Timothy Dwight but his brother Theodore who in
1801 referred to the "consummation of Democratic blessedness" with the
country governed by "knaves and blockheads," the ties of marriage severed, wives and daughters "thrown into the stews," and filial piety extin-
guished. And Theodore Dwight, as Robinson has showed, was referring
not to the United States of 1801 but to the imaginary state discussed by
William Godwin in his *Enquiry Concerning Social Justice*.

what they considered a decline in morals, is evident. Why
had not the Congregational clergy of the state taken vigorous action to prevent the development of the situation
which in the 1790's was deemed so alarming? To answer
this question it is necessary first to consider some hitherto
unmentioned factors which contributed to the general un-
rest and then to examine briefly some aspects of the history of Congregationalism in New England.

The American Revolution followed two disturbed decades during which the colonists were involved successively
in the French and Indian War and in political and economic controversies with the mother country. With attention centered on these secular affairs, there was little time
for religious matters. The Revolution itself Timothy
Dwight called a period that "unhinged the principles, the
morality, and the religion of this country more than could
have been done by a peace of forty years."[45] In his *History
of Connecticut* the Reverend Benjamin Trumbull penned
several poignant sentences undoubtedly born of his experiences during and after the struggle with Great Britain. "A state of war," he wrote, "is peculiarly unfriendly
to religion. It dissipates the mind, diminishes the degree
of instruction, removes great numbers almost wholly from
it, connects them with the most dangerous company, and
presents them with the worst examples. It hardens and
emboldens men in sin; is productive of profaneness, intemperance, disregard to property, violence and all licentious
living."[46]

Connecticut made the transition to statehood with little
difficulty, but the years after 1783 represented "troublous
times." Economic conditions were bad throughout the
country with the cessation of much of the trade formerly
carried on with Great Britain and her empire, the infla-
tion of the currency, and the inability of debtors to meet
their obligations.[47] The period of confusion under the

45. Quoted in Osborn, ed., *History of Connecticut*, I, 377.
46. Benjamin Trumbull, *History of Connecticut*, II, 18.
47. James T. Adams, *New England in the Republic, 1776–1850*, p. 139;

Articles of Confederation was followed by arguments over the Constitution, and after its adoption came the early days of a new experiment in government with all the distractions and contention inherent in such a pioneering venture. It seems reasonable to suppose, also, that the rejection of the English king and parliament and the establishment of a republic may have rendered authoritarian religion in general, and Connecticut Congregationalism in particular, distasteful to many who had participated in the political and social upheaval. Conditions were further disturbed by the extensive migration northward to Vermont and westward to New York and Pennsylvania which began even before peace was restored.

For an understanding of the religious situation in the 1790's a consideration of New England Congregationalism is also essential.[48] The early settlers in this part of America were for the most part strict Calvinists who set up their theocracies and struggled with the elements, the Indians, unfriendly fellow-colonists, and England. Difficulties of one sort and another soon began to plague the churches, and with the coming of age of the first generation born in America their memberships declined. Admission requirements were very severe. Many persons who had been baptized as the children of church members experienced no conversion in later life and were therefore not entitled to have their names on the church lists. What was to be done with them and their children? A compromise was the answer, the Half-Way Covenant of 1662, under which individuals who had received baptism but were not full members might, if they led upright Christian lives, sign the covenant and thereby obtain for themselves and their children the right to be "half-way" members. These offspring might be baptized and were considered within the covenant, although neither they nor their parents were

M. Louise Greene, *The Development of Religious Liberty in Connecticut,* pp. 344–345; Dwight, *A Discourse on Some Events of the Last Century* (1801), p. 11.

48. The story of Congregationalism is well told in Williston Walker, *A History of the Congregational Churches in the United States.*

permitted to go to the communion table, nor could they vote in church matters. As a result, the number of those who were nominally connected with the churches increased, but the spirit of New England religion was not revived. A Reforming Synod was convened in 1679 at which measures, aiming to restore the church to its pristine holiness, were adopted. Since the Half-Way Covenant which represented a retreat from earlier strictness was continued, and since any serious attempt to restore discipline would have meant losses in membership, the movement for reform was unsuccessful.

In the early decades of the eighteenth century New England Congregationalism appeared to be losing its hold on the people. Arminians were attacking it, members were dropping away in spite of the Half-Way Covenant, indifference was rife, and strict adherence to the doctrines and practices of Calvinism could not be obtained. In Boston and Cambridge the Mathers stormed and threatened, but offered no practicable plan for improvement. In Connecticut the Saybrook Platform, adopted in 1708, strengthened the form of church organization, but no religious awakening ensued. Stoddardeanism was a way out in several Congregational churches, but this merely meant a further dilution of fundamental doctrines and practices.[49] Reinvigoration did not follow this lowering of standards.

At this juncture Jonathan Edwards appeared on the scene. Edwards rendered many services to American religion by his preaching and writing; one of the greatest lay in his efforts to rescue New England Congregationalism from the desperate situation just described. He neither compromised as had the proponents of the Half-Way Covenant and Stoddardeanism nor indulged in pointless wrangling as had the Mathers. He taught relentlessly the need for complete surrender to the will of God and intro-

---

49. The Reverend Solomon Stoddard of Northampton, Massachusetts, Jonathan Edwards' grandfather, introduced the practice of admitting to the communion service people who had been baptized but had experienced no conversion. The Lord's Supper thus came to be viewed as a converting agency.

duced into New England the religious phenomenon known as the revival. A great boon to lifeless churches, the revivals began in Edwards' Northampton church in 1734 and swelled to flood tide six years later under George Whitefield.

The Great Awakening resulted. When the churches of New England and of other parts of the colonies were visited by what he considered outpourings of the Holy Spirit and thousands were converted, Edwards could view with pleasure the renewed strength of institutions which only a short time before had drooped and seemed close to death. Short-lived, however, was the triumph. The excesses which appeared in 1742 and 1743, the actions of itinerating evangelists which led to a reversal of the 1740 and 1741 practice of inviting them to fill the pulpits of settled ministers, the return of George Whitefield to England, and the natural weariness which follows a period of religious excitement brought the Great Awakening to an end in 1743. In 1750 Edwards himself was dismissed by the Northampton church, the people resenting his renunciation of Stoddardeanism and his efforts to exercise strict discipline within the church. He retired to preach to the Indians in the frontier town of Stockbridge.

Here, through his writings, Edwards made another great contribution. In the *Freedom of the Will*, published in 1754, *The Great Christian Doctrine of Original Sin Defended*, in the press when he died in March, 1758, and *The Nature of True Virtue*, published posthumously in 1765, Edwards completed a restatement of Calvinist doctrines as well as his own ethical system, which he rounded out with the doctrine of grace as expressed in *Decrees and Elections* and *Efficacious Grace*. For the purposes of this study the *Freedom of the Will* has special significance. Herein he carried to a high point his life-long assault on Arminianism; not only did he restate the Calvinist position but he also attacked vigorously the Arminian arguments. In so doing, he distinguished between will and inclination, writing that man was free to follow the dictates of his own mind although he had no control over the direction of his choice. "Strictly speaking," Professor Clarence H. Faust has written, "Edwards did not deny the freedom of the will. He merely defined it so as to limit it to the power of acting upon impulses in the generation of which the mind was wholly passive."[50] Miss Winslow asserts, "He had qualified freedom rather than denied it," and then continues,

In its application to man's salvation, this qualification of his freedom meant that those whom God had chosen might repent if they would, but the desire to do so came from God. Man's responsibility lay in acting on the choice, no matter whence the inclination toward that choice might come. To this extent only was man's salvation in his own hands. This was very useful ammunition for the practical pastor who had difficulty reconciling man's helplessness with man's responsibility.[51]

That Edwards went no further is understandable when one realizes that he was obliged to reconcile any concession to man with the doctrine on which he insisted above all others, the sovereignty of God. To his own satisfaction Edwards disposed of the Arminian opposition; he also introduced some idea of moral responsibility and human choice into New England theology.[52]

The ejection of Jonathan Edwards from the Northampton church was symbolic of developments in Connecticut during the half-century following the Great Awakening. Opponents of Edwards dominated the churches, men who belonged to what was known as the Old Divinity group[53]

50. Clarence H. Faust and Thomas H. Johnson, editors, *Jonathan Edwards, Representative Selections*, p. l.
51. Ola E. Winslow, *Jonathan Edwards, 1703–1758*, pp. 300–301.
52. See also discussions of the subject in Frank H. Foster, *A Genetic History of the New England Theology;* Williston Walker, *Ten New England Leaders;* Walker, *A History of the Congregational Churches in the United States;* Arthur C. McGiffert, *Jonathan Edwards;* Alexander V. G. Allen, *Jonathan Edwards;* William W. Sweet, *The Story of Religions in America.*
53. The characteristics of Old Divinity theory and practice are men-

and were theological descendants of the Old Lights of the Great Awakening controversies. Their policies had much to do with the situation which was causing alarm in the 1790's. These Old Divinity ministers opposed revivals on the grounds that they inevitably led to the unrestrained and objectionable excesses of 1742 and 1743; in most churches the use of the Half-Way Covenant was continued. To augment a declining membership no severe demands were made of those presenting themselves for admission, nor were the clergy willing to enforce discipline on back-sliders due to the fear that a further loss of members would result. Under such conditions the people did not rally to religion any more than they had in the early years of the century.

Engrossed in the multifarious concerns of the confused and active period which began with the French and Indian War in 1756, many people made no inquiries whatsoever about religion. Nothing was done about them by the Old Divinity ministers who from their pulpits preached sermons on hackneyed themes which frequently bored their listeners. No special efforts were made to stir up the interest of young people in religion, and family visits by ministers were practically suspended. Under such leadership, the churches had little to offer people harassed by the new philosophies, war, economic difficulties, and other perplexing problems. They had trouble holding their old members and were unable to win converts. Lacking boldness and aggressiveness, the Old Divinity group offered no strong defense against the spread of irreligion and immorality.

Timothy Dwight and most of the other Connecticut ministers whose opinions on conditions in the 1790's have

tioned in many places. See, among others, *The Literary Diary of Ezra Stiles*, III, especially pp. 343–344; William C. Fowler, *History of Durham*, p. 77; George N. Boardman, *A History of New England Theology*, pp. 30–31; L. Beecher, *A Sermon delivered at Woolcot [sic]*, . . . *at the Installation of Rev. J. Keyes* (1814), p. 8; L. Hart, "A View of the Religious Declension in New England," *Quarterly Christian Spectator*, V (1833), 220–229.

been cited were not Old Divinity adherents. A New Divinity group, which numbered no more than four or five in 1756, increased to forty or fifty by 1773, and included more than one hundred in 1796, had also developed among the New England clergy.[54] Of these Connecticut had probably the majority.

Outstanding among the New Divinity men were the Reverend Samuel Hopkins of Newport, Rhode Island; two Massachusetts ministers, Stephen West of Stockbridge and Nathaniel Emmons of Franklin; and four Connecticut clergymen, Joseph Bellamy of Bethlehem, John Smalley of New Britain, Jonathan Edwards the younger of New Haven, and Timothy Dwight.[55] All but one of these men were natives of Connecticut, all but one graduates of Yale. Erroneously the generic name Hopkinsian is frequently applied to the group. This implies an agreement in doctrines and a dependence on Hopkins which did not exist. Certainly the theology of Dwight, the New Divinity leader in Connecticut in the 1790's, differed markedly from that of Hopkins.[56] To designate the group as neo-Edwardean would be nearer the truth, for the source of what they practiced and preached was Jonathan Edwards, who by his determined stand against the forces that made for the decline of religion, his cogent reasoning, and his forceful writing won disciples as well as opponents. Hopkins and Bellamy were close friends of the older Edwards, Edwards of New Haven was his son, Timothy Dwight his grandson.

The Connecticut neo-Edwardeans looked with favor on revivals to build up the churches. They followed Dwight in telling people that reading Bibles, attending church

54. George P. Fisher, *A Discourse, Commemorative of the History of the Church of Christ in Yale College, during the First Century of its Existence,* pp. 80–82.
55. Walker, *A History of the Congregational Churches in America,* p. 280.
56. Dwight emphasized the agency of man more than did Hopkins. Furthermore, he advocated the use of means, whereas Hopkins contended that an unregenerate man committed a sin in making use of them. Dwight was a theological descendant of Bellamy rather than of Hopkins.

services, and praying might not be unconnected with their salvation, and Jonathan Edwards the younger in advocating the doctrine of a general atonement. Although they preached the sovereignty of God, they left room for the ability of man—but they were opponents of Arminianism.[57]

With these beliefs the New Divinity men combined strictness of discipline.[58] When converts presented themselves for membership in the churches, a careful inquiry into their experiences was made. Wherever it survived, the Half-Way Covenant was attacked. Backsliders were dealt with rigorously, and there was no winking at the malfeasances of professing Christians to stem defections. A healthy church, New Divinity ministers believed, was a stern church.

Since those who had rejected Jonathan Edwards were in no hurry to welcome his disciples, the rise of the New Divinity was slow. But these opponents of the "do-nothing" Old Divinity adherents preached effectively, wrote prolifically, and persisted in their efforts to win hearings. Of importance, too, was the fact that their homes were the theological seminaries of the period. Students for the ministry were attracted by their aggressive policies and forceful personalities, and as a result the candidates for Connecticut pastorates were in increasing numbers products of these "schools of prophets." Since the Old Divinity faction during the years following the Revolution was no more successful in combatting its ideological rivals than it was in curbing the spread of infidelity and religious in-

57. The best statement of the New Divinity principles which prevailed in Connecticut after 1795 will be found in the four volumes of T. Dwight, *Theology Explained and Defended, in a Series of Sermons.* See also *A Summary of Christian Doctrine and Practice,* published under the direction of the Missionary Society of Connecticut, 1804.

58. The Reverend Alexander Gillett, a New Divinity man, encountered difficulties in Wolcott, where he was pastor from 1774 to 1792, because he insisted on strict discipline. Samuel Orcutt, *History . . . of Wolcott, from 1731 to 1874* (Waterbury, 1874), p. 58. See also James M. Bailey, *History of Danbury, Conn., 1684–1896* (New York, 1896), p. 292.

difference, the number of pulpits captured by the neo-Edwardeans mounted.

In the 1790's the New Divinity men constituted a vociferous group among the Connecticut clergy who viewed with alarm the rising tide of heterodoxy and neglect of religion. They were keenly aware of the effects of the disturbed decades on this side of the Atlantic, of the spread of infidelity from its European sources, and of the failure of the Old Divinity men to meet the challenge to religion. Professor George P. Fisher has written, "The election of Dr. Dwight to the Presidency of Yale College marked the triumph in New England of the Edwardean theology."[59] This is too broad a statement, but certainly Timothy Dwight's election symbolized the New Divinity victory in Connecticut.

59. Fisher, *Church of Christ in Yale College*, p. 80.

III

COUNTER-REFORMATION

THROUGHOUT the country there were religious leaders who believed with Timothy Dwight that "where there is no religion, there is no morality," and that "with the loss of Religion, . . . the ultimate foundation of confidence is blown up; and the security of life, liberty, and property buried in ruins."[1] That a crisis had arisen they did not doubt when the ferment of the eighteenth century came to a dramatic climax in the French Revolution and Tom Paine wrote *The Age of Reason.* They undertook to combat the foes of orthodoxy, and the result was a general revival period, in varying degrees of intensity, not only in New England but also along the Atlantic seaboard to the south and on the frontier.

In Connecticut, one of the most important centers of revivalism, the awakening resulted from the conjunction of two forces in the 1790's. One was the widely voiced conviction that irreligion and immorality had so developed as to threaten the very foundations of society, sentiments that were underscored by developments in France after 1791. The other was the rise to power of the New Divinity group who felt that aggressive, vigorous measures must be taken to bring about an upturn in religion. That the alarm was widespread was pointed out in the preceding chapter, as was the ascendancy of the New Divinity, neo-Edwardean theology. A surprisingly large number of men with these leanings gained their pastorates in the 1790's.[2] At approximately the same time that Unitarianism was making

1. Dwight, *Travels,* IV, 403–404.
2. Ebenezer Porter in Washington, Asahel Hooker in Goshen, Azel Backus in Bethlehem, Dan Huntington in Litchfield, Bezaleel Pinneo in Milford, Edward D. Griffin in New Hartford, Abel Flint in Hartford, Daniel Dow in Thompson, and others.

headway in eastern Massachusetts, a group gained control in Connecticut who combined in a sense the two parts of the Puritan heritage to which Professor Perry Miller has referred, the tradition of regeneration and providence, of emotion and ecstasy, and the tradition of law and order, of regulation and control—even of reason and criticism.[3] And these neo-Edwardeans revitalized religion.

In spite of popular disapproval and the Old Divinity attitude, revivals did not disappear completely from Connecticut after the Great Awakening. The Reverend Ammi Robbins wrote of a revival in his Norfolk church in 1767, the Reverend Israel Day of another in Killingly in 1776, the Reverend Thomas Brockway of a third in Lebanon in 1781. In 1783 several towns in Litchfield County were "awakened," while the next year New Britain experienced a "fruitful" revival. "Precious harvests" were gathered in East Haddam and Lyme in 1792, in New Hartford and Farmington three years later, and in Milford in 1796.[4] The Reverend Edward Dorr Griffin later wrote that the modern revival period dated from 1792, but these scattered "appearances of the Holy Spirit" were only the forerunners of the awakening which began in 1797 and became widespread in 1798, significantly in Litchfield County where New Divinity strength was greatest.

The first period of the new revival movement lasted from 1797 through 1801, during which time what were called "outpourings of the Holy Spirit" were visible in many

3. Miller, "Jonathan Edwards to Emerson," *New England Quarterly,* XIII (1940), 600. It should be noted that while both Timothy Dwight and Nathaniel Emmons, a Massachusetts New Divinity leader, were neo-Edwardeans, Emmons followed the conservative Hopkins more closely than did Dwight, whose theology was "much more moderate and conciliatory." Walker, *History of the Congregational Churches in the United States,* pp. 300–303.

4. *Connecticut Evangelical Magazine,* I, 311–314; III, 226, 388–389; Trumbull, *Century Sermon* (1801), p. 18; Alfred Andrews, *New Britain, Genealogy, and Ecclesiastical History* (Chicago, 1867), p. 72; letters from Noah Porter and Edward D. Griffin in William B. Sprague, *Lectures on Revivals of Religion,* appendix, pp. 69, 151–152; T. Dwight, *A Discourse in Two Parts, delivered on the Public Fast, July, 1812,* p. 39.

parts of the state. In describing these events Griffin wrote, "I saw a continued succession of heavenly sprinklings at New Salem, Farmington, Middlebury, and New Hartford, . . . until, in 1799, I could stand at my door in New Hartford, Litchfield county, and number fifty or sixty contiguous congregations laid down in one field of divine wonders, and as many more in different parts of New England."[5]

In the pages of the *Connecticut Evangelical Magazine,* a publication which appeared first in July, 1800, are found accounts of many of these revivals. In West Simsbury, for instance, the awakening began suddenly and unexpectedly on the second Sabbath in October, 1798, with one young woman who became convinced that she was a sinner and was going to hell. She informed others of her convictions. "The next evening, at a conference," wrote the Reverend Jeremiah Hallock, "there was an unusual solemnity, and many were in tears. . . . On the ensuing sabbath, the work was visible in the house of God; and the conference in the evening was full and very serious. But one week before matters never appeared darker: but now the marvellous goings of the victorious Lamb were seen and felt." From this time on, the number of people affected increased. Conferences were set up in various parts of the parish; attendance at all religious meetings was large; weekly, and even daily, reports of hopeful conversions were received. Within a short time fifty-nine persons had made public professions.[6]

An increasing attention to religion was visible in Plymouth toward the end of 1798. Congregations were not only more numerous than usual but were more attentive to the sermons and to other parts of the service. Not until February, 1799, however, did anything further appear. Then "the spirit came like a mighty rushing wind, and seemed

5. Letter from E. D. Griffin, in Sprague, *Lectures on Revivals,* appendix, pp. 151–152.
6. *Conn. Evang. Mag.,* I, 136–142, 177–184.

to breathe on many at one and the same time." Sixty-one
persons were added to the church and about one hundred
baptized.[7] At Torrington an unusual solemnity was first
apparent at an evening meeting in December, 1798, when
the minister, Alexander Gillett, and two neighboring
clergymen were conducting the service. Here, it was reported, "some sinners, who had labored heretofore under
fears about their state, were more deeply and thoroughly
impressed," and inquired, "What shall I do to be saved?"
An increase in solemnity, concern, and conviction marked
the succeeding weeks, and the converts numbered forty-
five.[8]

The awakening in Northington originated in a group
of young people who invited the minister to attend a conference with them; while in Warren it began with religious
conferences which were held regularly on Sabbath evenings after March, 1799. In South Killingly the attention
dated from the visit of a former resident who brought reports of a religious stir in his New Hampshire home. In
Northington, "many confessed their sins, complained of
the hardness of their hearts, the abounding wickedness of
their lives; and appeared very sensibly to feel that it would
be just in God to cast them off forever." The revival in
Warren affected a number of people, "who before appeared to be far from the kingdom of God, were considered
very erroneous in their sentiments, and were supposed to
have imbibed opinions, which savored of Deism, and Universalism."[9]

Early in 1799 the Reverend Joseph Washburn of Farmington noticed "an uncommon attention and concern,
among the people of God, in view of the situation in their
Society, and . . . a disposition to unite in prayer for the
divine presence, and a revival of religion." Accordingly,
after advising with the deacons and the principal brethren
of the church, he decided to call a meeting for prayer and

7. *Ibid.*, II, 23–27, 60–67.   8. *Ibid.*, I, 131–136.
9. *Ibid.*, I, 100–101, 102–105; III, 225–231.

consultation. It was declared expedient to set apart times "for fervent social prayer that God would not pass us by." A revival resulted which brought sixty-one into the church within a year.[10] In a letter to his son the Reverend Ammi Robbins described the 1799 revival in Norfolk:

O my Son, the work of God increases marvellously among us —13 or 14 have obtained hope of mercy very lately. . . . The Conference last Thursday at the north Green (for not a third could get into the School house) was indeed attended with extraordinary manifestations of the *Presence* and *Power* of *Jehovah*—some sweetly rejoicing—others dreadfully distressed with a Sense of their horrible Guilt—and others awakened and in tears of distress—& others solemn & filled with astonishment—these my Son, are the Lord's Doings— every Day I am either attending Conferences in one part or another, or receiving visitants to talk about the State of their Souls—some who have hope—some in deep distress.[11]

Observers commented favorably on the improved conditions which they considered the results of these revivals. In one place, "Levity, balls and other similar diversions have been laid aside"; in another, "A general reformation of morals and sobriety of conduct are observable through the town"; in a third, "It [the awakening] appeared to make children more dutiful to their parents and respectful and kind to others and to one another." "Century Sermons" in 1801, which contained lengthy descriptions of the spiritual decline subsequent to the Great Awakening, closed on an optimistic note occasioned by the religious upturn. The first recognition of improvement in the General Association records appeared in 1800, when it was stated that "the report of the members of the Association happily evinces the State of religion and of our churches to be more encouraging than at any preceding period, for many years past; especially in regard to the awakening and renewing influences in the hearts of sinners in various places;

10. *Ibid.*, I, 378–386, 420–431.
11. A. Robbins to T. Robbins, June 1, 1799, Robbins Papers.

the purity of the work, and the harmony which is generally prevalent in our churches."[12]

Although the general religious enthusiasm in the state subsided somewhat in 1801, the next year a revival occurred at Yale College. For seven years Timothy Dwight had been lashing at infidelity and portraying the benefits of revealed religion.[13] Sometime prior to April 15, 1796, a group of undergraduates organized to improve moral conditions in the college, for on that day H. Belden, a Yale student, wrote to his friend, Thomas Robbins, "I have broken myself of the vulgar habit of swearing & the still more pernicious one of gambling. I expect at the next meeting of the Moralists I shall propose myself as a Candidate to enter."[14] In 1797 the Moral Society of Yale College was founded.[15] For a time, however, the membership of the college church showed no notable increase, and there was no revival until 1802. In the spring of that year a religious stir, viewed as the answer to the fervent prayers of a few, was felt among the students. "The salvation of the soul," wrote Professor C. A. Goodrich who made an exhaustive study of Yale revivals, "was the great subject of thought, of conversation, of absorbing interest; the convictions of many were pungent and overwhelming; and 'the peace in believing' which succeeded, was not less strongly marked." At no time during the awakening were the regular college exercises suspended, nor was preaching more frequent than usual. Of the two hundred thirty students then at Yale it was estimated that about one-third were converted. Sixty-three joined the college church,[16]

12. *Acts and Proceedings of the General Association of Connecticut, 1800,* p. 205.

13. Opposition to Dwight's theology in the Yale Corporation was sufficiently strong to prevent his appointment as professor of divinity until 1805, significantly the year when the Unitarian Henry Ware became professor of divinity at Harvard.

14. H. Belden to T. Robbins, April 15, 1796, Robbins Papers.

15. The MS. Journal of the Moral Society is in the Yale University Library.

16. Chauncey A. Goodrich, "Narrative of Revivals of Religion in Yale College," *American Quarterly Register,* X (1838), 295–296.

among them Benjamin Silliman, then a tutor, who wrote his mother, "Yale College is a little temple: prayer and praise seem to be the delight of the greater part of the students, while those who are still unfeeling are awed with respectful silence."[17]

These revivals in state and college marked only the beginning of a movement. A graph of its course in Connecticut during the succeeding quarter of a century would show not a sustained, straight line but a jagged curve representing the upward and downward trends natural to such a protracted period of religious attention. After 1802 high points were reached in 1807–1808, 1812, 1815–1816, 1820–1821, and 1825–1826. There was, however, no complete cessation of revivals during the three decades.

As the Reverend Bennet Tyler has pointed out, a remarkable uniformity may be observed in the origin and progress of these revivals, in the means employed to further them, in the behavior of the subjects both prior and subsequent to conversion, and in the "permanency of the fruits."[18] Brief extracts from a few of the multitudinous extant accounts will suffice, therefore, to give an adequate picture of the religious scene in Connecticut.

In 1807 and 1808, when it was recorded that the work of God was in evidence in practically every section of the state, the religious situation in Litchfield was among the most interesting. From the pens of both the town's minister, the Reverend Dan Huntington, and one of its leading laymen, Tapping Reeve, came descriptions of the "display of divine grace." Huntington wrote that for a number of months preceding the revival "the church had been gradually awakening from a state of slumber, and Laodicean lukewarmness, to some degree of Christian zeal in duty." Sometime in April or May, 1807, he preached a sermon to which unusual attention was given and which aroused a feeling of opposition to the character of God. This was considered a favorable omen. From this time a

17. G. P. Fisher, *Life of Benjamin Silliman,* I, 83.
18. Bennet Tyler, *New England Revivals,* p. vi.

deep attention to the great truths of religion developed, and at length it was decided to institute meetings for special prayer in the various districts of the society. "Scarcely had these prayer meetings travelled the circuit of the different districts in the society, before it was evident that God was visibly present among us." Sinners awakened to a sense of their danger and in the first stages of conviction were eager to do something to commend themselves to the favor of God. They soon learned that their strength was weakness, and that they must yield themselves to the disposal of sovereign grace. Then and then only could a conviction be followed by a hope, and this at the discretion of God. More than two hundred within a year were brought "out of the bondage of sin, into the glorious liberty of the children of God."[19]

Tapping Reeve described this Litchfield revival in a letter to his friend, Judge Boudinot of Newark. He wrote that while all who were awakened to a serious concern for their immortal interests were deeply impressed with a sense of the importance of religion and were well pleased to be in the hands of God, "there was a wide difference in the degree of distress which took place previous to the experiencing that submission of will to God, which all felt." Some violently opposed God's law and government while others did not; some were in distress for only a few days, while others were in sorrow for many months. Reeve saw few instances of sudden conversion. It was common for "subjects of this work" to complain that they were becoming stupid and had lost their convictions, and yet at this very time opposition to God disappeared. Unaware that their hearts were changed and uninformed by their hopeful friends, they observed "how widely different the exercises of their minds were, [and] finding . . . that what they used to hate they now loved, and what they used to love, they now hated, began to suspect that a real change had taken place; they hoped, however, with much trem-

19. *Connecticut Evangelical Magazine and Religious Intelligencer*, I, 155–157, 313–318.

bling, and gradually advanced to a steady, comfortable hope, with great caution and much examination."[20]

The New Haven churches, unaffected by the powerful awakening at Yale in 1802, experienced their first revivals in 1807 and 1808. Not until the summer of 1807 was it common to hear Christians express their hopes for an "outpouring of the Holy Spirit." That fall the two churches united to establish a monthly prayer meeting, and attempts were made to restore discipline. Conferences were inaugurated in December, and during the following February, March, and April attention to religion increased. In the smaller conferences there was free and familiar conversation on solemn and important subjects in which all were deeply interested. The larger conferences were more formal. "The exercises were prayer, the singing of psalms and hymns, the reading of the Scriptures, and conversations upon the passages of Scripture which were read. Sometimes a sermon, or some other religious production, were read instead of the Scriptures." As a result of the awakening one hundred forty persons were added to the First Church and one hundred seventy to the North (now the United) Church. One observer noted, "The converts were of all ages, and of all variety of characters which the town contained. Old and young, the moral and the profane, the enlightened and the ignorant, those who were favorably inclined toward revivals of religion and those who were vehemently opposed to them, speculative believers and determined Infidels, the regular and the vicious, were among the subjects of the work, and united most cordially in the reception and the profession of the same doctrines. They delighted in the same kind of preaching and united in seeking for happiness, whence alone it can be found, in the favor of God, as bestowed on man through the Divine Mediator."[21] After a delay which caused great anxiety to President Dwight, the awakening spread to the college. Of

20. Sermon preached by Joseph Eldridge, 1852, in *Proceedings of the North and South Consociations of Litchfield County*, pp. 141–142.

21. *Conn. Evang. Mag. and Relig. Intel.*, II, 96–104; *Panoplist*, VII, 113–118.

the thirty student converts, twenty-two of whom joined the college church, three-quarters went into the ministry after leaving college.[22]

On two other occasions during Dwight's presidency significant renewals of religious faith occurred at Yale. The first of these came in the winter of 1812–1813, when a number of undergraduates, many of them seniors, were led individually to reflect seriously on spiritual matters. What really brought on the revival was the remarkable change in one who, as Professor Goodrich has it, "though not openly vicious, had been to a high degree thoughtless and even profane; and whose warmth of feeling and energy of character, gave him great influence with most of the students." This was Elias Cornelius who, after graduation, as agent for the American Board of Commissioners for Foreign Missions and secretary of the American Education Society, was active in other phases of the Second Great Awakening. Nearly twenty students evidenced a genuine "change of heart" at this time.[23]

A more "fruitful" awakening began at the college in April, 1815. For four months secret prayer meetings had been held early every Sabbath morning at which earnest supplications for a manifestation of divine grace were made. At length it appeared that the prayers were answered. The immediate cause was the reading at evening prayers of a tract describing the death of Sir Francis Newport. Although not religiously inclined, the student to whom fell the duty of reading on that particular evening was so wrought up that he was in tears when he finished. The effect on the undergraduate body was immediate. "Nearly every individual in college, became anxious for the salvation of his soul; and those who had been most thoughtless seemed to be the most affected." Regular exercises were continued because it was considered unwise to lay aside ordinary employments, but more attention was

22. Goodrich, "Revivals of Religion in Yale College," *American Quarterly Register*, X (1838), 297–300.
23. *Ibid.*, pp. 300–301.

devoted to religious instruction. At one time it seemed that the entire college was under conviction, and approximately eighty experienced conversion.[24]

Shortly after the awakening had subsided at the college, and contemporaneously with a general attention to religion throughout the state, a remarkable "effusion of the Holy Spirit" occurred in the town of Salisbury. During the year 1816 the amazingly large total of one hundred seventy-two persons was received into the church. This was the more notable because the parish had had no settled minister since 1812. As in so many other cases, the "work" began in the hopes and prayers of a small group. By the first of September, 1815, it was evident that many were under conviction, and frequently the question, "What shall I do to be saved?" was heard. In the preliminary stages and during the early days of the revival the labor of ministers from nearby churches was adequate, but soon it became obvious that special assistance was needed. Therefore, the Reverend Asahel Nettleton, an active figure in Connecticut's Second Great Awakening of whom more will be said later, was invited to Salisbury. Here he sojourned for several months, and the number of converts testified to the effectiveness of his labors. In the account of the revival special emphasis was laid on the change which took place in its subjects, a change of life as well as of feeling. The people, it was asserted, became "better parents and better children, better husbands and better wives, and better in every situation in life. Many family altars have been erected, and many children have been instructed in religion, who, if they were before not taught, yet they were influenced by example, to walk in the paths of sin." This revival was distinguished, according to a contemporary, "for its stillness and solemnity, for deep conviction of conscience, for discriminating views of divine truth, for humility and subsequent stability of christian character."[25]

24. *Ibid.*, pp. 301–303.
25. *Religious Intelligencer*, I, 393–397; B. Tyler, *Memoir of the Life and Character of Rev. Asahel Nettleton*, p. 84.

Two further instances will suffice to illustrate the character of the revivals of Connecticut's Second Great Awakening. Among the many revivals of the years 1820 and 1821 perhaps the most remarkable occurred in New Haven and Farmington. In the former town the year 1820 began with no unusual interest in religious matters. Not until a Bible class was formed at Yale in April was a spirit of inquiry aroused. By the early part of July appearances were so favorable that a meeting was held for those who were anxious about their own salvation, and although only seventeen people assembled, the effects were immediate and powerful, and a series of such conferences was arranged. "These meetings," wrote the New Haven ministers, Nathaniel Taylor and Samuel Merwin, "were usually opened with a short address, after which all knelt and united in a short prayer. The ministers present then proceeded to converse with every individual, in a low tone of voice, so as not to interrupt each other, or break the solemn stillness of the scene. The meeting was then closed with suitable exhortation and a prayer. It is impossible to convey to those who have not witnessed such an assembly, an adequate idea of its impressive solemnity. There was evidently much emotion, although no noise—there were many tears, although no outbreaking of the agony of the mind, save in the expressive look and the half-stifled sigh." Meetings were held in private houses; conferences in the churches were frequent at which the object was "to impress the simple truth on the conscience; to show sinners, from the word of the living God, that they are guilty, condemned, lost, and must be miserable for ever without a change of heart; and that it is their duty immediately to submit to God, and become reconciled to him through the efficacy of atoning blood." Asahel Nettleton was present for several weeks, and the Reverend Lyman Beecher of Litchfield was very active. The life of the entire community was affected. "The profane swearer," wrote Taylor and Merwin, "has been struck dumb by a sense of guilt, and his oaths and curses given place to prayer and praise to God and the

Lamb. The scoffer has been taught to admire the grace he once despised, and the supercilious, sarcastic infidel prostrated at the foot of the cross, imploring mercy, as a ruined hell-deserving sinner." About one hundred eighty persons were added to the two Congregational churches.[26]

Even more "fruitful" was the revival in Farmington where two hundred twenty-four people made public professions of their faith. In the summer of 1820 the Reverend Noah Porter experienced some feeling of hope, but not until the following February did he sense a serious attention to religion. Thereupon Porter invited first a deputation from New Haven and then Asahel Nettleton to visit his church. At an "anxious meeting" on February 26, about one hundred seventy persons were present. By March 19 Porter knew of more than ninety of his flock who enjoyed hopes of conversion. The life of the town underwent a change. "From the various meetings which were attended," the Farmington minister recorded, "the people were accustomed to retire with little communication with each other, directly to their own fire-sides. Visiting for merely social purposes was suspended, and business, not immediately indispensable, was generally postponed. The great subject of attention among the body of people, appeared to be their salvation; in attending to this great concern they were generally disposed to be much alone; and were led spontaneously to take the pure word of God for their guide. The *Bible* was preferred to every other book, and was searched daily, and with eager enquiry." The attention to religion spread rapidly among all classes, and the awakening became one "which for its suddenness, its power, its extent, its purity, and its happy effects, has, it is believed, been rarely exceeded in our country."[27]

Following the 1820–1821 "outpourings of the Holy Spirit" there were intermittent revivals in Connecticut which reached another high point five years later. The revivals did not cease after 1826; indeed, in 1831, a brilliant

26. *Relig. Intel.*, V, 668–671.
27. Noah Porter, *Memorial of a Revival*, pp. 8, 18–21.

"display of divine grace" occurred. During the late 1820's, however, the successes of Charles Grandison Finney, the Presbyterian revivalist, in western and central New York brought to the attention of Connecticut people the methods which he employed to arouse religious interest. These were the celebrated New Measures, which included protracted meetings, the extensive use of "anxious seats," prayer for individuals by name, and the encouragement of women to talk in assemblies.[28] Since it was felt that such innovations would harm the revival movement, their introduction into New England was opposed. Lyman Beecher and Asahel Nettleton led the fight against Finney and his methods. They headed a delegation which met with the advocates of the New Measures in New Lebanon, New York, in 1827. They expressed their views in the pulpits, in letters, in the press, and in pamphlets. Beecher went so far as to issue an ultimatum to Finney. "I know your plan, and you know I do," the New England champion thundered. "You mean to come into Connecticut, and carry a streak of fire to Boston. But if you attempt it, as the Lord liveth, I'll meet you at the State line, and call out all the artillery-men, and fight every inch of the way to Boston, and then I'll fight you there."[29] In spite of this opposition the New Measures penetrated into Connecticut. Four-day meetings were held throughout the state in 1831 with great success.[30] A new era in revivalism was under way.

It is now in order to inquire more deeply into the origins of these revivals and to ask why they continued as they did for three decades. For many people of the time the answer was simple. The awakening, they felt, was the work of God, who moved in a mysterious way to revive drooping Christianity in Connecticut. Let one contemporary speak for the rest. "Thus the Lord, in his infinitely free and sov-

28. Emerson Davis, *The Half Century*, pp. 355–361; *Relig. Intel.*, XII, 456–459, 463–468, 513–517, 527–533.
29. Beecher, *Autobiography*, II, 101.
30. *Relig. Intel.*, XVI, 8, 62, 76–77, 237.

ereign grace, hath remembered us in our low estate, when iniquity was abounding, and the love of many was waxing cold. When the enemy was coming in among us like a flood, the spirit of the Lord hath set up a standard against him. This is the Lord's doings, and it is marvellous in our eyes."[31] Without being irreverent, one must scrutinize matters more carefully.

The determination of New Divinity ministers to do something about what they considered an alarming situation has been discussed. Since these neo-Edwardeans agreed with the Reverend Ammi Robbins, who remarked "that if God's people really desire he should grant them a gracious visit, they must humbly *ask* for it,"[32] in 1794 and 1795 there was state-wide consideration of a proposal, evidently originating with the Reverend David Austin and the Reverend Walter King, for concerts of prayer for revivals.[33] The Tolland County Association voted in October, 1795, "That this Association being anxiously impressed with the apparent decline of religion, unanimously agree to meet on the second Tuesday of each month, beginning with next November, for the purpose of special prayer for the outpouring of the Holy Spirit, and for other religious exercises."[34] Other county associations took similar action, and in 1797 a general revival period began. During the ensuing years the New Divinity group became increasingly dominant, for after the Old Divinity practices and practitioners had been once dislodged, their complete collapse was rapid. Accordingly, every effort was made to continue the revivals.

The fact that this New Divinity group was composed of remarkably able men helped to account for the awaken-

31. From the Reverend Peter Starr's account of the revival in Warren. *Conn. Evang. Mag.*, I, 101.

32. *Conn. Evang. Mag.*, I, 340.

33. Records of the Hartford County North, Fairfield County West, and Fairfield County East Associations, Congregational House, and of the New Haven County West Association, Yale University Library.

34. Records of the Tolland County Association, Congregational House.

ing. Timothy Dwight was the recognized leader until his death in 1817. Azel Backus evidenced such striking ability at Bethlehem that in 1812 he was called to the presidency of Hamilton College. Norfolk had Ammi R. Robbins, the town's first pastor, until 1816. The devoted shepherd of his affectionate flock, he was also the master of a school in his home to which many lads came for college preparation. Robbins' successor, Ralph Emerson, after declining the presidency of the newly organized Western Reserve College in Ohio, became in 1829 a professor in the Andover Theological Seminary. At Torringford was Samuel J. Mills, vigorous, effective, witty, and the father of a son who attained high rank among American Protestant saints. In 1791 Asahel Hooker was installed at Goshen where he preached "fruitfully" and instructed numerous candidates for the ministry until his health failed near the close of the first decade of the nineteenth century. His successor was the aggressive Joseph Harvey. To the town of New Hartford in 1795 came the dynamic Edward D. Griffin. After a colorful ministry here he preached in Newark and Boston, did pioneer work at the Andover Theological Seminary, and rescued Williams College from what seemed certain extinction while serving as its third president, 1821–1836. Ebenezer Porter labored valiantly in Washington until he was called to the Andover Seminary, of which institution he subsequently became president.

Lyman Beecher came to Litchfield in 1810 from a distinguished pastorate in East Hampton, Long Island. On him fell the mantle of leadership when Dwight died. There was also Heman Humphrey of Fairfield, later to be president of Amherst College and destined to strengthen this institution as Dwight strengthened Yale and Griffin Williams. Connecticut could boast, too, of Abel McEwen of New London, Nathan Strong, Abel Flint, and Joel Hawes of Hartford, Nathan Perkins of West Hartford, Noah Porter of Farmington, Samuel Merwin, Moses Stuart, and Nathaniel Taylor of New Haven, Calvin Chapin of Rocky

Hill, Wethersfield, Belazeel Pinneo of Milford, Moses Welch of Mansfield, Jeremiah Hallock of West Simsbury, and many others.

The one laborer in the awakening who was not a settled minister was the Reverend Asahel Nettleton.[35] A Yale graduate with the class of 1809, Nettleton early determined to devote his life to the cause of religion. He planned a missionary career, but because of his remarkable success as a revivalist in Connecticut, he was ordained as an evangelist to labor throughout the state. He possessed none of the characteristics which one frequently associates with evangelists. Not in any sense a haranguing, ranting enthusiast, he preached always the soundest of doctrines in the sternest of sermons. A contemporary who knew Nettleton well said of his addresses that they "were too plain to be misunderstood, too fervent to be unheeded, and too searching and convincing to be treated with indifference."[36] He insisted that people should gather quietly for meetings, that they should be quiet in their assemblies, and that they should disperse quickly and without disturbance. He never roused his listeners with passionate appeals, but rather inspired them with a desire for a new religious life by his intense sincerity. Of Nettleton one writer has said, "The central element and impelling force in his character was an uncommonly constant and firm belief of the realities of the invisible world, . . . and of the absolute necessity of regeneration and sanctification in order to save the soul. . . . He had comparatively no interest but in this one thing, the salvation of the soul."[37]

Nettleton was held in high regard by the Connecticut clergy, who soon learned that his appearance was almost the signal for a revival and who accordingly issued many invitations to him to visit their churches. In vacant par-

35. For the story of Nettleton's career, see Tyler, *Memoir of the Life and Character of Rev. Asahel Nettleton.*

36. Letter from N. Porter, in Sprague, *Lectures on Revivals,* appendix, p. 73.

37. Letter from the Reverend Edward Beecher, in W. B. Sprague, *Annals of the American Pulpit,* II, 553.

ishes, as well, his work was invaluable. The revival in Salisbury in 1816, to which reference has been made, was a striking example of his success. From 1812 to 1822, when his health failed, he labored in many parts of the state to promote a new interest in religion.

It is necessary to examine more than the roll of distinguished ministers, their attitude toward revivals, the doctrines which they preached, and the circumstances which prompted them to act, in order to explain the awakening. One should recall, first of all, the religious, economic, and social conditions in Connecticut which were discussed in the first chapter—a general conservatism, a long-settled, agricultural civilization, a strong religious tradition, an established church, a tightly organized Congregationalism dominant over relatively weak Episcopalian, Baptist, and Methodist sects. These combined to create a climate of opinion in which revivals could flourish.

The nature of the Connecticut revivals also helps to account for their continuance. During the Great Awakening the revivals, at first applauded, soon incurred popular disapproval, and the General Court of the colony as well as the General Association were impelled to take action against the revivalists. When these phenomena reappeared in the closing years of the eighteenth century, the widespread apprehension revealed the intense feeling which had been aroused a half-century earlier.[38] But the revivals of Connecticut's Second Great Awakening were of a different sort. They were quiet and subdued, unaccompanied by exuberance and physical manifestations. References to these characteristics were made in practically every revival account. The religious leaders, thoroughly acquainted with the Great Awakening, succeeded in avoiding the developments which had marred the earlier period.

Meetings were held in churches or in the homes of the faithful; neither the outdoor gatherings of the Great

---

38. The fear and distrust exhibited when the revivals began in the last decade of the eighteenth century are mentioned in Samuel W. S. Dutton, *The History of the North Church in New Haven, 1742–1842*, p. 106 note.

Awakening nor the three- and four-day camp meetings of the frontier occurred among Connecticut Congregationalists at this time. The groves did not become God's temples. In all gatherings there was an insistence on calm, austere behavior. People assembled quietly and dispersed in the same manner. The ministers indulged in no haranguing, no emotional appeals, no oratorical pyrotechnics. In a dignified manner they preached the neo-Edwardean doctrines.

No special group of evangelists took the field to labor for revivals. With one exception, as has been indicated, the work was entirely in the hands of settled ministers. Sometimes the pastors of parishes in which there was an attention to religion were invited to churches in which a spiritual stir seemed imminent. Sometimes three or four ministers labored, by invitation, in a nearby community where an awakening was under way, their combined efforts being needed to converse with those who were seeking the road to salvation. There were no lay preachers, no itinerants, no ministers from outside the state. Although Connecticut revivals were not spectacular, they were very effective. They were approved by legislators, clergymen, and people in all strata of society; everything possible was done to prolong these "visitations of divine grace" which were adding vitality to Connecticut's religious life.

That the Connecticut revivals were part of a general awakening both in the United States and in England was also a factor explaining them. The Second Great Awakening must be regarded as an important chapter in the history of cultural relations between Europe and America. Its origins, as has been demonstrated, lay in part in the reaction against Europe's Age of Reason and certain aspects of the French Revolution. There was also a connection with the British Evangelical Revival of the eighteenth century. For example, revivals in England were followed by revivals in the United States, and, as will be shown later, missionary activities in England by missionary activities in the United States, and the British and Foreign Bible Society by the American Bible Society. Nor did culture-borrowing end here. Political independence, fortunately, did not mean cultural independence. Within the United States religious phenomena such as revivals tended to be very contagious. From religious magazines, religious news in secular papers, letters, and visitors, people learned of awakenings in widely scattered parts of the United States as well as in their own state. Frequently, the knowledge that there was a revival in a nearby town turned attention to spiritual subjects and caused the faithful to pray for a similar development in their own community. Revivals took on the characteristics of an epidemic, a fact of which ministers were not unaware.

A final cause of the long revival period lay in the fact that this Awakening was not merely a series of these religious phenomena. As will be pointed out in later chapters, the new religious spirit found expression, among other things, in missionary activities, the distribution of Bibles, and humanitarianism, which in turn furnished impetus for the continuation of the revivals.

In connection with the revivals it should be inquired whether there was any relation between them and political, economic, and military developments in Connecticut. The Embargo, 1807–1809, seriously affected the state's commerce and provoked vigorous protests in many quarters, but the revivals flourished without interruption or diminution in zeal. Although the War of 1812 broke out in a year of numerous "outpourings," its imminence did not prevent their appearance nor did the commencement of hostilities put a stop to them. No such religious setback occurred as was the case during the eighteenth-century wars. Peace in turn brought a boom which culminated in the panic of 1819. Still, the years 1815–1816 saw many revivals, while the inauguration of the *Religious Intelligencer* and the beginning of religious news columns in secular newspapers in 1816 testified to the public interest in the subject of religion. Perhaps there is some significance in the fact, already noted, that high points in the revival movement came in 1807–1808, 1812, 1815–1816, and 1820–1821. In such disturbed periods people may have been more disposed to give attention to religious matters. But it should be observed that revivals were plentiful in other years and that in general the sermons preached contained no references to the problems of the day.

The struggle between Republicans and Federalists took place in Connecticut during this period. That the Congregational clergy were Federalists and that they viewed Republicanism with alarm because it was linked in their minds with the rise of infidelity has already been shown. Influenced in their political thinking by their religious beliefs, these men opposed Republicanism and worked for revivals. In this sense only was the threat of Republicanism a factor in causing the Connecticut awakening; there is no evidence for believing that religious means were used for political ends. Religion must be kept in mind when attempting to explain Federalism—in Connecticut at any rate.

Although the Federalists remained in power in Connecticut for a longer period than elsewhere, they disappeared as a party soon after the Republican victory of 1817. The following year a constitution supplanting the charter of 1662, which had been the state's basic law, was framed and approved by the voters. By this constitution religion was disestablished; no longer were people required to contribute to its support. This raises two interesting questions. How did it happen that disestablishment occurred contemporaneously with a growing interest in religion? What was the relationship between disestablishment and the revivals?

Much of the story of the struggle for constitutional reform would have to be retold if this apparent paradox, separation of church and state at a time when the Congregational churches were being strengthened, were to be explained fully. This is manifestly impossible here, but one point which throws light on the situation will be discussed briefly. The Congregational clergy do not seem to have participated to any great extent in this contest which resulted in disestablishment.

In the last decade of the eighteenth century and the early years of the nineteenth, Connecticut ministers entered the political arena and from their pulpits assailed Republicanism. They were fighting for revealed religion against opponents who in their estimation were the supporters of infidelity. There is practically no evidence to show that the clergy were similarly active in the years of conflict prior to the 1818 reform, when the established church was at stake. The records of the General Association and of the county associations reveal no discussion of the proposed separation of church and state, no resolutions, no campaign strategy. There seem to have been practically no sermons on the subject, and no pamphlets even in an age of pamphlets. The Federalist newspapers whose columns were open to the ministers contained almost nothing from their pens. Nothing appeared in the *Religious Intelligencer*. An examination of available correspondence has yielded nothing. Thomas Robbins, who abhorred Republicanism, deplored the situation in his *Diary* but noted no agitation or action. About the sole evidence of clerical activity, except for that in Beecher's *Autobiography*, was penned by the Reverend S. W. S. Dutton in *Contributions to the Ecclesiastical History of Connecticut*. He wrote that he had lately read a sermon preached by Beecher during the period when the new constitution was pending in which the Litchfield pastor eloquently described the plan of leaving religion to voluntary support "as one which would open the floodgates of ruin on the state."[39]

In *The Development of Religious Liberty in Connecticut*, Miss Greene wrote of "the clergy, led by President Dwight, Simon Backus, Isaac Lewis, John Evans, and a host of secondary men who turned their pulpits into lec-

39. *Contributions to the Ecclesiastical History of Connecticut*, p. 122. The present writer has been unable to locate Beecher's sermon and does not know its date.

ture desks and the public fasts and feasts into electioneering occasions."[40] Dwight was certainly a leader and his actions at the turn of the century would warrant Miss Greene's comments. Evidence is lacking, however, to show that the Yale president, although a staunch Federalist and no friend of disestablishment, performed in this manner for at least a decade prior to his death in 1817. Indeed, preaching in 1812 Dwight lamented the way in which politics had engulfed religion. "My friends and brethren," he queried, "will party politics carry you to heaven? Has Christ said, '*He that is a Federalist, he that is a Democrat, shall be saved?*' . . . Believe me: this preference of politics to Religion *is not of the Father, but of the world.*"[41] Revealing is the letter written in February, 1844, by John Cotton Smith to the Reverend W. B. Sprague in reply to the latter's request for information about Dwight. Smith had been the last of the so-called "Puritan governors," the Federalist who was defeated by the Republican-backed Wolcott in 1817. Had Dwight been the great politician that he has been pictured, his association with Smith would have been frequent and close. Yet Smith declared that he was unable to furnish any new information about the former Yale president. "My intercourse with him was official, rather than intimate and confidential," the ex-governor wrote. "When the Legislature sat at New Haven, it was during the autumnal vacation at Yale College, and the doctor was generally absent on an excursion for his health. . . . Our intercourse became more frequent, while I occupied the executive chair of the state, and was, ex-officio, a member of the [Yale] corporation; but you are sensible there is more of form than of familiarity in meetings of such bodies. Still we occasionally corresponded, and I have been in various ways favoured

40. Greene, *The Development of Religious Liberty in Connecticut*, p. 435.

41. T. Dwight, *A Discourse in Two Parts, delivered on the National Fast, August, 1812*, pp. 42–44.

with the means of forming a high estimate of his character."[42]

Isaac Lewis, Simon Backus, and John Evans were the others cited by Miss Greene as those who led the clergy. Isaac Lewis of Greenwich was a preacher of some distinction, but he was not one of the aggressive leaders. Simon Backus had no standing whatsoever in Connecticut. True, in 1804 he published a pamphlet entitled *A Dissertation on the Right and Obligation of the Civil Magistrate to take care of the Interest of Religion, and provide for its support,* but at the time he was a minister without a charge, for he had been dismissed in 1801 from his small North Bristol (now North Madison) church. He died in 1816, having been supported by contributions from his fellow-ministers during his latter years.[43] The name of John Evans does not appear among the Congregational ministers listed in *Contributions to the Ecclesiastical History of Connecticut.*

Richard J. Purcell has discussed the political activities of the Congregational ministers in his *Connecticut in Transition, 1775–1818.* While no one would deny that these men were strong supporters of Federalism and probably of the established church and that they must have had something to say on political subjects, it should be noted that Purcell has only two references to ministerial writings or actions in the years immediately preceding 1818. And about both these references questions must be raised.

The Reverend Abel Flint of Hartford in 1816, Purcell writes, urged the legislature to preserve unimpaired "those civil and religious institutions for which the state is so long and justly celebrated." This injunction, according to Purcell's footnote, was contained in the *Connecticut Cou-*

42. *The Correspondence and Miscellanies of the Hon. John Cotton Smith,* p. 172.

43. F. B. Dexter, *Biographical Sketches of the Graduates of Yale College,* II, 571–572.

rant for April 30, 1816. A careful examination of this issue of the *Courant* reveals nothing from the pen of the Hartford minister. The words attributed to Flint do appear, however, in a sermon which he preached on May 9, 1816. He was not engaged in any electioneering against disestablishment. He was preaching the annual Election Sermon, and he expressed sentiments common to all such sermons for at least three decades. "May the Honorable Council and House of Representatives adopt, from time to time," Flint counselled, "such regulations as shall be wisely calculated to restrain the wicked,—to discountenance iniquity of every kind,—to promote truth and justice between man and man,—and to preserve, unimpaired, those civil and religious institutions, for which this state has been so long and so justly celebrated."[44]

The second reference was to Lyman Beecher. Beecher was apparently more of a politician than most. In November, 1812, he wrote to his friend, the Reverend Asahel Hooker, "I am persuaded the time has come when it becomes every friend of this state to wake up and exert his whole influence to save it from innovation and democracy."[45] Two years later one of his congregation recorded, "Thanksgiving Day—As usual *Dr. Beecher* gave us an excellent sermon a little dashed with politics." And again a few days later, "Thursday 15 A general concert of prayer on account of the setting of the convention at Hartford—*Mr. Beecher* had meetings in our school two of the best political addresses I ever heard—he ran over in a masterly manner—the causes of our misfortune—the dangers that presented themselves and the means of preventing them."[46] In April, 1817, Beecher wrote at length to Nathaniel Taylor. "How do you do in these days of Tol-

44. Purcell, *Connecticut in Transition,* p. 340; Abel Flint, *A Sermon, preached at the Anniversary Election* (1816), pp. 20–21.

45. Beecher, *Autobiography,* I, 257.

46. Emily N. Vanderpoel, compiler, *More Chronicles of a Pioneer School, from 1792 to 1833, being added History on the Litchfield Female Academy kept by Miss Sally Pierce and her Nephew, John Pierce Brace* (New York, 1927), pp. 111–112.

eration?" he inquired. "I am more and more convinced
that we must attack and defend by tracts. These are
anonymous; and call no names; cheap, and easily multi-
plied; short, and easily read; plain, and easily understood; numerous, and capable of being spread everywhere." Then even Beecher went on, "But, on the whole, I
have concluded to give up the ship, not to enemies who
have determined to take it, but to Christ, who, I doubt
not, will save it from being buried in the waves, and from
being boarded and borne away in triumph by the wicked."[47]

Beecher's *Autobiography* is the chief source for all those
who portray the Connecticut clergy as ardent politicians,[48]
especially a paragraph in which, referring to developments about 1812, he wrote, "The ministers had always
managed things themselves, for in those days the ministers
were all politicians. They had always been used to it from
the beginning. On election day they had a festival. All the
clergy used to go, walk in procession, smoke pipes, and
drink. And, fact is, when they got together, they would
talk over who should be governor, and who lieutenant governor, and who in the Upper House, and their counsels
would prevail."[49] This is far from the truth, for a governor usually remained in office until his death when he was
succeeded by the lieutenant governor, while the latter office was ordinarily filled from the upper house or council.
This was the key to the Connecticut Standing Order and
was one of the reasons why ambitious young men seeking
more rapid political advance than was possible in the state
moved in such large numbers to the frontier. Beecher himself in paragraphs immediately following the statement on
which historians have relied so heavily describes how in

47. Beecher, *Autobiography*, I, 336–337.
48. See, for example, Adams, *New England in the Republic*, p. 318;
Greene, *The Development of Religious Liberty in Connecticut*, p. 402;
Morse, *A Neglected Period of Connecticut's History*, p. 3; Purcell, *Connecticut in Transition*, p. 323; George Stewart, *A History of Religious
Education in Connecticut to the Middle of the Nineteenth Century*,
p. 234.
49. Beecher, *Autobiography*, I, 259.

1811 that friend of the ministers, John Treadwell, in a manner most untraditional was set aside by the lawyers after serving somewhat over one term as governor and a more congenial candidate nominated and elected to the governorship.[50] Beecher's *Autobiography*, written several decades after the events, must be used with greater care than has frequently been the case.

How is this relative indifference to the struggle over disestablishment to be explained? No definitive answer can be given, but several points will be mentioned which undoubtedly were contributing factors. The *American Mercury* declared in 1803 that the clergy had subsided in obedience to a dictum from "Pope" Dwight who felt that his subordinates had been more zealous than discreet.[51] This statement by the chief Republican organ in the state cannot be taken too seriously. Lyman Beecher, writing long after 1818, declared that "there was a considerable period in which the Congregational ministers agreed to hold back and keep silent till the storm blew over," but he gave no reason for this action.[52]

Perhaps after the American Revolution the Congregational ministers were not the arch-politicians that they have been pictured. Three legislative acts of the 1790's indicate that they had no stranglehold on politics. The first of these was the grant of funds to Yale in 1792 on condition that the governor, the lieutenant governor, and the six senior assistants in the Council should be ex-officio trustees or fellows. Those who controlled the destinies of the college at the time were pleased to obtain the much-needed money, and they could observe that the lay politicos thus introduced into the Yale corporation were orthodox Congregationalists who would want to strengthen and perpetuate traditions rather than to revolutionize, and that moreover this lay element constituted a minority.[53]

50. *Ibid.*, I, 260.
51. Quoted in Purcell, *Connecticut in Transition*, p. 318.
52. Beecher, *Autobiography*, I, 346.
53. *The Literary Diary of Ezra Stiles*, III, 457.

But it should be noted that the ministers received the grant for Yale only by yielding some of their control over the college.

Two events of greater import were crowded into the May, 1795, meeting of the state legislature.[54] One of these was the repeal of an act, passed in October, 1793, by which the money to be received from the sale of western lands was to be set aside as a permanent fund for the support of ministers and "schools of education." Opposition to this act had arisen immediately after its passage, for many people disliked this concession to the clergy, especially those who saw that the Congregationalists would get the lion's share. At both the spring and fall legislative sessions in 1794 the lower house reversed its 1793 vote, but on both occasions the Council demurred. Timothy Dwight preached eloquently for a continuation of this measure in his Thanksgiving Sermon for 1794.[55] Nevertheless, the anticlerical forces won the day in 1795, and the money was set aside for the support of schools only. Little solace was found in the "sop" thrown to the religious elements in an article which declared that the funds could be diverted to the support "of the christian Ministry of the public worship of God" by a two-thirds vote of any society.[56]

By this same act of 1795 a new method of supervision for the schools of the state was authorized. Since 1712 the parishes or ecclesiastical societies had directed the public educational institutions, which had meant that people con-

54. *Acts and Laws of the State of Connecticut, 1784–1795*, pp. 487–489. This matter is fully discussed in Henry Barnard, "History of the Legislation of Connecticut respecting Common Schools, down to 1838," *Annual Report of the Superintendent of Common Schools of Connecticut, 1853*, pp. 5–167.

55. Quoted in *ibid.*, pp. 97–100.

56. Only one society, Kensington in the town of Berlin, seems to have voted such a diversion of funds, and the legislature negatived its petition. Connecticut Archives, Ecclesiastical Affairs, Second Series, 1666–1820, I, 27, Connecticut State Library. Article Eight of the 1818 Constitution which dealt with the School Fund contained no such clause. See *The Public Statute Laws of the State of Connecticut, Revision of 1821*, p. 30.

nected with the churches had hired the teachers and set the courses, and that ministers had had much to say about school matters. By the 1795 law, however, the state was divided into special school societies, composed of all the voters within their limits, to which were entrusted the powers formerly exercised by the parishes. This transfer of control, made more complete by a supplementary law in 1798,[57] was a blow to the clergy, the more so since the 1795 act specifically stipulated that ecclesiastical societies at their meetings might "transact any business relating to the ministry and the public worship of God, according to the law; but shall have no power to act on the subject of schooling." Had it not been for the Second Great Awakening, one wonders, in view of these developments, whether disestablishment might not have come at an earlier date than it did.

The ministers attacked Republicanism as a part of their campaign against infidelity, but the Republicans soon demonstrated that they were not determined to destroy public order and moral principles. Perhaps the Awakening with its revivals and numerous organizations and enterprises may have engrossed the ministers so completely that they had little time for political exertions. Calvin Chapin, one of the state's leading clergymen, in March, 1818, considered turning down an appointment to the Board of Examinations of Yale. "There is now an excitement among my people," he wrote to Jeremiah Day, then president of the college, "which demands every moment of my time. I do not call it, as yet, a revival—but there seems to be an uncommon preparation for such an event. Should this continue, I doubt whether it will be possible for me to attend the examination in May."[58] Long-continued Republican successes in the national field may have had some effect, as well as the increase in their numbers within the state, some of whom undoubtedly contributed to the many

57. *Acts and Laws of the State of Connecticut, 1796–1799*, pp. 481–484.
58. C. Chapin to J. Day, March 30, 1818, Day Papers, Yale University Library.

religious enterprises of the time. The ministers realized that they were accused of being too politically minded and may have decided to restrain themselves. The Hartford Convention of 1814 discredited the Federalists, and the preachers may have felt that under the circumstances silence was the better part of valor. Perhaps they saw that disestablishment was inevitable and did not want to fight in a losing cause. After all, church and state had been separated in every other state except Massachusetts.

The fact that a number of churches no longer relied on taxes for their support has been mentioned.[59] Furthermore, as will be indicated in later chapters, the Awakening developed extensively the principle of voluntary support of religious institutions, and as a result of the new religious spirit the ministers had every reason to feel that the churches could face the future without fear. Certainly the First Church of Hartford seems to have been unconcerned about the effects of disestablishment when in 1817 it was faced with an unusually heavy financial burden in pensioning the veteran Nathan Strong and hiring his successor at a good salary.[60] Aeneas Monson, Jr., a layman of New Haven, in writing to David Daggett in April, 1816, asserted, "I am more concerned about the *State* than *Church* the Latter is in Prosperity like a City on a Hill—but the former seems to be threatened with the angry passions of Jacobinic fury—fomented by artful and designing men thursting [*sic*] for office."[61] Perhaps it was not so much of a paradox to have had disestablishment at a time when religion was strong. Even the orthodox Congrega-

59. See page 9 above. In 1814 Beecher said, "The vital principle of our system, that every man shall pay according to his property, somewhere, for the support of religious instruction, as a public civil benefit, and for the preservation of morals, and good order, in the state, is gone." Beecher, *A Sermon delivered at Woolcot . . . at the Installation of Rev. J. Keyes,* p. 12.

60. George L. Walker, *History of the First Church in Hartford, 1633–1883,* pp. 364, 370–371.

61. A. Monson, Jr., to David Daggett, April 1, 1816, Daggett Papers, Yale University Library. Samuel Merwin, New Haven minister, wrote a number of letters to Daggett but said nothing about politics.

tional minister, Ebenezer Porter, in a letter of April 29, 1817, to Jeremiah Day wrote, "Do not the prospects of Yale College brighten with the election of O. Wolcott?"[62] Wolcott, it will be remembered, was the Toleration Party's candidate for the governorship who defeated the Federalist, John Cotton Smith, in 1817.

After this rather lengthy consideration of the fact that disestablishment took place during a revival period, it is necessary to turn to the second question and to examine other aspects of the relationship between disestablishment and the revivals. There is no reason to believe that the Congregational ministers inspired revivals either to defeat their opponents or to increase church membership and thus provide a cushion in case compulsory support of religion should be discontinued. In all the bitter struggle waged by Republicans, disgruntled Federalists, Episcopalians, Baptists, and Methodists for constitutional reform no such charge was brought against the Congregational clergy.

Disestablishment became a fact in 1818. A recent writer on Connecticut history has asserted that the powerful revivals of 1820–1821 were called into being by the ministers both to repair the damage done to the Congregational churches by the constitutional change, and to prevent the other sects from making inroads upon their membership. "The dread of infidelity," he writes, "brought about a temporary and unsuccessful attempt to maintain some measure of the special bond that had once connected church and state."[63] Such a position is untenable. These revivals were simply part of a movement which began in the closing years of the preceding century. Nothing new as to procedure, nature of meetings, or manner of preaching was introduced. If these revivals had been connected with disestablishment, somewhere in prayers, sermons, or accounts of revivals would appear thanks to God for thus

62. E. Porter to J. Day, April 29, 1817, Day Papers.
63. Morse, *A Neglected Period of Connecticut's History*, p. 125.

having rescued His churches from the hands of those who would have destroyed them. Such sentiments were not expressed. Disestablishment seems to have been taken very calmly, and even Lyman Beecher later wrote that separation of church and state was the best thing that could have happened to Connecticut.[64]

That the Connecticut revivals were part of a general awakening tends to allay more completely any suspicions that might be directed against the Congregational ministers. As has been indicated, revivals appeared throughout the country. Furthermore, within the state the Baptists and Methodists had revivals and, along with the Episcopalians, made substantial gains. These religious phenomena were not the special creation of the Congregational clergy for their own benefit.

As a result of the revivals a new interest in spiritual matters evidenced itself in Connecticut, and to a large extent the fears of orthodox Christians were dispelled. How many Congregational churches were affected during the three decades, how many people were added to them, it is impossible to determine. Nearly every church in the state must have experienced a religious stir to some extent. Figures already given afford some information regarding the number of converts. A few more figures will be of interest.[65]

In June, 1810, reports to the General Association indicated that during the preceding year about sixteen hundred persons had joined the churches.[66] The 1816 report breathed enthusiasm about a year which had been distinguished by extensive revivals. Eleven of the sixteen parishes in the Fairfield County West Association had been "refreshed," while in the Litchfield County North Association twelve hundred had been "brought into the king-

64. Beecher, *Autobiography*, I, 344.

65. It is essential to remember that these gains occurred during a period when there was no great increase in the state's population, which was 251,002 in 1800 and 297,675 in 1830.

66. *Extracts from the Minutes of the General Association, 1810*, p. 12 note.

dom" of whom six hundred had already made confessions.[67] In the year 1821 between eighty and one hundred of the somewhat over two hundred Congregational churches were "signally blessed." In the Hartford County North Consociation alone nineteen of the twenty congregations were "visited with divine favor," as a result of which one thousand members were added, and three or four hundred more hopefully converted. Powerful revivals appeared in the eastern part of the state during the following two years. Asahel Nettleton wrote that sixteen or eighteen churches were affected and that more than thirteen hundred people experienced a "saving change."[68]

Gains made by various churches reveal the power of the revivals. In five "outpourings" at the Canton church during the ministry of Jeremiah Hallock, 1785–1826, 268 persons made public professions. Exactly the same number were added to the Goshen church in seven revivals between 1799 and 1828, while during this period a total of 488 became church members in Norfolk.[69] During Samuel Merwin's ministry in the North (now the United) Church in New Haven, 1805–1831, 932 accessions were made as compared with 524 during the much longer period, 1742–1805. Joel Hawes, who became pastor of the Hartford First Church in 1818, wrote in 1832 that 550 people had joined the church in those fourteen years, no fewer than four-fifths of whom were "fruits" of revivals.[70]

Some other figures may be given to advantage. The church in Killingworth which had a membership of 207 in 1818 increased by 107 in the 1821 awakening. To the 216 members of the Norfolk church in 1816 were added 103

67. *Proceedings of the General Association of Connecticut, 1816,* pp. 13–18.

68. Letter from N. Porter, in Sprague, *Lectures on Revivals,* appendix, p. 71; *Relig. Intel.,* VI, 406–410; VIII, 462–463.

69. *Ibid.,* XII, 651–652, 731; MSS. notes in the Congregational House, compiled by the Reverend William H. Moore, secretary of the Missionary Society of Connecticut, 1864–1899.

70. Dutton, *History of the North Church in New Haven, 1742–1842,* p. 127; letter from Joel Hawes, in Sprague, *Lectures on Revivals,* appendix, p. 57.

by a revival in the same year. The Farmington church
had its membership of 200 more than doubled by the
1820–1821 revival. The membership of the Old Saybrook
church was 69 in 1783, 196 in 1818, and 326 in 1832, the
increase in large part being due to extensive revivals in
1810, 1827, and 1830. The Sharon church had 94 members in 1804 and 215 in 1835; a revival in 1822–1823 had
added 150.[71]

These revivals constituted only one phase of Connecticut's Second Great Awakening. The other aspects, which
will be discussed in succeeding chapters, were the result, in
part at least, of the religious spirit which they engendered.

71. The Reverend W. H. Moore's MSS. notes.

IV

GOING OVER INTO MACEDONIA

DISTINGUISHED by the way in which the revived religious spirit was translated into varied activities and permanent institutions, the Second Great Awakening marked the beginning of the Protestant missionary movement in the United States. Throughout the settled areas of the country people were moved both to make efforts to convert the heathen and to answer the age-old cry of those who want spiritual assistance, "Come over into Macedonia, and help us."[1]

Missionary endeavors were by no means innovations in the closing years of the eighteenth and the early years of the nineteenth century, nor were they indigenous to America. From its earliest days the Christian religion had been a missionary venture, and its widespread dissemination was the result of missionary labors. The earliest voyages of discovery in the fifteenth century possessed a missionary flavor, while zealous Catholic fathers played an important rôle in exploring the innermost parts of the American continent in the sixteenth and seventeenth centuries. In 1649 the same Parliament which voted the beheading of Charles I established the first English Protestant missionary society by creating what was known as "The President and Society for Propagation of the Gospel in New England." After the Revolution of 1688 three new ventures were launched, the Society for Promoting Christian Knowledge (1698), the Society for the Propagation of the Gospel in Foreign Parts (1701), and "The Associates of Dr. Bray" (1723). These were designed to keep the Anglican fires burning among the American colonists and to encourage "the Christian education of our

1. Acts 16.9.

Negro and Indian children." Of the three, the second, the famous S.P.G., did the most extensive work.

During the colonial period other phases of missionary activities appeared in America.[2] The Moravian work represented a chapter in itself. There were also the missions to the Indians led by John Eliot, "apostle to the Indians," who received help from the society founded in 1649. Connecticut shared in these endeavors among the aborigines. In the seventeenth century the Reverend James Fitch of Norwich labored among the neighboring Mohegans after mastering their language, while in the following century Connecticut produced the melancholy and introspective David Brainerd, who after brief sojourns among the Indians in Massachusetts and New York moved on to pioneer ventures in New Jersey. From Connecticut came also Samuel Kirkland, who founded in Clinton, New York, Oneida Academy which in time became Hamilton College, and Eleazar Wheelock, who conducted in Lebanon (now Columbia), Connecticut, an Indian school which when later transferred to New Hampshire was known as Dartmouth College.[3]

Missionary in spirit was the frequent supplying in vacant parishes by neighboring ministers, eager to help congregations without the "means of grace." As early as 1774 the Connecticut General Association gave attention to the new settlements which were springing up to the north and west,[4] but the outbreak of hostilities with England the next year made it impossible to send out the two men whose appointment had been approved. During the Revolution the subject was discussed but no action was taken.

Against this background the American Protestant missionary movement was inaugurated in the late eighteenth

2. See chapter I of Oliver W. Elsbree, *The Rise of the Missionary Spirit in America, 1790–1815,* for an account of these pioneer missionary societies.

3. The Society in Scotland for Propagating Christian Knowledge, founded in 1709, assisted these eighteenth-century ventures among the Indians. See Elsbree, *Rise of the Missionary Spirit,* pp. 16–17.

4. *Records of the General Association, 1738–1799,* pp. 79–81.

and early nineteenth centuries. The Connecticut chapter, one of the most important in these pioneer endeavors, may be written in terms of three societies, the Missionary Society of Connecticut (1798), organized to send missionaries to the new settlements and to the Indians; the American Board of Commissioners for Foreign Missions (1810), which was concerned with work in the foreign field and which took over the Indian enterprise; and the Domestic Missionary Society of Connecticut (1816), founded for the purpose of building up hitherto neglected "waste places" within the state.

The organization of the first of these societies, the Missionary Society of Connecticut, came after an active decade following the state's ratification of the federal Constitution in 1788. That interest in the new settlements had been evidenced by the General Association in 1774 and 1780 has already been indicated, but not until 1787 and 1788 was there definite action. Then, in response to appeals from settlers recently moved to the frontier, the county associations appointed missionaries for brief tours in New York and Vermont. To Vermont went the Reverend Seth Williston and the Reverend Amos Fowler, sent by the New Haven County West Association. The New Haven County East Association dispatched Branford's minister, Samuel Eells, to New York where he made his way westward as far as Fort Stanwix. While the Reverend Achilles Mansfield was sent to Vermont by the Middlesex County Association, the Reverend Nathan Perkins fulfilled a ten weeks' mission to the north for the Hartford County North Association. Supported by the Litchfield County Association the Reverend Jeremiah Day spent two weeks in Vermont. All these early missionaries were settled ministers whose churches were cared for during their absences by neighboring pastors.[5]

After four years without organization, it was felt that

5. Edwin P. Parker, *Historical Discourse in Commemoration of the One Hundredth Anniversary of the Missionary Society of Connecticut,* pp. 8–9.

greater efficiency would result if the General Association assumed a supervisory capacity, and if a general appeal for financial aid were made. Accordingly, in 1792 the General Association appointed a Committee on Missions, consisting of Ezra Stiles, Jonathan Edwards, Jr., and Nathan Williams, to direct the missionary enterprise.[6] To secure the necessary funds permission was obtained from the state legislature to have annual contributions in the churches for a period of three years. Such legislative approval was needed because without it the circulation of a brief for funds in a town or society was prohibited "unless it be on some special Occasion, for any distressed or afflicted Person of their own inhabitants."[7]

Thus constituted, and financed by a contribution taken in May, 1793, whereby £382 9s. 1¼d. ($1,274.86) was raised in 165 churches, including one Baptist and two Episcopal congregations, the Committee on Missions went to work. In 1793 nine missionaries were employed in Vermont and eastern New York. The following year, when £409 4s. 4d. ($1,364.71) was collected, thirteen men worked in the areas just mentioned as well as in northern Pennsylvania and western New Hampshire. During the six years of its existence this Committee sent twenty-two different men to the frontier settlements, some of whom received more than one appointment. It continued the policy, instituted by the county associations, of appointing as missionaries for two-month or four-month tours ministers who were settled in Connecticut churches.[8]

In the last decade of the eighteenth century there occurred in England developments which profoundly af-

6. *Records of the General Association, 1738–1799*, pp. 138, 141.

7. *Acts and Laws, Revision of 1796*, p. 58. This law was not repealed until 1825. Miss Greene gives the following inadequate explanation of the "appeal" to the legislature: "The Association hesitated to take up such a collection in all the churches, dissenting or Established, without such permission." Greene, *The Development of Religious Liberty in Connecticut*, p. 386.

8. *Report of the Directors of the Missionary Society of Connecticut for the Year 1880*, pp. 8–9; *Records of the General Association, 1738–1799*, pp. 154–166.

fected the Connecticut missionary movement.[9] In 1792 the Baptist Missionary Society was founded under the leadership of the famous William Carey, who sailed to India the following year as the first Protestant missionary to that section of the world. American interest in Carey was great, but New England was stirred even more deeply when in 1795 the English Independents, Presbyterians, and Episcopalians established the London Missionary Society. Then took place one of the many examples of culture-borrowing which featured the Second Great Awakening. The news of the English activity, added to the realization that the demands of the frontier were becoming excessive for the Committee on Missions, led to the next step in Connecticut in 1798.[10] This development, significantly, was practically simultaneous with the beginning of the revivals.

In 1797 the General Association had published in pamphlet form an address on the subject of a missionary society, which not only contained extracts from accounts of English missionary activities and called attention to the inadequacy of the Committee on Missions, but also requested the county associations to deliberate on plans for more satisfactory support of missionaries.[11] Immediately, the Hartford County North Association established a missionary society.[12] Action was therefore expected when the General Association held its 1798 meeting in Hebron, and the supporters of the movement were not disappointed. The General Association voted to become the Missionary Society of Connecticut, and a constitution was approved.[13]

9. See *An Address of the General Association of Connecticut to the District Associations on the subject of a Missionary Society* (1797), pp. 5, 8–10.

10. Three societies antedated the Missionary Society of Connecticut, the American Society for the Propagation of the Gospel among the Indians and Others in North America, formed in Boston, 1787; the New York Missionary Society, 1796; and the Northern Missionary Society in the State of New York, organized in January, 1797.

11. *Address* mentioned in footnote 9.

12. Records of the Hartford County North Association, Oct., 1797, Congregational House.

13. *Records of the General Association, 1738–1799*, pp. 177–179.

"To christianize the Heathen in North America, and to support and promote Christian knowledge in the new settlements, within the United States," was the object of the new organization. Funds were to be obtained, not from membership dues, for this society was not organized on a membership basis, but by annual contributions in all the Congregational churches of the state in accordance with an act of the legislature which had to be renewed every three years. Twelve trustees were appointed to supervise the enterprise, six laymen and six clergymen. "The precedence given to 'civilians' in this resolution," one writer has observed, "and the precedence of their names in the list of trustees seem to signify the General Association's graceful recognition and honor of the lay-element thus welcomed to participate in the management of missionary affairs."[14]

Among the first trustees were two laymen who had long and intimate associations with the society, Lieutenant Governor John Treadwell of Farmington and Jonathan Brace of Hartford. Treadwell, a devout man and the society's first president, was closely connected with several phases of the Second Great Awakening, lending the prestige of his distinguished name and position to the cause of religion. Continuing as president until 1816, he attended meetings regularly and played no small part in shaping the society's policy. His successor was Jonathan Brace, lawyer, member of Congress, mayor of Hartford, judge, land agent, Federalist, staunch Congregationalist, and one of Connecticut's leading citizens. Brace's activities on behalf of the Missionary Society exceeded those of any other trustee, for he served faithfully on most of the committees which conducted the society's business.

Also outstanding among those who directed the affairs of the Missionary Society was the Reverend Abel Flint, pastor of Hartford's Second Church and secretary of the society from 1798 until 1822. In this post he kept the minutes of all trustee meetings, carried on the voluminous

14. Parker, *Historical Discourse,* p. 14.

correspondence with the missionaries in the field, communicated with other missionary societies, and dealt with the countless details that were constantly arising. One regrets that this busy man counselled the missionaries to confine their letters to their actual deeds to the exclusion of their thoughts,[15] but the complete records of the Missionary Society of Connecticut testify to his assiduous application to his task.

After 1798 intrepid missionaries in the employ of this pioneer society made their way from settlement to settlement on several parts of the American frontier, bringing the longed-for "means of grace" to many a believer, carrying the banner of revealed religion against the forces of irreligion, endeavoring to soften the harsh tone of life. Soon they were sharing the enterprise with representatives of other societies, but the Missionary Society of Connecticut long remained one of the most active and effective organizations of its kind.

Shortly after the society was formed, the trustees voted a change in procedure, one necessitated by the fact that the old method of sending out settled ministers as missionaries had proved unsatisfactory. Not only were ministers reluctant to go but churches were also unwilling to spare their spiritual leaders. Much time was wasted in journeying to and from the frontier settlements. Henceforth, the society hired men ordained as evangelists to serve as missionaries.[16] Seth Williston, whose subsequent career as missionary and minister was long and distinguished, was the first of the new type. He and his co-workers, appointed usually for a year, were expected to spend this length of time in the territory designated.

To meet more satisfactorily the needs of the frontier, the policy was soon modified again. The trustees decided to permit missionaries to settle as part-time pastors in

15. Amasa Loomis to Abel Flint, May 4, 1818. All letters mentioned in the footnotes of this chapter, together with all other MSS. records of the Missionary Society of Connecticut and the Domestic Missionary Society of Connecticut, are in the Congregational House.
16. Flint to Williston, May 31, 1799.

frontier communities from which they received a partial share of their support.[17] These men then gave the remainder of their time to work in nearby settlements still financially unable to employ ministers of their own. For this the Missionary Society of Connecticut recompensed them. On this basis, which combined the principle of settling and self-help with that of itinerating and financial support from Connecticut, the society carried on most of its work. Some itinerating was required of all missionaries, for the frontier was extensive and the ministers few in number. Not until 1829 was there any further change in procedure.[18] Then, according recognition to the changed conditions in that part of the West where the Connecticut society was concentrating its efforts, the trustees voted that a missionary might limit himself to one congregation whenever the circumstances seemed to warrant it, even though the people could afford to give him only partial support. Although it was realized that there would be only a small amount of itineracy under the new system, the trustees declared that while "the itinerating method is best adapted to the wants of the most recent, and scattered, and indigent settlements, experience teaches the propriety of different arrangements for the benefit of others."[19]

A study of the territories to which the Connecticut society sent missionaries reveals the story of the advance of the American frontier. In 1798 men were assigned to Vermont, western New Hampshire, and eastern New York along the Mohawk and Hudson rivers, while one man was instructed to extend his tour to the eastern end of Lake Ontario. Appointed to Onondaga County in New York early in 1799, Seth Williston was also commissioned to labor in the other western counties of the state. Jedidiah Bushnell, Salmon King, and Williston did some work in northeastern Pennsylvania during the same year.[20] The districts aided were those to which the early emigrants

---

17. Flint to Williston, Feb. 16, 1800.
18. *Proceedings of the General Association, 1829*, p. 10.
19. *Ibid., 1827*, p. 13.
20. Records of the Board of Trustees, 1798–1799.

from Connecticut had moved. When the movement farther west came, the missionary followed close behind the pioneer. Joseph Badger began his remarkable missionary career as the society's first representative in that section of Ohio known as the Western Reserve in 1801, at a time when the Reserve's population did not much exceed thirteen hundred persons. In May, 1804, the society had three men in this part of Ohio, while Seth Williston was laboring in southwestern New York and northern Pennsylvania. At the same time the trustees voted to send missionaries to northern Vermont, to the towns south and west of Lake George, to the settlements west of Lake Champlain and on the Oswegatchie River, to the Black River and its vicinity, and to the Susquehanna country in northern Pennsylvania and southern New York.[21] Before the War of 1812 some work was being done by Connecticut missionaries in Ohio south of "New Connecticut," and during the war Samuel J. Mills, Jr., and John F. Schermerhorn were sent on their famous journey through the West.

When, following the Peace of Ghent, the frontier was pushed farther west by the new flood of migration, the Missionary Society of Connecticut for a time tried to keep pace.[22] In 1815 the trustees commissioned Daniel C. Banks to Ohio and Kentucky, gave Nathan Derrow permission to "missionate" in Indiana, and appointed Cyrus Kingsbury to Tennessee. On the 25th of December of that year Salmon Giddings left his home in East Hartland, Connecticut, and began a wearisome horseback journey to the Missouri Territory; he was the first Protestant missionary west of the Mississippi River. Timothy Flint, destined to gain fame as a magazine editor and chronicler of life on the Mississippi, joined Giddings in late 1816. When Elias Cornelius spent three months in New Orleans in 1817 and helped to prepare the way for the establishment of the first Presbyterian church in this southern city, he was in

21. *Ibid.*, May 29, 1804.
22. *Ibid.*, May 10, 1815; records of the Committee on Missions, Oct. 6 and Nov. 27, 1815.

the joint employ of the Missionary Society of Connecticut and the American Board of Commissioners for Foreign Missions. Thus did the representatives of the Connecticut society, along with those of similar societies, make a gallant effort to follow the frontier. In the 1820's the task became too great for these individual organizations, and, as will be noted below, a national society was formed.

It will be remembered that the constitution of the society called for work among the Indians as well as in the new settlements. Faithful to their duty, the first trustees shortly after their appointment set about making inquiries as to ways of dealing with the Indians.[23] One letter was sent to Timothy Pickering, then Secretary of State under President John Adams. The prompt reply must have been discouraging to the supporters of work among the Indians. Pickering thought that little could be done with the aborigines. He cited several reasons for the failure of missions to the Indians, two of which are especially interesting. Too much of the work had been directed to tribes nearest the whites. "It is a lamentable reflection," wrote Pickering, "but true as lamentable, that the vicinity of the whites, of professed Christians, to the Indians, while it gives the latter some idea of civilized society, increases their intemperance and debauchery." Furthermore, the English and their descendants were too averse to matrimonial connections with the Indians. Pickering concluded, "I am therefore pleased to find that the institution of your Society embraces a second object—'to support & promote Christian knowledge in the New Settlements within the limits of the United States.' *There* missionaries are wanted, and thither they may be usefully sent."[24]

Nothing daunted by these comments the trustees early in 1800 appointed a young licentiate named David Bacon

23. At the 1799 meeting of the General Association Jonathan Edwards moved that one-half of the funds on hand should be appropriated for the express purpose of evangelizing the heathen. The Association voted that this be done; or if more than half of the funds had already been appropriated, that all remaining money be used for this purpose.

24. Pickering to Flint, June 29, 1799.

to work among the Indians in the vicinity of Sandusky Bay or among the other tribes south and west of Lake Erie. Bacon immediately made a preliminary journey to Detroit, travelling much of the four hundred miles from Hartford to Buffalo on foot. By the 30th of December Bacon was back in Connecticut, for on that day he met with the trustees of the Missionary Society and was ordained as an evangelist to the Indians. Early the following year he set out again for Detroit, taking with him his bride and her brother. After spending several months in Detroit where he taught school, in the spring of 1802 Bacon investigated the possibility of establishing a mission in the Upper Miami country. Deciding against this location he finally turned to the Chippewas of Upper Michigan and in the summer of 1802 began, at what was then known as Michilimackinac, the labors to which he had been assigned. Then followed two fruitless years at this advanced post on the American frontier. The experiences of the Bacon family were trying; the venture was heroic as well as foolhardy. But the net result was negligible. Even the Indian boy whom the Bacons took to live with them returned to the religion and customs of his fathers.[25]

The Indians were long a difficult problem for the missionary forces of the white men, and probably no mission in Upper Michigan could have been successful at the time when Bacon made his attempt. Nevertheless, the Connecticut missionary must bear some of the blame for the disappointing failure. On his first trip to the west he was directed to consult at New Stockbridge, New York, with John Sergeant, who had had extensive experience with Indian missions and who was one of those to whom the Missionary Society of Connecticut had written for suggestions. This Bacon failed to do, and for this disregard of instructions he offered a weak excuse.[26] In addition, Ba-

25. See the Bacon correspondence for the story of this mission.
26. Bacon was informed that Sergeant was absent from New Stockbridge. He did not bother to check up on this, but went on without visiting New Stockbridge. His excuse was that he had received unfavorable

con had been commissioned to work among the Ohio Indians, but after what seems a superficial study he again disobeyed orders and chose to establish his mission in a more remote area among a tribe which was certain to oppose his enterprise vigorously.[27] Finally, Bacon never really started his work, in large part because of his poorly managed efforts to secure an interpreter.[28] His correspondence with the society shows Bacon to have been on the one hand enthusiastic and zealous and on the other inexperienced, impractical, and imprudent.

During the entire period of Bacon's mission the trustees were dissatisfied with both the methods he adopted and the results he achieved;[29] but sympathetic because of the difficulties of the task and hopeful that some progress would be made, they tolerantly kept him in the field until 1804. Then, influenced by the fact that somewhat over $2,500 had been expended on this mission and convinced that any success was impossible, they voted that Bacon should move to the new settlements in northeastern Ohio.[30] This failure, which taxed the resources of the Missionary Society so heavily, put almost a complete stop to its Indian work.[31]

The Missionary Society of Connecticut early exhibited a special interest in the Western Reserve, quite naturally since this area was settled in large part by Connecticut people. Joseph Badger, the first missionary sent to Ohio, has already been mentioned. To a remarkable extent this man, who was mechanic as well as preacher, and who helped in raising houses and laying out roads as well as in saving souls, entered into every phase of life on the Reserve and was soon recognized as one of its leading citi-

reports of the interpreter Sergeant proposed to give him. Bacon to Flint, Sept. 4, 1800.

27. Bacon to Nathan Strong, Jan. 1 and July 2, 1802.

28. Bacon to Flint, May 18 and Sept. 27, 1803.

29. See, for example, letters written by Flint to Bacon, Jan. 12 and July 22, 1802.

30. Records of the Board of Trustees, Jan. 9, 1805.

31. The trustees gave $100 to Joseph Badger in January, 1809, for his mission among the Wyandotte Indians, but beyond this nothing was done.

zens. The Reverend Calvin Chapin wrote of him in 1806, "As a guide in Mechanics, Agriculture & Religion he [Badger] found himself regarded & treated as nearly infallible."[32] Ezekiel Chapman joined Badger in 1801, but his well-meaning enthusiasm was outweighed by a childish simplicity and ingenuousness which rendered him ineffective in communities which expected much from the representatives of eastern civilization. To take Chapman's place Thomas Robbins was dispatched to the Reserve in 1803.

Two years later a crisis developed. The general cause of the difficulty was the rise of bad feeling among the missionaries, especially between Badger and Robbins, but each man had a special grievance as well. Badger was disgruntled because of a salary reduction which the society had put into effect,[33] and decided to accept an offer to work among the Ohio Indians. Ill health led Robbins to feel that missionary life was too strenuous for him, and he returned to less arduous work in Connecticut. Bacon encountered difficulties with the people of Hudson who employed him half-time as well as with the trustees and concluded that it would be better for all concerned if he left the employ of the society. Accordingly, the Reserve was without missionaries in 1806.

Even before it was realized that things would come to such a pass, the trustees, who were acquainted with the difficulties in this area, had appointed the newest and youngest of their number, the Reverend Calvin Chapin of Rocky Hill, Wethersfield, to make a tour of inspection. Informed of the situation in the Reserve by Robbins whom he met along the way, and therefore not surprised when he reached his destination, Chapin arrived in "New Connecticut" in June, 1806. The trustees' representative then made a careful inquiry into the causes of the missionary debacle and prepared a long report which he presented to his colleagues.

32. Chapin's Report to Trustees, 1806.
33. Badger to Flint, July 19, 1803.

In starting over again on the Reserve the Connecticut society found it necessary to employ missionaries who were not New Englanders and who were Presbyterians rather than Congregationalists. Among the first of this new group were Jonathan Leslie, Abraham Scott, and Nathan Derrow. The first two were natives of Pennsylvania and graduates of the Presbyterian college in Cannonsburg, while Derrow went to Ohio from a ministry in Homer, New York. Soon, however, it was possible to return in large part to the practice of employing Congregational ministers who wanted to move to the West or young men of New England who desired to begin their careers in Ohio. In 1812 the society had nine missionaries in the district which it considered its special field,[34] and after the War of 1812, when the work was being extended farther to the west, emphasis on this section of Ohio continued. In the 1820's the Connecticut organization, finding that its resources were decreasing and feeling that the national society established in 1826 could take care of the needs of the rapidly extending frontier, concentrated even more heavily in the Reserve. Twenty-three of the society's twenty-six missionaries were in "New Connecticut" in 1828.[35]

Under the joint auspices of this society and the Massachusetts Missionary Society Samuel J. Mills, Jr., and John F. Schermerhorn made their memorable tour of the western country in 1812 and 1813.[36] Deputized to conduct a survey of religious conditions in the West, the two young men passed through Ohio, touched Kentucky, and then went on into Indiana, Illinois, and Tennessee. From this latter state they travelled down the Mississippi River with

34. *Narrative . . . of the Missionary Society of Connecticut, 1813,* pp. 4–9.

35. *Proceedings of the General Association, 1828,* p. 11.

36. Letters from Mills are in the files of the Missionary Society of Connecticut. See also Thomas C. Richards, *Samuel J. Mills,* chapter VI; John F. Schermerhorn and Samuel J. Mills, *A Correct View of that Part of the United States which lies West of the Allegany [sic] Mountains, with regard to Religion and Morals* (1814).

General Andrew Jackson and his troops. In March, 1813, Mills and Schermerhorn reached New Orleans. Wherever they travelled, they made observations and talked with leading citizens, including the governors of the various states and territories. Not only did they gather information but they were also active in organizing Bible societies, hoping thereby to stimulate an increased interest in religion among the people in the new settlements.

The reports of this tour which were printed and widely distributed brought to the people of the East a clearer conception of the religious needs of their countrymen to the west than they had previously possessed. In vivid terms the young observers enumerated the areas where ministers were sorely needed and described the alarming shortage of Bibles. They inspired the inhabitants of the old settlements, particularly in New England, to make greater efforts than ever to send the gospel and its heralds to the newer parts of the country. One contemporary remarked that the results of this journey, and of a subsequent one made by Mills in company with Daniel Smith, "can never be duly appreciated."[37] A later comment was that the reports "had more influence, probably, than any measure of the period, in awakening public attention to the bearing of that valley on the future destinies of our country."[38] Certainly there was a direct connection between the expedition of Mills and Schermerhorn and the establishment in 1814 of new missionary fields in Kentucky, Missouri, and Louisiana by the Missionary Society of Connecticut.[39]

In the missionary activities carried on under the auspices of this society, many people in the state took a keen interest. Their attitude was natural since they had numerous relatives, friends, and erstwhile neighbors in the new settlements. They not only received many calls for help from those who missed the religious privileges which had

37. G. Spring, *Memoirs of the Reverend Samuel J. Mills*, p. 94.
38. *Contributions to the Ecclesiastical History of Connecticut*, p. 168.
39. Records of the Board of Trustees, Jan. 12, 1814.

been theirs in their old homes but also had special induce-
ments to furnish the desired aid.[40]

There was a second reason for Connecticut's interest in
missionary activities. Apprehensive because of the spread
of infidelity and indifference to religion within the state
borders, the people were quite naturally afraid that amid
the wild, unsettled conditions on the frontier religion would
tend to disappear altogether. The rise of revivalism also
inspired the friends of religion to support a movement
which aimed to quicken spiritual life on the frontier. They
were ready to aid the new settlements where the cry, "Come
over into Macedonia," was being raised.

Each May contributions were made in the Congregational churches of the state in accordance with acts of the
state legislature, members of which indicated their approval of the missionary movement by renewing this legislation every three years. From 1798 to 1830, in only three
years, 1809, 1810, 1811, were the contributions omitted,
the reason given for this action being that the society had
sufficient funds for its work.[41] In 1799, $2,018.25 was
contributed by the Connecticut Congregational churches.
During the next four years a steady increase occurred until in 1803 the sum of $3,069.96 was reached. The average
for the following four years was about $2,800. In 1808,
probably due to the effects of the Embargo, the total receipts dropped to $2,192.32. Contributions were then sus-
pended for three years, and when renewed in 1812, the sum
of $3,255.99½ was collected. Two years later, during the
war with England, the churches made the best showing in
the early history of the society, contributing $3,973.85½.
The decline thereafter was gradual. At the beginning of
the next decade the annual contribution was $2,338.71; in

40. It was the policy of the Missionary Society of Connecticut from
the beginning to pay particular attention to those parts of the new settlements where emigrants from Connecticut were most numerous. See
quotation from T. Dwight's address to these emigrants in Parker, *Historical Discourse*, p. 20.

41. *Conn. Evang. Mag. and Relig. Intel.*, I, 238, 273.

1826 when the American Home Missionary Society was organized, $2,224.94½ was received. The last contribution before the status of the Missionary Society was changed in 1830 amounted to but $1,832.83.[42]

All parts of Connecticut joined in supporting the missionary enterprise. The annual financial statements show that during the three decades under consideration Hartford, the most populous as well as the wealthiest county, made the largest contributions, with Litchfield County next in order followed by New Haven County and Fairfield County. From 1799 until 1830 no significant changes took place in the relative standings of the state's eight counties.[43]

No strenuous campaigns were instituted to raise money at the annual contributions. A simple announcement was made one Sabbath, and on the next the minister preached an appropriate sermon, at the conclusion of which the collection was made. Probably there were some substantial gifts, but Thomas Robbins' accounts of the collections in his church at East Windsor indicate that there were many small givers, anxious that their less fortunate countrymen in more remote sections should enjoy the "means of grace."[44] No special contributions at irregular times were ever made. The method of raising money was as orderly and restrained as the revivals of the Second Great Awakening.

In addition to the annual collections the Missionary Society of Connecticut received special gifts of money and books from interested persons, among whom General Jedediah Huntington of New London and Benjamin Beecher of Cheshire are to be noted. It was also the beneficiary of several bequests of land and money, the largest coming from the estate of Dr. Solomon Everest of Canton, who

42. These figures are in the published *Narratives* of the society for the years mentioned.

43. See published *Narratives*, 1799–1830.

44. Robbins, *Diary*, I, 819, 859, 893, 926, 965. The town line has been changed with the result that Robbins' church, in East Windsor during his ministry, is now in South Windsor.

died in 1822.[45] The profits of the *Connecticut Evangelical Magazine*, and its successor, the *Connecticut Evangelical Magazine and Religious Intelligencer*, periodicals published by men closely connected with the missionary venture, were turned over to the society. The total received during the fifteen years (1800–1815) in which the magazine appeared amounted to $11,520.07. A small sum, averaging no more than $250 annually, was contributed by the people in the new settlements. A permanent fund was created at an early date and invested, interest on this increasing the income of the society. From 1799 to 1829 the receipts of the society, incorporated in 1802, totalled more than $150,000.[46] For many years Andrew Kingsbury, who was long the state treasurer, served the Missionary Society in a similar capacity and gave it sound financial direction.

During the three decades under discussion a total of approximately $135,000 was expended. Before 1814 the amount spent annually exceeded five thousand dollars only twice, $5,235.40 in 1810 and $5,041.81 in 1813. In the eleven years after 1813, however, expenditures exceeded six thousand dollars annually except in 1819, while in 1818 they soared to $7,244.57. In 1826 only $3,419.90 was spent and in 1829, $3,879.31. Almost all the money was used to support missionaries. Some was spent for religious books to be sent to the frontier, but practically no expenses were incurred in Connecticut.

From 1793 until 1798 the General Association's Committee on Missions made a weekly allowance of nine dollars to its missionaries, half for the man employed and half to supply his pulpit during his absence. After the society was formed and settled ministers were no longer employed, the weekly salary became six dollars. Although Joseph Badger, by special vote, was granted seven dollars

45. *Report of the Directors of the Missionary Society for the Year 1880*, p. 21. Dr. Everest's estate totalled somewhat over $16,000, of which one-quarter went to the Missionary Society. This resulted in the establishment of the Everest Fund.

46. *Ibid.*, pp. 14–15.

a week when he began his work in the Western Reserve, his wages were reduced to six dollars in 1803 on the grounds that a uniform rate for all men employed by the society was desirable. In 1806 the weekly salaries were twice raised, first to seven dollars and then to eight, the last amount being paid to missionaries during the next quarter of a century. They thus received about the same remuneration as did most settled ministers in Connecticut. It became customary, also, to give travel allowances to those going to distant places.

In 1798 the society employed six missionaries. A decade later when work in the Western Reserve was resumed, nineteen men were in the field. The largest number supported by the Missionary Society in any one year was forty-four, this total being reached in 1814 and again in 1820. Neither war nor a financial panic, it appears, interfered with the religious ventures which were part of the Second Great Awakening. In 1826 the society employed twenty-five men, in 1830 thirty-three. During the years 1798–1830 the Missionary Society of Connecticut made 862 appointments.[47]

Many have written about the influence of the frontier on the older sections of the United States. Of importance, too, has been the influence of the East on the West, a subject to which less attention has been given. Under new and exacting conditions on the frontier a civilization developed which differed in many ways from that of the older areas. It is probable that the difference would have been greater, had not certain modifying influences of eastern origin been steadily at work. Among these were the representatives of the Missionary Society of Connecticut and other such organizations who became the media through which the religious and social customs of the older settlements were transferred to the sparsely settled areas to the north and west.[48]

47. *Ibid.,* p. 14.
48. This conclusion is reached as the result of examining hundreds of letters from missionaries.

On the frontier, where the economic situation was usually such as to preclude the possibility of employing a minister, religious services could not be held regularly and the restraints of religion ceased to operate. It is true, as Frederick Jackson Turner has written, that "at the frontier, the environment is at first too strong for the man." Into this environment came the missionaries, supported either wholly or in part by the inhabitants of the older, settled regions. These heralds of the gospel conducted religious services in areas that would have been destitute of the word of God. They brought Bibles and other religious books and tracts. They baptized children, thereby comforting parents who would otherwise have been seriously concerned about the future welfare of their unbaptized offspring. They administered the Lord's Supper, which brought new courage and inspiration to those who partook. They comforted the distressed, visited and cared for the sick, conducted funeral services, and prayed with those who mourned. Since the missionaries lightened the burdens of both life and death, it is not surprising that people in the new settlements welcomed them and invited them to repeat their visits.

The missionaries organized churches which, in the new settlements as in the old, became social centers around which developed a community and group spirit.[49] After organizing new churches, the missionaries admitted new members. When a church could afford the partial support of a minister, the Missionary Society continued to employ the man chosen on a part-time basis, and as soon as the entire support of a pastor could be managed, the society released him and used its resources to aid more needy areas. The Missionary Society of Connecticut thus introduced many ministers into the western country.

The representatives of the Connecticut society influenced the frontier areas in other ways. They brought to

49. The missionaries of the Missionary Society of Connecticut founded about four hundred churches, 1798–1829. Proceedings of the General Association, 1829, p. 10.

these western settlements the spiritual quickening which characterized the Second Great Awakening. Revivals were stimulated, not the noisy, tumultuous exhibitions which flourished elsewhere on the frontier,[50] but awakenings as quiet and as effective as those described in the previous chapter. After the settlements grew a little older, they established their own missionary societies as well as Bible societies, tract societies, education societies, moral societies, Sunday schools, and charitable societies. Religious culture moved westward with the missionaries.

Since Connecticut Congregationalism placed great emphasis on an educated ministry, the missionary society of the state employed only men who had received thorough training. Most of its representatives were college graduates whose education had been supplemented by theological study, and all were ordained before they became missionaries. Therefore, they took with them to the frontier the point of view of educated men who encouraged the establishment of schools and the hiring of competent teachers. Not only were they frequent visitors in schools where they catechized the students, but in several instances, after they were settled part-time, they organized schools in their homes. Almost as soon as Joseph Badger reached the Western Reserve he began to think in terms of a college for that pioneer section, and drawing up a constitution for such an enterprise, he agitated for its incorporation by the territorial legislature.[51] Badger was far ahead of his time. Academies were indeed established in the Reserve, in part under missionary influence, but not until 1826 was Western Reserve College founded in Hudson, Ohio. Then it was not only the embodiment of Badger's scheme conceived more than two decades earlier, but also the direct outcome of work done in the 1820's by employees of the Missionary Society of Connecticut, who wanted an insti-

50. Revivals in Kentucky and Tennessee are described in Cleveland, *The Great Revival in the West, 1797–1805.*
51. Badger's narrative, July 29, 1801.

tution that would educate the ministers needed in that section of Ohio.[52]

The Connecticut missionaries brought their ascetic moral code to the frontier, where, they believed, morals were certain to degenerate. Since the Sabbath was commonly disregarded, the Connecticut spiritual agents labored to make it more like the New England Sabbath, a day for rejuvenation of the soul and body rather than for a continuation of work or for dangerous relaxation after a strenuous week of struggle with the wilderness. And since intemperance and profanity were common on the frontier, the missionaries used their influence to check these habits. To some extent, it would seem, they were successful.

There were other effects of the missionary movement.[53] Within Connecticut the interest in missionary activities contributed to the general religious quickening which occurred at the time. It appears, as well, that the enterprise was of importance in developing national unity in the United States. The men sent to the frontier helped to bind the Old East to the New West. Furthermore, when people in different states and various sections of the country participated in the same venture, even though divided in their several individual societies, common interests developed which furthered the nationalizing process. The effects of this increased when the national societies were formed. People in areas outside New England had opportunities to become acquainted with something more than "Yankee tricks." Connecticut folk, in turn, during a period when dissatisfaction with the national government, rampant as

52. Giles Cowles, a missionary settled part-time in Austinburg, was particularly active. See his letters to Flint.

53. The Missionary Society of Connecticut was accused of being politico-religious in its purposes, as were also the state Bible Society, Tract Society, Moral Society, and other organizations which will be discussed later in this study. Since these charges came from Republican sources, they must be carefully scrutinized. They seem to be invalidated by a study of the activities of the various societies. It must be remembered that these organizations were parts of an Awakening which was not limited to Connecticut.

a result of the Embargo, the Non-Intercourse Act, and the unpopular War of 1812, culminated in the Hartford Convention, had something in common with people in other sections which served to counterbalance the forces that were moving against national unity.

An example of such coöperation was evidenced in the Plan of Union, drawn up by the Connecticut General Association and the General Assembly of the Presbyterian Church in 1801.[54] These two bodies first exchanged delegates at their annual meetings in 1790. When the missionary enterprise began, they saw that joint action would be far superior to needless conflict. Accordingly, the Plan of Union was framed, its main object being to promote harmony between the inhabitants of the new settlements holding Presbyterian convictions and those holding Congregational. All missionaries were instructed to work for a mutual forbearance and a spirit of accommodation. The churches of the Congregational order might settle Presbyterian ministers and still retain the Congregational form of government, while Presbyterian churches were accorded the same privilege in regard to Congregational ministers. Both Presbyterians and the Congregationalists of Connecticut and of other states which accepted the Plan of Union heartily subscribed to this arrangement at the time, but later the Plan was abrogated, Congregationalists objecting to it because, to quote the words of a speaker at the Albany Convention in 1852, "they have milked our Congregational cows, but have made nothing but Presbyterian butter and cheese."[55]

The Plan of Union, correspondence among the several missionary societies in various parts of the country, and informal coöperation in a common venture during the first quarter of the nineteenth century, were forerunners of a national missionary institution. In May, 1826, a group of interested clergymen and laymen met in New York City

54. The terms of the Plan of Union are given in Walker, *Creeds and Platforms of Congregationalism,* pp. 530–531.
55. Quoted in *ibid.,* p. 533.

and drew up a constitution for the American Home Missionary Society. Presbyterian, Congregational, Reformed, and Associated Reformed churches participated in this joint enterprise.[56]

No representative of the Missionary Society of Connecticut attended this meeting in New York City, but its secretary wrote a congratulatory letter to the corresponding secretary of the new national organization in which he expressed the belief that further correspondence would be mutually beneficial.[57] The society, however, took no immediate steps to work out a national affiliation. In spite of the fact that the financial situation of the past few years had been none too satisfactory, the decline in contributions being in large part attributed to the many calls that were being made upon the charity of the people and to the feeling that the inhabitants of the new settlements should do more to help themselves, the trustees preferred to maintain an independent existence. It was clear that such a situation could not long continue. In 1828 the General Association appointed a committee to consider a union with the American Home Missionary Society. The committee made an unfavorable report the following year, having been unable to agree on a workable compromise in a situation complicated by the existence of the Domestic Missionary Society of Connecticut.[58] In 1830 and 1831, however, a satisfactory settlement was arranged under which the Missionary Society of Connecticut henceforth should have no contributions but should carry on its operations so far as it could on the income from the permanent fund. To the Domestic Missionary Society, affiliated with the national organization under the name of the Missionary Society of Connecticut, auxiliary to the American Home Missionary Society, was assigned the task of build-

56. Joseph B. Clark, *Leavening the Nation*, pp. 61–62.
57. H. Hooker to Corresponding Secretary of the American Home Missionary Society, Aug. 28, 1826.
58. *Proceedings of the General Association, 1828*, pp. 6–7; *ibid., 1829*, p. 8.

ing up the "waste places" in Connecticut. It would also contribute to the American Home Missionary Society which would carry on the main part of the work in the West in which the old Missionary Society of Connecticut had engaged.[59]

The American foreign-missionary movement was a second phase of the evangelical developments of the early years of the nineteenth century and was a part of the Second Great Awakening. Its origins lay in the new religious spirit roused by the age of revivals, in the home-missionary activities described above, and in the pioneering endeavors made by the British. Its early history belonged jointly to Connecticut and Massachusetts.

Samuel J. Mills, Jr., has been aptly called the "missionary pathfinder" by his biographer. The son of Torringford's esteemed minister, he was reared in a home where missionary affairs were frequently discussed. Not only was his father one of the first of Connecticut's settled ministers who undertook a mission to the new settlements under the auspices of the General Association's Committee on Missions, but also in 1806, at the time when the son entered Williams College, the older Mills became a trustee of the Missionary Society of Connecticut. Young Samuel had become a church member during the end-of-the-century revival at Torringford, and he had read about the English activities in the mission field in the copies of the *Connecticut Evangelical Magazine* which came to his home. As a result he went to Williams with his heart set on a missionary career.

When Mills reached college, he found a revival in progress, one, incidentally, for which students from Litchfield County were responsible. Then occurred the famous Haystack incident, when lives were dedicated to service in the foreign-mission field, and the society known as the "Brethren" was organized. Upon his graduation from Williams, Mills together with several of his college associates went to

59. *Ibid., 1830*, pp. 8–9.

the Andover Theological Seminary, where discussion of plans for the Christianization of Asia continued and the "Brethren" was reorganized. When the Hawaiian youth, Obookiah, appeared in New Haven and was brought to Andover, the young zealots were fired with new enthusiasm, for here was heathendom in the flesh.[60]

In June, 1810, four Andover students, Adoniram Judson, Samuel Nott, Jr., Samuel J. Mills, Jr., and Samuel Newell, presented a petition to the recently organized General Association of Massachusetts. After stating their deep interest "in personally attempting a Mission to the Heathen," the young men inquired, "Whether with their present views and feelings, they ought to renounce the object of Missions as visionary or impracticable; if not, whether they ought to direct their attention to the eastern or western world; whether they may expect patronage and support from a Missionary Society in this country, or must commit themselves to the direction of a European Society; and what preparatory measures they ought to take previous to actual engagement?"[61] The Association heartily approved the proposed plan and appointed a board consisting of five men from Massachusetts and four from Connecticut who should devise ways and means for spreading the gospel into heathen lands. In September, 1810, five of these men held in Farmington, Connecticut, the first meeting of the American Board of Commissioners for Foreign Missions.[62] They drew up a constitution, elected officers, Governor John Treadwell being the first president, and prepared an address to the Christian public. "In the present state of the world," it concluded, "Christian missions cannot be executed without pecuniary support. Shall this be wanting? When millions are perishing for lack of knowledge, and the young disciples of the Lord are waiting with ardent desires to carry the gospel to them, shall

60. Obookiah had been brought to New Haven by a sea captain of that town whose boat had stopped at the Sandwich Islands.
61. Richards, *Samuel J. Mills*, p. 72.
62. This institution will henceforth be referred to as the A.B.C.F.M.

those millions be left to perish and that ardent desire be disappointed?"[63] So hearty was the response that the first missionaries sailed for India in 1812. Thus began a story which has continued to the present time, a narrative filled with much heroism and devotion to a cause, as well as denominational bickering and a tendency at times to confuse Christianization with Americanization.

There were no ulterior motives in the early years of the foreign-mission movement, no contemplation of territorial or economic aggrandizement. The sole purpose of the youths who at Williams College and the Andover Theological Seminary initiated the enterprise, of the missionaries who courageously went to the foreign field, of the commissioners who authorized their going, and of those whose contributions made possible the missionary operations in distant places, was to extend the knowledge of Christ and the gospel to the so-called heathen. In view of the religious climate of opinion of the time, changed so decidedly in somewhat over a decade, it was natural that this interest in the spread of Christianity should have developed, the more so since England had made gallant beginnings.

Some opposition to the new venture appeared. When the A.B.C.F.M. applied to the Massachusetts legislature for an act of incorporation, one member asserted during the debate that he opposed any action which facilitated the export of religion, for the country had none to spare. He probably derived small solace from the reply that "religion was a commodity of which the more we exported the more we had remaining."[64] Some questioned the advisability of foreign missions on the grounds that they would adversely affect home-missionary activities.[65] Others felt that the cost of the work would be so great as to make it unwise.

63. Richards, *Samuel J. Mills,* p. 75.

64. William E. Strong, *The Story of the American Board,* p. 141.

65. As did Thomas Robbins. See a memorandum entitled "On Foreign Missions" in his papers (Miscellaneous, Box II) in the Connecticut Historical Society.

During its first two decades the A.B.C.F.M. established stations in widely scattered parts of the world. The first missionaries, as has been mentioned, went to India, and the earliest mission stations were set up at Bombay and on the island of Ceylon. In 1819 Pliny Fisk and Levi Parsons began their memorable work in Palestine. Two missions were sent to the Sandwich Islands, the first in 1819 and the second three years later. From the beginning the Board planned to support work among the American Indians, and this was started in January, 1817, when the Reverend Cyrus Kingsbury inaugurated a Cherokee mission in the northern part of Tennessee. A little later missions were opened among the Choctaws and Arkansaws. In 1820, a year when the expenditures of the Board totalled $57,420.93, approximately one-half was used for Indian work. The A.B.C.F.M. continued to expand its efforts in the 1820's; and a further step was taken in 1826 when it effected a union with the United Foreign Missionary Society, which, with headquarters in New York City, had been the agent of the Presbyterian, Dutch Reformed, and Associated Reformed churches for work among the Indians. The enlarged A.B.C.F.M. assumed control of these endeavors and also took under its care the remaining Stockbridge Indians and the Chickasaw mission which the Presbyterian Synod of South Carolina and Georgia had initiated. In 1828 the expenditures of the Board which had been averaging about $50,000 a year soared to $108,-676.25.[66]

Although the A.B.C.F.M. with headquarters in Boston and support from all parts of New England, as well as from other sections of the country, was not a Connecticut organization as was the Missionary Society of Connecticut, the state's contributions in both men and money reveal the interest of the people in this phase of the mission-

66. Strong, *The Story of the American Board*, pp. 36, 56–57, 62, 80; *Minutes of the General Assembly of the Presbyterian Church, 1826* (Brace Variety, v. 18), p. 20; *Report of the American Board of Commissioners for Foreign Missions* (1828), p. 126.

ary movement. The prominent part played by young
Mills in the early proceedings, the holding of the Board's
first meeting at Farmington, the inclusion of the son of
Franklin's venerated minister, Samuel Nott, in the first
missionary group—these facts roused the zeal of people
whose religious spirit was renewed by revivals and who
were already supporting home missions. The Litchfield
County Foreign Mission Society, formed in 1811, was the
first auxiliary of the A.B.C.F.M., and when it is realized
that of the $11,361.18 received in the spring of 1813,
$1,354.11 came from this one county, it seems reasonable
to believe that Dr. Samuel Worcester, secretary of the
Board, exclaimed, "I bless God for making Litchfield
County."[67] Auxiliaries sprang up in various parts of the
state, and in the fifth annual report of the A.B.C.F.M.
twelve of the thirty auxiliaries and seven of the Female
Foreign Missionary Societies listed were in Connecticut.

From 1811 through 1820 Connecticut's contributions
to the A.B.C.F.M. amounted to $34,859.76; during the
next decade they totalled $123,991.60.[68] Figures for the
Litchfield County society show that with one exception
this auxiliary raised more than one thousand dollars in
each of its first fourteen years. In 1822 and again in 1823
the amount contributed exceeded two thousand dollars.
For the fourteen years the average was $1,427.57, a large
sum for a single county as a comparison with the receipts
of the Missionary Society of Connecticut will show.[69]

The generous support of the A.B.C.F.M. testified both
to the general interest in the enterprise and to the effectiveness of the propaganda employed. Auxiliary societies
were formed whose members paid annual dues of fifty
cents upward. Gifts and bequests, larger and more numerous than those to the home-missionary society, together
with interest on invested funds swelled the total. A number

67. Alain C. White, *The History of . . . Litchfield . . . 1720–1920*,
pp. 184–185; *Semi-Centennial of the Litchfield County Foreign Mission
Society*, p. 25.

68. *Ibid.*, p. 35.   69. *Relig. Intel.*, XI, 489.

of ingenious plans for raising money were introduced. For example, people were urged to set apart pieces of land known as missionary fields to be tilled and the proceeds turned over to the auxiliary societies.[70] Missionary boxes were placed in convenient locations where people could drop in their contributions. Undoubtedly, judging from similar boxes used in Pennsylvania, these bore appropriate verses from the Scriptures combined with reminders such as, "Do you feel for the poor heathen? O then feel in your pocket, and give what you can spare, and even deny yourself to assist sending the gospel to them."[71] The *Connecticut Courant* on June 24, 1823, referred to the "Missionary Wheel" on which clothing might be spun for the heathen. "Young ladies!" the editor clarioned, "who spend your long mornings in useless slumbers,—awake! and pass the precious hours before breakfast in this laudable employment—say not that you know not how to spin,— 'You are not too old to learn.' Teachers, Wheels, and materials for spinning are provided at several houses in this City; Persons so disposed may call at any time of day most convenient to themselves. For further information enquire at this office." The attention of Connecticut people was called to one enthusiast who purchased two logs, had them cut into boards and sent to Philadelphia, and then gave the profit as well as the original purchase money to the A.B.C.F.M. "It will be done," he wrote, "not only by missionary fields and missionary logs, but it can be done by missionary apprentice boys, missionary horses, cows, sheep, fowl, eggs, machines, wheels, spindles, savings, profits, retrenchments, &c. in a thousand ways."[72]

There was a glamour to the foreign-mission movement which home missions were never able to provide. The American Indian, living close to the white man, had long been viewed with interest and concern by the Christian forces, and it was dramatic and romantic to help in con-

70. *Ibid.*, V, 752, 800; VI, 48; VII, 223–224.
71. *Connecticut Courant*, May 4, 1819.
72. *Relig. Intel.*, VI, 63.

verting the heathen in distant places. One could be sure that he was performing his Christian duty. Accordingly, a profound and widespread interest in foreign missions abounded in Connecticut. In the columns of the *Connecticut Evangelical Magazine and Religious Intelligencer*, the *Religious Intelligencer*, and the *Panoplist*, the people read reports of the A.B.C.F.M. and the auxiliary societies, news items regarding the foreign field, and letters from missionaries. Even such secular newspapers as the *Connecticut Courant* and the *Connecticut Mirror* contained much religious news. Not only did the readers learn what the missionaries were doing, but they also became more intimately acquainted with the heathen world which they yearned to bring to Christ and with heathen customs which they became more anxious to extirpate. Such publications as the *Memoirs of Harriet Newell*, Buchanan's sermon entitled *Star of the East*, and the pamphlet expressively called *The Claims of Six Hundred Millions, or the Conversion of the World*, were widely read.[73]

Two representatives of heathendom became familiar to Connecticut people, a young Hawaiian named Obookiah and a Cherokee Indian girl who was called Catharine Brown. Obookiah was brought to New Haven in 1809, and for the next nine years, most of which he spent in Connecticut, he represented his whole unfortunate race—and the heathen millions in general. His presence spurred missionary efforts. When he was converted, he symbolized what Christianity could and must do. A little later someone wrote of him that "he appeared as one redeemed from that cruel bondage in which millions of the heathen, and all who are ignorant of God, may be found."[74] In 1818 Obookiah died. Like many another, he was even greater in death than he had been in life. Lyman Beecher is reported to have remarked "that if the churches of New England

---

73. In 1819 the members of the Fairfield County West Association were requested to read publicly in all churches the last of these publications. *Contributions to the Ecclesiastical History of Connecticut*, p. 302.

74. *Relig. Intel.*, VII, 635.

had chartered a ship to go to Owyhee and bring Obookiah that he might be converted and die as he has, they would be amply recompensed."[75] Obookiah was raised to sainthood by the New England zealots. Many copies of a *Memoir of Henry Obookiah*, prepared by E. W. Dwight, one of those who had befriended the brown-skinned youth when he first appeared in New Haven, were sold in Connecticut and in other parts of the country. Obookiah's death prevented his return to his native land, but from his grave on a Cornwall hillside he inspired the missions which went to the Sandwich Islands. Listen to the instructions of the A.B.C.F.M. to Thomas Hopoo, when he sailed from Boston in 1819! "You will never forget Obookiah.—You will never forget his fervent love,—his affectionate counsels,—his many prayers and tears for you, and for his and your nation. You saw him die;—saw how the Christian could triumph over death and the grave;—saw the radiant glory in which he left this world for heaven. You will remember it always; and you will tell it to your kindred and countrymen who are dying without hope."[76]

Great was the interest when Hiram Bingham and Asa Thurston, the leaders of the first mission to the Sandwich Islands in 1819, were ordained in Goshen, and when the marriage of Bingham to Sybil Moseley was solemnized in Hartford on the eve of their departure for Hawaii. Even greater was the excitement when the second mission to these Pacific Islands set sail from New Haven in 1822.[77] When they learned of the marriage of Thomas Hopoo, who had lived in Connecticut, the people rejoiced. "This event is remarkable," the A.B.C.F.M. reported, "as the first marriage ever solemnized at these islands, according to the usages in Christian countries. Every friend of happiness and virtue must anxiously desire, that an institu-

75. *Connecticut Journal*, March 31, 1818.
76. Instructions to the members of the mission to the Sandwich Islands, printed with Heman Humphrey, *The Promised Land, a Sermon delivered at the Ordination of the Rev. Messrs. Hiram Bingham and Asa Thurston*, p. xv.
77. *Relig. Intel.*, IV, 336, 344–345, 390–391, 430–432; VII, 414–415.

tion so indispensable to domestic enjoyment may be universally regarded as sacred."[78]

Catharine Brown never visited Connecticut, but she was well known there, since the A.B.C.F.M. considered her its first Indian convert. Not only did a lengthy description of her conversion appear in a Brainerd Mission report, but practically every subsequent report mentioned her. People were told that she was beautiful and that she was the equal of genteel young ladies in New England. They became familiar with her piety, for did they not read that she voluntarily presented her jewelry to the A.B.C.F.M. and that she confounded an infidel whom she encountered in Huntsville, Alabama? Desolate with her when she was forced to leave Brainerd because her family was moving westward, they approved her spirit of obedience. They rejoiced with her when she was able to return to the mission station where she gave valuable assistance to the white missionaries.[79] In 1819 a "missionary drama," depicting the affecting circumstances of her departure from Brainerd, was presented at Woodbridge. "The plan of an exhibition of this kind, novel in itself, succeeded beyond expectation," wrote a correspondent to the *Religious Intelligencer*. "The young people entered with ardour into the business and acted the dialogue and other pieces well. Their parents and others were induced to attend, and the house was crowded."[80]

Like Obookiah, Catharine Brown died young, and news of her death evoked tears in many a Connecticut home. Several ladies with whom she had corresponded felt that they had lost a personal friend, and Lydia Huntley Sigourney, "the sweet singer of Hartford," was inspired to compose a long narrative poem about the young Indian girl. A *Memoir of Catharine Brown* soon appeared. "Let the life of Catharine Brown," her biographer wrote, "op-

78. *Report of the A.B.C.F.M.* (1823), p. 112.

79. The story of Catharine Brown is told in Rufus Anderson, *Memoir of Catharine Brown*, and in the *Relig. Intel.*, *passim*.

80. *Relig. Intel.*, III, 792.

erate as an appeal to the benevolence of the Christian community. Though dead, she speaks; and oh, let her voice fall with persuasive and irresistible eloquence upon every ear."

Because of a rather remarkable experiment conducted from 1817 until 1827, Connecticut had a special interest in the foreign-missionary movement. In the former year a school was established in the town of Cornwall where natives of the various heathen races were to be educated and, if possible, converted to Christianity.[81] Obookiah was the inspiration for this venture, for difficulties had been encountered in trying to educate him. In the hope that it would benefit the missionary cause by supplying educated, Christian natives who would act as missionaries to their own people, the A.B.C.F.M. set up this Cornwall School. Upwards of one hundred representatives of heathendom were domiciled here, some for only a few weeks, others for a period of years. Indians, Hawaiians, Chinese, Negroes, and others assembled in the gambrel-roofed building on the Cornwall plain to learn of the white man's religion and his culture, and with this group studied several zealous Connecticut youths who felt that thus they could best prepare themselves for missionary careers. Under the successive direction of three principals, Edwin Dwight, Herman Daggett, and Amos Bassett, a veritable Tower of Babel arose which attracted the attention of people in Connecticut and other parts of the United States and even drew foreign travellers.

The death of Obookiah in 1818 led the supporters of the infant enterprise to increase their exertions. At his grave they rededicated themselves to their task. Connecticut people responded nobly with contributions of money and clothing for the strangers within their gates, and for a time this pioneer venture flourished. Reports of the agents or supervisors reflect an enthusiasm that was probably

81. The best accounts of the Cornwall School will be found in Starr, *A History of Cornwall;* Edwin W. Dwight, *Memoir of Henry Obookiah;* Ralph H. Gabriel, *Elias Boudinot, Cherokee, & His America.*

real. Then, with dramatic suddenness, the school was closed in 1827.

Three reasons may be advanced for this action. In the first place, to conduct such an institution was no easy task, and the difficulties increased with the years. Furthermore, the conviction grew that more satisfactory results could be obtained if the heathen youths were educated in their own habitats and not brought into the white man's environment. Support for this belief came from an English missionary of wide experience who visited Connecticut in 1825 and counselled the transfer of the work at Cornwall to the Indian country, Hawaii, India, and elsewhere, where there were enough missionaries to conduct the schools. Finally, two marriages between Indian students and Cornwall girls roused much opposition to the school. The second of these marriages, between Harriet Gold, daughter of one of Cornwall's leading citizens, and Elias Boudinot, a Cherokee, created a considerable stir. An angry mob demonstrated against the marriage on the Cornwall Green, the exasperated agents of the school took a firm stand against the union, and Isaiah Bunce, the vigorous editor of Litchfield's *American Eagle*, gave the matter much attention.

Although the experiment failed, the Cornwall School aided the missionary cause. While it existed, the school undoubtedly stimulated interest in missionary activities; when it was abandoned, people believed that the work, transferred to more favorable environments, would flourish and produce more satisfactory results. After the flurry of opposition in Cornwall to the Gold-Boudinot marriage, a reversal of feeling occurred which removed much of the bitterness from the episode. Furthermore, several of the students later rendered distinguished services to their people. Thomas Hopoo was a member of the first mission to Hawaii, while David Brown, brother of Catharine, had a useful career among the Cherokees. Elias Boudinot was employed for a time by the A.B.C.F.M. and was a coworker and close friend of the famous missionary, Samuel

Worcester. His newspaper, the *Cherokee Phoenix*, was published in both Cherokee and English and had as one of its objects the keeping alive of New England interest in the Cherokee missions. Boudinot also helped his people in negotiations with the United States government regarding their lands.[82]

The third aspect of the missionary movement had to do with work within Connecticut. As early as 1783 the New London County Association asked the General Association, "What shall be done respecting our destitute Churches and congregations whose resettlement in the enjoyment of gospel ordinances is improbable?" Two decades later, after missionaries had begun to work in the new settlements, attention was again called to Connecticut's needs, the New London ministers in particular pleading for the vacant parishes in their part of the state. To the appeal for assistance the trustees of the Missionary Society of Connecticut replied that the charter gave them no right to divert funds for work in the state, and nothing was done. People had their attention fixed on the more fascinating endeavors in the West.

Matters drifted along until 1814 when Lyman Beecher took advantage of the installation of the Reverend John Keyes at Wolcott to preach a sermon on the "waste places of Connecticut." After discussing the vacant parishes, Beecher pointed out that the religious decline which had occurred in the eighteenth century had caused a deplorable situation. Although parts of the state had been very successful in restoring religion after the decline, certain areas remained desolated. It was the duty of the prosperous churches, the Litchfield minister declared, to help the less fortunate ones, not only to save them but also to pre-

---

82. Professor Gabriel demonstrates that Boudinot did not betray his people but encouraged migration because he felt that the expulsion of the Indians from their Georgia lands was inevitable in the face of the onrush of the whites.

vent their further decay from undermining, ultimately, civil and religious order in the state. To remedy the situation he recommended not only occasional itineration by settled ministers but more strongly the establishment of a society which should employ missionaries to work among the feeble and destitute congregations. Beecher's call was heard throughout the state, with the result that at its 1816 meeting the General Association resolved itself into the Domestic Missionary Society of Connecticut.

Since the object of this new society was merely "to build up the waste places of Connecticut and its vicinity, by furnishing the destitute with religious instructions," its scope was limited and its plan of operation simple. As the trustees said in an early report, "the demand is not for the conversion of six hundred millions of pagans; nor for the transportation of twenty millions of Africans to a foreign land; nor for the establishment of a large number of printing institutions to fill the world with Bibles: but, simply, to restore fifteen or twenty of our own parishes, almost able, and very anxious to help themselves, to the enjoyment of the regular institutions of religion."[83]

Twelve trustees, six ministers and six laymen, were appointed to direct the society's affairs. Funds were raised in the Congregational churches of the state by contributions held annually on the first Sabbath in September. The sums raised were not large, $1,263.63 in 1817, $1,651.66 in 1818, $938.02 in 1820, and $1,344.00 in 1826, and on several occasions the trustees complained because only a small proportion of the state's 210 Congregational parishes made remittances, 75 in 1820 and 88 in 1826.[84] Because of the purely local nature of its work the Domestic Missionary Society received practically no gifts or bequests, about the only exception being $2,000 from the

83. *Fourth Annual Report of the Directors of the Domestic Missionary Society of Connecticut* (1820), pp. 5–6.
84. The figures are from the society's *Annual Reports*. See also *Relig. Intel.*, XI, 538–540.

estate of a Mrs. Lewis of New London.[85] Each year the society spent about what it received; in fact, it based its expenditures on its receipts. As a result, no permanent fund
could be established.

Informed of the needs of the state either by delegates to
the General Association or by the county and half-county
associations, and the recipients as well of applications direct from the vacant parishes, the trustees employed as
many missionaries as funds would permit. In the first year
after its establishment the Domestic Missionary Society
had twelve men in twelve of the seventeen parishes reported as being without regular preaching. Nine missionaries were in the society's employ in 1819 and six in 1821,
of whom four labored among their own people who were
unable to give them complete support. In 1824 assistance
was given to fifteen parishes, three on condition that they
settle ministers.[86] The trustees noted in 1825 that they had
received a number of new applications for assistance and
at the same time appointed a committee to confer with the
trustees of the Missionary Society of Connecticut on "the
practicability and expediency of uniting the operations of
the two societies for the purpose of obtaining funds." In
1826 the committee reported that no conference had been
held. That the society's funds were insufficient was shown
in May, 1828, by the report of a committee appointed to
consider "what measures can be adopted to increase the interest taken in the cause of Domestic Missions by the
people of this State."[87] Since there was dissatisfaction with
the way in which both the Missionary Society of Connecticut and the Domestic Missionary Society were function-
ing, the General Association discussed the problems and
began the negotiations with the American Home Missionary Society which resulted in the reorganization of the

85. Dom. Miss. Soc., *3d Rept.* (1819), p. 6.
86. The figures are from the society's *Annual Reports.*
87. Records of the Domestic Missionary Society, Sept., 1825, May,
1826, and June, 1828.

Domestic Missionary Society as an auxiliary of the national body.

During the Awakening interest in missionary activities had waxed strong in Connecticut, and indeed throughout the United States. Many people had displayed great zeal in their efforts to provide "the means of grace" for those who were without them and to convert the heathen in foreign countries. The missionary movement had become an American institution.

V

ORTHODOXY FORGES NEW WEAPONS

THE more aware one becomes of the many tangible manifestations of the new religious spirit which characterized the first quarter of the nineteenth century, the stronger becomes the conviction that the Second Great Awakening—in Connecticut and elsewhere—deserves a place in American history not hitherto accorded it. The missionary movement was but one of these tangible manifestations. There were, too, Bible societies, tract societies, education societies, and Sunday schools.

Soon after the Awakening began, there appeared a consciousness of a Bible shortage. In the old settlements Bibles were desired by those who sought to rouse people from their indifference and to rout infidelity. The revivals increased the number of those who wanted to own the Scriptures. When missionaries began to penetrate the new settlements and to venture into the foreign field, the demand greatly exceeded the supply.

In addition to pioneering in the missionary endeavors, the people of Great Britain were the first to cope with this shortage. They organized the British and Foreign Bible Society in 1804, which immediately began to raise money and to arrange for the publication and distribution of a large number of Bibles.[1] Soon the project of translating the Scriptures into as many languages as possible was under way. This pioneer society expended more than $54,000 in 1808, the year when Americans organized their first Bible society in Philadelphia.[2] The Bible-society movement spread rapidly throughout the country. In 1809 organizations similar to the one in Philadelphia were formed in

1. *Conn. Evang. Mag.*, VI, 319–320.
2. *Address, Constitution, and Subscription Proposal, of the Connecticut Bible Society* (1809), pp. 2–3.

Connecticut, Massachusetts, New York, and Maine, while each succeeding year saw an increase in the number of societies and in the enthusiasm for the project.

Connecticut had the second Bible society in the United States. The laws of the state required that every family have a Bible, that every apprentice and indented child on becoming of age should be given a Bible, and that the Scriptures should be constantly used as a textbook in the common schools.[3] But these laws could not be strictly enforced. Even if a universal desire to possess Bibles had existed, there would have been neither a sufficient quantity to go around nor enough money to purchase them. Accordingly, on May 11, 1809, a group of laymen and clergymen met in Hartford and organized the Connecticut Bible Society. John Cotton Smith of Sharon, later governor of the state, was elected president, while General Jedediah Huntington of New London was one of the vice-presidents along with three Congregational clergymen, Samuel Nott of Franklin, Azel Backus of Bethlehem, and Samuel Merwin of New Haven. The indefatigable Abel Flint was agent for purchasing and distributing Bibles. After paying tribute to the pioneering efforts of the British and Foreign Bible Society, the Connecticut society, which had as its sole object "the circulation of the Holy Scriptures," directed attention to the need for Bibles on this side of the Atlantic. Later in 1809 the directing committee announced that the field of the society's operations had no bounds except such as pecuniary ability should fix, but that those "destitute of Bibles in Connecticut and its vicinity will be among the *first*—though, by no means, the *only*, or the *principal* objects of the institution." Annual dues for members were set at three dollars, while a contribution of forty dollars constituted the subscriber a member for life.[4]

Immediately, the directors of the society took steps to

---

3. *Acts and Laws, Revision of 1796*, pp. 429–430.
4. *Report of the Directing Committee of the Connecticut Bible Society* (1810), p. 3; Conn. Bible Soc., *2d Report* (1811), pp. 4, 7, 9; *Conn. Evang. Mag. and Relig. Intel.*, II, 383–386.

raise money and to secure Bibles for distribution. Not only did they issue an address to the people of the state,[5] but they saw to it that many articles portraying the progress of Bible societies appeared in the *Connecticut Evangelical Magazine and Religious Intelligencer.* Societies established in many churches in response to appeals from the pulpit sent in contributions, and a gift of £50 was received from the British and Foreign Bible Society. In its first annual report the Connecticut Bible Society announced that its receipts totalled $1,360.70 of which $560 had been appropriated to establish a permanent fund, and that 723 Bibles had been purchased, of which 220 had been delivered to subscribers, 307 had been distributed gratuitously, and 196 were still on hand.[6] Early in 1811 Lyman Beecher wrote to his friend, Asahel Hooker, "We are succeeding remarkably in [Litchfield] county in getting subscribers to the Connecticut Bible Society, especially in this town. Judge Reeve is the agent here, and manifests his usual zeal and activity, and meets with more than his usual success. . . . Churchmen and Democrats, Christians and men of the world, all fall into the ranks on this occasion. The thing is the most popular of any public charity ever attempted in Connecticut."[7]

During the War of 1812 the Bible societies received a powerful stimulus. The Mills-Schermerhorn tour of the West under the auspices of the Missionary Society of Connecticut and the Massachusetts Missionary Society has already been described. Shortly after his return Mills led another expedition through the same territory, supported this time by the Massachusetts and Philadelphia Missionary societies and the Philadelphia Bible Society, and accompanied by the Reverend Daniel Smith who soon afterward was installed as pastor in Natchez, Mississippi. The reports on these two journeys revealed a shortage of Bibles

---

5. *Address, Constitution, and Subscription Proposal, of the Conn. Bible Soc.* (1809).
6. Conn. Bible Soc., *Rept.* (1810), p. 4.
7. Beecher, *Autobiography,* I, 241.

which alarmed the friends of religion. "It is our sober conviction," wrote Mills, "that at least 76,000 Bibles are necessary for the supply of the destitute; and the number is every year increasing. . . . The existing Societies have not yet been able to supply the demand, in their own immediate vicinity. Some mightier effort must be made. Their scattered and feeble exertions are by no means adequate to the accomplishment of the object. It is thought by judicious people, that *half a million of Bibles* are necessary for the destitute in the United States. It is a foul blot on our national character. Christian America must arise and wipe it away."[8]

Christian America made a valiant effort to do just that. Existing Bible societies increased their activities and a national society was formed. To determine who should have credit for the national organization is difficult. As early as 1810 the secretary of the British and Foreign Bible Society seems to have broached the subject to the New York and Philadelphia Bible societies only to receive a negative answer. One of Timothy Dwight's amanuenses referred to Dwight as the pioneer in this important development; while in 1813 and 1814 several articles on the subject appeared in the *Panoplist*. Certainly to Mills and his companions on his two journeys great credit must be given. Mills concluded one of his reports with a call for a national society. "The existing Societies," he wrote, "are not able to do it. They want union;—they want co-operation; —they want resources. If a National Institution cannot be formed, application ought to be made to the British and Foreign Bible Society for aid." Lyman Beecher called Mills "the primary agent in this movement," and according to his first biographer, Mills gave some thought to the possibility of having the General Assembly of the Presbyterian Church bring forward the idea in 1814 but was deterred by the consideration that it "should originate with no one ecclesiastical body, but with some one of the State

8. Quoted in Spring, *Memoirs of the Rev. Samuel J. Mills*, p. 93.

Bible Societies, who could give it currency with the least suspicion of local or party views."[9]

The New Jersey Bible Society issued the invitations for the gathering at which the American Bible Society was formed. To this meeting, held in New York City in May, 1816, Connecticut sent no commissioned delegates, but the Reverend Lyman Beecher of Litchfield, the Reverend Nathaniel W. Taylor of New Haven, and Mr. Ichabod Skinner of North Coventry, all of whom were connected with the Connecticut Bible Society, represented the state. Beecher served on the committee which drew up the constitution for the national institution, while John Cotton Smith, then governor of Connecticut, became one of its vice-presidents. An address issued to the people of the United States indicated that the American Bible Society would use the British and Foreign Bible Society as its model.[10]

Exhibiting the desire to remain independent which characterized societies in the state, the Connecticut Bible Society did not immediately become an auxiliary of the national organization.[11] Although in complete sympathy with the larger body, the trustees felt that in independence lay greater strength. There were, however, many ties between the people of the state and the American Bible Society. By 1818 nine auxiliaries had been established, and in 1819 five Connecticut men, the three who had attended the 1816 meeting together with the Reverend Heman

9. *Ibid.*, pp. 93–96; W. B. Sprague, "Timothy Dwight," in Jared Sparks, ed., *American Biographies*, Second Series, IV, 338–339; *Panoplist*, IX, 356–358; X, 117–123.

10. *Relig. Intel.*, I, 11.

11. In several instances Connecticut societies exhibited a reluctance to affiliate themselves with national organizations. This was due in part to legal difficulties connected with charters and funds and in part to a sincere conviction that independent action would produce more satisfactory results. Perhaps it may also be attributed to the existence of the state-rights doctrine in a field other than the political, to the sense of primacy and superiority which Connecticut Congregationalists definitely felt, and to a distrust of the theology of those with whom they would be obliged to coöperate. The nation as such was very young when these societies were formed.

Humphrey of Fairfield and the Reverend Isaac Lewis of Greenwich, were life directors of the society. Furthermore, ninety of the state's Congregational ministers had been constituted life members of the American Bible Society by their congregations.[12] Connecticut was giving material assistance to the national organization, which in 1820, after four years of operations, could report a total of $138,464 collected, somewhat over ninety-seven thousand Bibles and Testaments distributed, and 207 auxiliaries formed.[13]

In 1817 the Marine Bible Society of New Haven was organized as an auxiliary to the Marine Bible Society of New York, its sole object being "to encourage the circulation of the Holy Scriptures, without note or comment, among Seamen." The realization that the actions of American sailors in foreign ports did much to lessen the effectiveness of missionary labors had stimulated an interest in this group. The editor of the *Religious Intelligencer* issued the following plea in 1818: "Surely then none stand in greater need of the Bible—none have more leisure to read it—none can be more strengthened by its consolations, and none are so often called to trust their all to that Anchor to the soul which it reveals"; and the New Haven society reported 144 members and receipts of $128.[14]

Although the organization of Bible societies anywhere interested Connecticut people, developments in Russia occasioned special comment. When in October, 1813, it was announced that "a *Bible Society* has lately been established in Russia, under the patronage of the *Emperor Alexander*," there was much rejoicing, and the Reverend Joseph Harvey of Goshen in a missionary sermon declared triumphantly, "A glorious light has dawned upon the vast empire of Russia." Several years later, in 1822, the editor of the *Religious Intelligencer* expressed an opinion which

12. *The Second Annual Report of the Board of Managers of the American Bible Society* (1818), p. 29; Amer. Bible Soc., *3d Rept.* (1819), pp. 36–38, 41–53.

13. *Quarterly Register and Journal of the American Education Society,* II (1829), 31.

14. *Relig. Intel.,* II, 104, 749–751.

revealed the crusading spirit of the Second Great Awakening. He had noted reports that Constantinople would soon fall into Russian hands. "If Constantinople falls," he wrote, "what is then to stay the legions of Russia from overrunning the plains of Asia! Alexander is the patron of learning and the friend of religion—wherever his armies go they will carry the Bible. They will open the way for the missionary of the Cross into every part of Asia, and the Sun of Righteousness will again shine on that country which first received his cheering beams!" Shortly thereafter Alexander's religious policy changed and the Bible society was suppressed. Accordingly, the editor of the *Religious Intelligencer* reversed his position and in 1826 hailed the news of Alexander's death, declaring, "That in him, the main head of this many headed Cerberus [the Holy Alliance], that guards the pass to bewildered Europe, is amputated, is surely matter of rejoicing to the world as well as to the church."[15]

After the establishment of the American Bible Society, the Connecticut Bible Society continued its independent existence. This society received $1,995.40 in 1817, announced the formation of several auxiliaries and the distribution of nearly three thousand Bibles, and in addition issued a circular in which it declared, "The present has been emphatically styled *'The Age of Bibles.'* The zeal excited throughout the christian world for diffusing the Scriptures, constitutes a memorable era. It is the earnest and the means of a moral revolution among men, a thousand times more stupendous than all the political changes which have occurred. Our own country has caught the holy flame."[16] Evidence for this last statement is found in the 750 societies which were at work in the land, most of them directly connected with the American Bible Society as auxiliaries.

15. *Conn. Evang. Mag. and Relig. Intel.*, VI, 375; Joseph Harvey, *A Sermon, preached before the Foreign Mission Society of Litchfield County* (1815), p. 20; *Relig. Intel.*, VI, 576; X, 598.

16. Conn. Bible Soc., *8th Rept.* (1817), pp. 8–10, 21; *Connecticut Courant*, Feb. 25, 1817.

The 1818 report of the Connecticut society showed that the preceding year had been one of its busiest. Not only had it distributed more Bibles than in any year since 1812 and collected more money than in any previous year except 1812 and 1814, but the total number of Bibles sent to the needy in Connecticut, in the West, and in foreign countries passed the twenty thousand mark. From this time on, however, the society declined. Receipts of $2,173.73 in 1818 dwindled to $474.87 in 1821.[17] Nevertheless, a committee appointed to consider an alteration in the relationship with the American Bible Society recommended no change on the grounds that satisfactory evidence had not been discovered "that the Society of Connecticut could do more, or even as much, by relinquishing its independence, and becoming auxiliary, in any other sense than that in which all such Societies are auxiliary to each other."[18]

Naturally, the decline in revenue occasioned much concern and led to lengthy discussions of its cause. Several explanations were offered. The national society was attracting much attention and a state organization could not hope to secure much support. So numerous had the objects of benevolence become that pocketbooks were too frequently tapped. Perhaps the methods used in raising funds could be improved. Finally, it was suggested that "another cause, however, which has operated to diminish our efforts, doubtless is, the declining state of that *fervency of spirit*, with which we ought to serve our LORD in every department of labour to which we are called in His Kingdom."[19] Probably each of the reasons cited contributed to the waning importance of the Connecticut Bible Society.

Throughout the 1820's the question of a closer tie with the national institution was intermittently discussed. Finally, at the 1829 meeting it was voted that the Connecti-

17. Conn. Bible Soc., *9th Rept.* (1818), pp. 7–8, 16; *12th Rept.* (1821), p. 16.
18. *Ibid.,* p. 11.
19. Conn. Bible Soc., *15th Rept.* (1824), p. 5; *16th Rept.* (1825), p. 5.

cut Bible Society should become an auxiliary of the American Bible Society and that it should participate in the national society's plan to furnish a copy of the Scriptures to every family in the country willing to receive it. In connection with this undertaking the new auxiliary, as its initial act, proposed to raise $10,000 in the four northern counties of the state, and probably a similar amount in the four southern counties.[20]

Tract societies had their origin in Europe, the impetus coming from both England and France. In France Voltaire and others had employed tracts in their attacks on religious, political, and social conditions. Why should not the defenders of the Christian faith wield against infidelity the very weapon which its champions had used to drive revealed religion from the minds of many who had been believers? A writer in the *Religious Intelligencer* declared, "Voltaire may be said therefore, without much violence of expression, to have blown the trumpet of salvation. He invented an engine for the demolition of Christianity, which has proved the downfall and destruction of his own infidelity."[21]

Not only did the English teach Americans how to write religious tracts and furnish many which were used on this side of the Atlantic, but they also organized the first tract societies. Hannah More, undoubtedly the greatest tract writer of her time, turned to this form of literature in 1792 in an effort to counteract French religious ideas which during the French Revolution were enjoying a certain vogue in England. Her first tract, entitled *Village Politics*, was such a phenomenal success that she was led to publish a series known as the *Cheap Repository Tracts*.[22] From Miss More and others of her countrymen Americans

20. Conn. Bible Soc., *21st Rept.* (1830), p. 3; records of the Tolland County Consociation, 1829, Congregational House; records of the New Haven County Bible Society, Conn. State Library, p. 22.

21. *Relig. Intel.*, II, 350.

22. Marion Harland [Mrs. M. V. Terhune], *Hannah More* (New York, 1900), *passim*.

learned the art of tract-writing, and three of the tracts most widely used in the United States, *The Dairyman's Daughter*, *The Swearer's Prayer*, and *The Shepherd of Salisbury Plain*, were English compositions. In 1799 the London Tract Society was formed.

Americans followed the British lead by forming in 1803 the Massachusetts Society for Promoting Christian Knowledge, the first tract society in this country.[23] Connecticut people soon became interested in this project. In 1805 the Tolland County Association voted to request the General Association to adopt measures for the publication and distribution of small religious tracts, "calculated for the defence of the christian religion & the promotion of vital piety amongst the inhabitants of this State." The General Association immediately took action through a committee which approved the Tolland County proposal and suggested that subscription papers be issued. In 1806 the committee reported that $200 had been received and that 3,611 tracts had been delivered.[24]

Timothy Dwight was president of the Connecticut Religious Tract Society which was established in New Haven the following year. "The sole object of the Society," it was declared, "shall be the promotion of evangelical religion; and nothing shall ever be published in the tracts, which shall give any just cause of offence to any particular denomination of Christians."[25] This society then proceeded to publish a series of twenty-six tracts, but very little else has been discovered about its career.

Other societies followed, of which the New England Tract Society, organized in Boston in 1814 by a group among whom the Reverend Ebenezer Porter and the Reverend Justin Edwards of the Andover Theological Seminary were leaders, was the most important. Very shortly

23. Daniel Dorchester, *Christianity in the United States*, pp. 417–418.
24. Records of the Tolland County Association, Congregational House; *Extracts from the Minutes of the General Association, 1805*, pp. 2, 7; *ibid., 1806*, p. 5.
25. *Panoplist*, III, 187–189.

after its establishment the society reported the distribution of three hundred thousand tracts, and during its first five years it received a total of $3,145 as donations and $7,913 from the sale of tracts.[26] In June, 1815, Jedediah Huntington, John Treadwell, and Calvin Chapin, members of the Connecticut corresponding committee of the New England Tract Society, suggested in the *Connecticut Mirror* that each branch of the Connecticut Moral Society would do well to constitute itself an auxiliary tract society. Nothing came of this; but earlier in the year such an auxiliary had been set up at Yale College.[27]

Meanwhile, interested groups were endeavoring to establish a satisfactory tract society in the state. In 1814 a committee appointed by the Hartford County North Association reported that since the New Haven organization could no longer prosecute its charitable designs and since tracts were badly needed, the General Association should act. The General Association as such did nothing, but in 1816 a group of ministers and laymen formed the Hartford Evangelical Tract Society. Auxiliaries appeared in various parts of the state, among them one organized by the young men of New Haven, which during its first year distributed 3,348 tracts to vessels sailing from the harbor and to people of the town.[28] In Thompson and Killingly 122 ladies enrolled as members of the United Female Tract Society, which flourished for two years and then became an auxiliary Bible society.[29] Thomas Robbins noted in his *Diary* on January 7, 1818, that he paid ten dollars to become a member of the Hartford Evangelical Tract Society and that in the evening he attended the society's annual meeting.

When by an act of the Massachusetts legislature in

26. *Ibid.*, X, 232–234; Davis, *The Half Century*, pp. 329–330.

27. *Connecticut Mirror*, June 5, 1815; Journal of the Moral Society of Yale College.

28. Records of the Hartford County North Association, Congregational House; James H. Trumbull, ed., *The Memorial History of Hartford County . . . 1663–1884*, I, 537; *Relig. Intel.*, II, 171–172.

29. Larned, *History of Windham County*, II, 435–436.

1823 the New England Religious Tract Society, with its headquarters in Andover, became the American Tract Society, the Hartford society enrolled as its Connecticut branch.[30] The American Tract Society reported in 1824 that during the previous year it had printed 777,000 tracts and had established twenty-eight new depositories of which fourteen were west of the Alleghenies. In addition, it had pictures in nearly half of its tracts, had commenced the publication of the *American Tract Magazine* to be issued bi-monthly at a cost of fifty cents a year, had begun a new series of children's books, was printing the *Christian Almanack* in seven of the principal towns of the United States, and had 117 depositories in nineteen states and nearly 250 auxiliaries. Little wonder that the Hartford Evangelical Tract Society, whose activities had not been very extensive, had been ready to become auxiliary to this institution which was second only to the London Tract Society! In 1825 the Massachusetts American Tract Society merged with a society of the same name, recently organized in New York City, to form a national American Tract Society.[31]

Regarded as valuable aids in the efforts to revive religion and improve morals in the older settlements, and to insure the survival of the faith and preserve moral standards in the newly opened regions, tracts were extensively used. Bibles were, of course, fundamental, but tracts, cheap and therefore easily obtained, short and therefore quickly read, brought a message both to those who did not possess Bibles and to those who had them but who needed the succinct, simple language of a tract to catch their attention. Tracts were always brief, sometimes consisting of but a single page. Written with an obvious moral which the most untutored could scarcely fail to grasp and in a manner deliberately calculated to attract those who had strayed from grace, they were distributed in homes, they were presented to children in schools, and they were fre-

30. Davis, *The Half Century*, p. 330; *Relig. Intel.*, IX, 234–235.
31. *Ibid.*, IX, 282, 680.

quently left in taverns where it was hoped sinners might
see them and be led to change their ways.

The subjects treated in tracts were varied. *The Swearer's Prayer* has already been mentioned. Several tracts
were written on the subject of intemperance, and in 1826
the American Tract Society offered a prize of fifty dollars
for the best tract on "The Ruinous Consequences of Gambling." The writer of *Common Errors* surveyed the entire
field of human failings. One minister wrote *On the duty of
professors of religion, and especially those who have wealth,
to consecrate their property to the spread of the Gospel*
and received a prize for his efforts. Many found comfort
in *Hopes for Eternity, God a Refuge, Contentment in
Humble Life,* and *On Walking by Faith,* while one tract
was significantly entitled *Anecdotes, illustrating the Usefulness of Tracts.*[32]

Tracts were of importance in various phases of the Second Great Awakening. Constant references to their services appeared in the columns of the religious periodicals.
During revivals in Connecticut ministers used them to direct attention to religious truths and to excite a desire for
religious renewal in those who had previously been unyield-
ing. In vacant parishes they were widely distributed. Letters from representatives of the Missionary Society of
Connecticut teem with references to tracts and their effectiveness in rousing and maintaining religious interest
among people in the new settlements.

While efforts were being made to supply people with
Bibles and tracts during the first quarter of the nineteenth
century, the shortage of educated ministers caused considerable alarm. The mere growth in population along with
the steady expansion of the frontier would, of course,
have caused the demand to exceed the supply. But the renewed interest in religion in both the old and the new settlements and the demand for men to serve as missionaries
intensified the problem.

32. *Ibid.,* X, 540; XI, 28; *Connecticut Courant,* Aug. 17, 1824.

Outside Connecticut conditions were bad. Letters from missionaries testified to the need for ministers in the newly settled areas. In no uncertain terms Mills and Schermerhorn called attention to the shortage in the territory through which they travelled, while Mills and Smith emphasized the same point a year later. Articles giving statistics which portrayed graphically the country's destitution appeared frequently in the religious publications of the day.[33]

Particularly in Congregational New England was this inability to secure an adequate supply of educated ministers alarming. To the Congregationalists, education was essential for those whose duty it was to preach the gospel. Preaching by uneducated men was suspect. Blessed was an educated ministry, it was believed, for theirs it was to lead people into the kingdom of heaven!

The inability of the Missionary Society of Connecticut to secure a sufficiently large number of missionaries during its first decade, and to some extent in succeeding years, evidenced the lack of ministers.[34] The need was clearly brought out in the deliberations which preceded the formation of the Domestic Missionary Society and in the reports of missionaries employed by this society after its organization. From time to time discussions of the subject took place at meetings of the county associations and the General Association, while frequent references to it occurred in the annual reports on the condition of religion in the state.

To meet the shortage concerted efforts were made in Connecticut to establish places where young men could receive training for the ministry and to furnish financial aid to those who needed it. Various measures were taken to

33. Schermerhorn and Mills, *A Correct View; Relig. Intel.*, III, 644–645; *Panoplist*, XI, 475–481. See also Ebenezer Porter, *A Sermon delivered in Boston, on the Anniversary of the American Education Society* (1820); H. Humphrey, *Sermon preached at Lenox, Mass., at a Meeting Called for the Purpose of Forming a County Education Society* (1818).

34. See numerous letters written by Abel Flint, secretary of the Missionary Society of Connecticut, Congregational House.

carry out the first part of this program, some of which were not at all new. Certain clergymen who were particularly gifted as teachers were encouraged to increase their efforts and train more youths in their homes. Ministers and their "schools of prophets" were already well known throughout the state. Until his death in 1803, the Reverend Charles Backus of Somers conducted one of the most famous of these schools. Lyman Beecher studied with Timothy Dwight in New Haven, Thomas Robbins with Stephen West in Stockbridge, Massachusetts. Friends pressed the Reverend Asahel Hooker of Goshen to give as much instruction as time allowed to young men desiring to become ministers.[35]

That these individual endeavors were inadequate, was apparent, and the remedy was obvious—the founding of a theological seminary in Connecticut. Soon after the nineteenth century began, an unsuccessful attempt was made to set up such an institution in West Hartford under the auspices of the Hartford County North Association.[36] For several years after this no further efforts were made in Connecticut, but the establishment of the Andover Theological Seminary in 1808 helped to satisfy the needs. Connecticut ministers approved this citadel of orthodoxy, especially since several of their number became members of the faculty. Edward D. Griffin, who had left New Hartford in 1801 to go to Newark, New Jersey, became Professor of Pulpit Eloquence. Ebenezer Porter went from his church in Washington, Connecticut, to succeed Griffin in 1811 while Moses Stuart was called to the seminary from the First Church in New Haven. Not a few Connecticut ministers secured their training at Andover, and the Missionary Society of Connecticut frequently turned there for men to labor in the West.

35. Mills Day, Asahel Gaylord, Moses Gillett, Gordon Hall, Luther Hart, Heman Humphrey, Abel McEwen, Noah Porter, Bennet Tyler, and others studied under Hooker. Augustine G. Hibbard, *History of the Town of Goshen* (Hartford, 1897), p. 91.
36. Records of the Hartford County North Association, 1800.

In spite of the fact that Andover was educating ministers and that there was no cessation of theological study in ministers' homes, the shortage continued. In 1822 the Yale Divinity School was established. Still the demand far exceeded the supply, for the country was very young and the day when any one of the professions would be crowded lay in the distant future.

A second aspect of the effort to provide adequate, educated religious leadership is found in the education societies which came into existence at this time, designed to aid "pious but indigent young men" who desired to enter the ministry. It was not new for such young men to be helped by individuals, but the education-society movement was another phase of the group activity which characterized the Second Great Awakening. In September, 1809, the North Consociation of Litchfield County resolved itself into a charitable society "for the purpose of aiding pious, indigent young Men, in obtaining education, for the work of the Gospel Ministry," and urged that females establish cent societies and that funds be solicited from others "for promoting the great objects of this Society." Evidently the South Consociation coöperated in this endeavor. One article in the constitution, to which Asahel Hooker was opposed on the grounds that young men should not be thus burdened, provided that grants should be in the form of loans and not outright gifts. Very little has been discovered about the activities of this society. In 1816 agents were appointed to explain its claims on public charity; two years later it merged with a charity school at South Farms.[37]

The General Association in June, 1813, discussed the need for ministers and voted "that it be earnestly recommended to the several Associations belonging to this Body, that they promote, by all practicable means, the forma-

37. *Conn. Evang. Mag. and Relig. Intel.,* II, 424–425; "Memoir of the Reverend Asahel Hooker," *The Adviser; or Vermont Evangelical Magazine,* March–April, 1815, pp. 76–77; records of the Litchfield County North Consociation, Congregational House.

tion of Female Charitable Associations for the education of indigent and pious youth for the gospel ministry." In accord with the spirit of this vote although not in direct response to it, a Benevolent Society was formed at Yale College the following month "to assist young men, of good talents, and unblemished moral character, in obtaining an education at this College." The movement in the state, and for that matter in the country, had its real beginning, however, with the organization of two education societies in New Haven in 1814 and 1815. By the men the "Charitable Society for the education of indigent pious young men for the Ministry of the Gospel" was formed in September, 1814, while six months later the ladies established the Female Education Society of New Haven. Men from many parts of Connecticut and even from other states joined the first of these societies, which during its first year did practically nothing because of limited funds. It was a different story the second year when receipts totalled $2,374 and grants to the extent of $1,094 were made to twelve students at Yale College. In the year 1816–1817 appropriations increased to $1,605, which was distributed among thirteen Yale students.[38]

The Female Education Society endeavored to clothe the young men to whom the Charitable Society gave financial assistance. By September, 1816, it had as members 182 ladies, each of whom paid annual dues of fifty-two cents, and the 1816 report showed among its auxiliaries a Ladies' Praying Society in Greenwich, an Education Society in Norwich, and a Female Cent Society in North Guilford. Similar societies soon appeared in various parts of the state, in Hartford, Litchfield, Goshen, Stratford, Colchester, and Middletown among other places, to assist the New Haven ladies. During its first year and a half the New Haven society received clothing valued at $264.60 and $790.02 in money. On the grounds that it was "the aggregate of small sums from numerous contributors, which

38. Conn. Evang. Mag. and Relig. Intel., VI, 302; Panoplist, X, 312–313; Relig. Intel., I, 377–379; II, 268–269, 281–282.

sustains the important operations of most of the Missionary and Bible Societies in Europe and America," an appeal was made for small contributions.[39] The Female Education Society and the men's Charitable Society naturally concentrated their efforts at Yale College, where figures showed that for forty years an average of only nine ministers a year had been graduated.[40]

In 1819 nearly thirty students enjoyed the patronage of the Charitable Society, but its resources were so limited that the committee on appropriations found it necessary to borrow more than four hundred dollars. The next year this Charitable Society, henceforth known as the Connecticut Education Society, became a branch of the American Education Society, which had been established as the Massachusetts state organization in 1815 and was rapidly assuming the characteristics of a national society. Immediately, the new auxiliary began to flourish, its total receipts reaching the high level of $2,648 in 1821, which it distributed among forty-three beneficiaries. According to the 1823 report of the American Education Society, however, the funds of the Connecticut society were "in a very languishing state."[41]

Since the Connecticut Education Society continued to languish, a new branch of the American Education Society was organized in 1826.[42] This reinvigorated auxiliary was thus ready to participate in the national society's drive under the direction of its recently appointed agent, Elias Cornelius. The drive was for a large number of scholarships, only the income of which could be used for the society's beneficiaries.

39. *An Account of the Receipts and Disbursements of the Education Society of Connecticut and of the Female Education Society of New Haven* (1816), pp. 10–15.

40. Yale should have been turning out eighty ministers a year, it was felt. *An Address of the Charitable Society for the Education of Indigent Pious Young Men, for the Ministry of the Gospel,* [1814], p. 12.

41. *Christian Spectator,* I (1819), 103–104; *Relig. Intel.,* IV, 503; VI, 255; *Eighth Annual Report of the American Education Society,* p. 46.

42. Records of the Connecticut branch of the American Education Society, Congregational House.

In the meantime, the Female Education Society continued its independent existence, relying on various types of auxiliaries throughout the state. In 1822 the ladies reported receipts of $501.67 in money together with goods and clothing valued at $1,169.05, with which they aided forty young men at Yale. Because of a subsequent decline in contributions the society in December, 1824, issued an appeal to the ladies of Connecticut, but none the less the 1825 report revealed a decrease of almost half the amount received in 1822. In a sermon preached at the fourteenth anniversary of the society's founding, Professor Eleazar Fitch of Yale College noted that, whereas the Connecticut Education Society was to furnish young men with tuition and board, the Female Education Society was "to supply the place of maternal care and kindness over them in regard to their wants of clothing." And he made a special plea that while the American Education Society and its branches were being supported, the ladies' organization should not be forgotten.[43]

During the early 1820's two other developments occurred which were parts of the education-society movement. In 1822 the members of the North (now the United) Church in New Haven formed an Education Society to support one or more beneficiaries at Yale at the rate of one hundred dollars a year for each student helped.[44] That year, also, saw the death in the town of Canton of Dr. Solomon Everest, whose estate, which eventually proved to be worth over $16,000, was willed to the A.B.C.F.M., the Missionary Society of Connecticut, and the General Association.[45] The last of these organizations, which received one-quarter of the total, set aside the income for use in aiding the young men in whom the education societies were interested.

43. *Relig. Intel.*, VII, 126–127, 142; IX, 474–475; X, 142; Eleazar Fitch, *A Sermon, delivered on the Anniversary of the Female Education Society of New Haven* (1829), pp. 25–27.

44. *Relig. Intel.*, VI, 735–736.

45. *Report of the Directors of the Missionary Society of Connecticut for the Year 1880*, p. 21.

In the period of revivalism during which missionary, Bible, tract, and education societies first appeared, the modern Sunday-school movement also began. To find its origins is not easy, for records are incomplete and there is lack of agreement as to what constituted a Sunday school. As early as 1669, it seems, what was called a Sunday school existed in Plymouth, Massachusetts, while Roxbury in the same state had another in 1674.[46] During his long pastorate, 1740–1790, at Bethlehem, Connecticut, the Reverend Joseph Bellamy was accustomed to meet the young people of his congregation on the Sabbath, "not merely for a catechetical exercise but for a recitation from the Bible, in connection with which he communicated, in a way admirably adapted to the capacities of the young, much important instruction." A school of the same type was operating in Washington, Connecticut, in 1791, and another in Litchfield in 1805.[47]

From no consideration of Sunday-school origins can the name of Robert Raikes be omitted. He was an Englishman who in 1781 established in Gloucester schools for the unfortunate children of the streets to whom no other opportunity for education was available. Raikes' schools and those copied from them had certain distinct characteristics. They were usually not connected with churches, many of the teachers were paid, the children belonged to the most ignorant classes, and the services were not religious in nature but tended to center upon the spelling-book.[48] In 1791 a Sunday school of the Raikes variety was opened in Philadelphia.

Modern Sunday schools in Connecticut, which date from about 1816, appeared in profusion during the ensuing decade. For the most part they were not of the Raikes

46. Marianna C. Brown, *Sunday-School Movements in America,* pp. 19–20.
47. Letter from T. Robbins, in Sprague, *Annals of the American Pulpit,* I, 410; Harry K. Eversull, *The Evolution of an Old New England Church,* p. 116; Stewart, *History of Religious Education in Connecticut,* p. 318.
48. *Ibid.,* p. 316.

type but resembled the earlier New England schools. In a state where industrialism had not appeared to any extent to create wretched conditions among the children, where facilities for elementary education, at least, were available for all, and where Sunday schools were established primarily to perpetuate religion, this was to be expected. That the Connecticut schools were designed not to teach the youth to read but to give them special opportunities to become acquainted with religious and moral truths is shown by the following "Rules & Regulations" of the Sunday school set up in Haddam in 1819:

1. The Children are to attend meeting every Sabbath morning, with hair combed, hands, face, and clothes clean, and sit together.
2. To be at the School Room at half past 12 o'clock.
3. To take their seats immediately on entering the School.
4. To say, together, the Lord's Prayer after the Superintendent.
5. To have some lesson learnt, to say to their Teachers, and to say it in a low voice.
6. To behave well in School, and neither laugh nor whisper.
7. To be grateful and attentive to their Teachers.
8. To love one another, and avoid contention and quarreling.
9. Never to swear, or tell a lie, or call names.
10. To go to meeting in the afternoon in procession, and behave with solemnity.[49]

A writer in the *Religious Intelligencer* for April 27, 1822, pictured vividly and accurately what seems to have been in the minds of those who fostered the movement:

Sunday Schools seek the improvement of both soul and body. The habits of industry, order, and sobriety, obedience to

49. E. E. Lewis, *Historical Sketches of the First Congregational Church in Haddam*, p. 50.

parents, respect to authority, personal cleanliness, and kindness of disposition to one another, which the children are taught in these schools, are blessings which more immediately regard the present life, and which tend to soften and ameliorate the general features of society. But Sunday School instruction, taking a higher direction from this, leads the blind and ignorant to the Bible, the foundation of light and knowledge, and is often blessed by God to the conversion of the individual. The salvation of the immortal soul is the ultimate and grand object of all Sunday School instruction.[50]

There were, indeed, a few schools in Connecticut modelled after those of Raikes. In a school for white and Negro boys in Norwich, established in 1816, reading was one of the exercises. Similar secular instruction appeared in the curricula of what were known as African Sabbath schools in Hartford and New Haven,[51] and in scattered communities in isolated areas the Sunday school did supplement the elementary educational endeavors. In all such cases, however, the chief object was the "salvation of the immortal soul."

Like the other schools in Connecticut, the Haddam Sunday School, mentioned above, was conducted from the middle of May until the end of August. Both girls and boys attended, 160 in all, who were divided into classes of five under teachers who volunteered their services. Emphasis was placed on learning and reciting Bible verses, verses of hymns, and answers contained in the various catechisms, and a careful record was kept of each child's accomplishments. "Punctuality, Good Behaviour, and Proficiency in learning," it was announced, "will be rewarded by Tickets and Premiums."[52] Ordinarily these premiums took the form of books, tracts, or religious magazines. In the Ledyard Sunday School rewards were figured at the rate of a penny

50. *Relig. Intel.*, VI, 768.
51. Alvan Bond, *A Historical Discourse, delivered at the Hundredth Anniversary of the Second Congregational Church, Norwich*, p. 36; *Connecticut Courant*, Dec. 25, 1821.
52. Lewis, *Historical Sketches*, pp. 47–50.

for ten Bible verses and the same for twenty hymn verses. Three little girls in this school who had each recited one thousand verses from the Scriptures received Bibles.[53]

In the early years of the Sunday-school movement, it was felt that this system of premiums stimulated attention to religious matters, but about 1826 a change of opinion occurred which led to a widespread reform. The officers of one school reported in 1827, "We believe, further, that the system of rewards, hitherto practised, is wrong in *principle*, as it encourages *selfishness, ambition*, and *envy*,— and in its effects, highly injurious to the moral feelings of the children."[54] Many schools began to develop libraries, and the privilege of drawing books became the reward for faithful performances. In one instance difficulty was encountered because the library system was introduced too suddenly for children accustomed to premiums. In 1826 the General Association voted that "Sabbath School Libraries are an important part of the system of Sabbath School instruction; and that it is desirable a library should be instituted in connection with every Sabbath School in the State."

The organizational side of the Sunday-school story may be treated very briefly. Beginning about 1816 these schools appeared in various churches throughout the state, New Britain, Norwich, Torringford, Derby, Hartford, Farmington, Meriden, Colchester, and Danbury being among the towns where they were first organized.[55] The movement spread with great rapidity, and the next step was union on a small scale, frequently with interdenominational cooperation among the Congregationalists, Episcopalians, Baptists, and Methodists. In 1818 a Sunday School Union, with four schools (two Congregationalist, one Bap-

53. W. T. Cook, *A Sketch of the Life of Rev. Timothy Tuttle*, Ledyard (Congregational House), pp. 8–9.

54. *Third Annual Report of the Connecticut Sunday School Union* (1827), p. 32.

55. Osborn, ed., *History of Connecticut*, III, 402; *Relig. Intel.*, X, 74; *Torringford: in Connection with the Centennial of the Settlement of the First Pastor, Rev. Samuel J. Mills*, pp. 36–37 note.

tist, and one Episcopalian) containing five hundred children under its supervision and with the ubiquitous Abel Flint as its president, was organized in Hartford. Several churches in the northwest corner of Litchfield County formed a union during the winter of 1819, under the auspices of which a school was set up in each society in the vicinity. The New Haven Sunday School Union came into existence during the summer of 1822.[56]

It was natural to expect that a state union and a national union would soon be created. In October, 1824, five months after the establishment in Philadelphia of the American Sunday School Union and auxiliary to it, the Connecticut Sunday School Union was formed.[57] The General Association, which had favored the movement from its inception, bestowed its blessing on the two unions and supported the intensive campaign launched to induce all Connecticut schools to join the state union. The advantages to be derived from such action were emphasized—the opportunity to learn about the condition and progress of the many schools connected with the state and national unions; the chance to exchange experiences with other teachers and supervisors and to become acquainted with new methods; the possibility of saving money by buying books at the American Union prices.[58] In 1826 the Connecticut Union had fifty-two auxiliaries in which there were about 1,200 teachers and 7,000 students. The following year the union had eighty auxiliaries which included 1,600 teachers and 10,000 students. In 1830 the General Association was coöperating with the national organization in its drive to establish within two years a Sunday school in every neighborhood in the Mississippi Valley.[59]

The Sunday-school movement had an interesting corollary. After these institutions had functioned for a short period, it became apparent that although they worked well

56. Trumbull, ed., *Memorial History of Hartford County*, I, 537; *Connecticut Courant*, June 6, 1820; *Relig. Intel.*, IX, 26–27.

57. *Ibid.*, IX, 473.   58. *Ibid.*, X, 90.

59. Conn. Sunday School Union, *3d Annual Rept.*, p. 13; *Proceedings of the General Association, 1830*, p. 7.

for children until they were thirteen or fourteen years old, the youths in their later teens still presented a perplexing problem. Bible classes were the answer. Inaugurated in Connecticut about 1825, they were really Sunday schools on a higher age level into which it was hoped young people would advance "easily and cheerfully." In the Bible classes, which ministers and deacons conducted, the Bible was studied rather than memorized. The aim was to continue religious instruction, but the approach was more mature. In its third annual report (1827), the Connecticut Sunday School Union announced that several Bible classes had been instituted with gratifying results. "It would be happy for our country," the report continued, "if Bible classes were universally established; but as ministers and churches are becoming more awake to their importance and utility, we expect, with confidence, that in a few years they will be found planted by the side of Sabbath Schools, in most of our towns and villages."

It now remains to account for the development of Sunday schools and Bible classes. When the Awakening became general in the state during the early years of the nineteenth century, the friends of religion, intent on making permanent their victory over the forces of infidelity and indifference, realized that this was contingent on their success with children and young people. Something akin to Sunday schools already existed in a few churches; the work of Raikes was known. What was more natural than the establishment of these institutions wherein the desired religious instruction could be given?

Of importance, too, was the fact that, following the passage in 1795 and 1798 of the school laws which increased secular control of educational matters, the public schools were visited and catechized less regularly.[60] In 1814 Lyman Beecher declared that the Bible and catechism had been exiled from the schools. He undoubtedly

60. T. Robbins, "A Century Sermon," in Theron W. Crissey, *History of Norfolk . . . 1744–1900* (Everett, Mass., 1900), p. 153; Beecher, *A Sermon delivered at Woolcot, . . . at the Installation of Rev. J. Keyes,* p. 9.

overstated the case, but there must have been some grounds for this contention. As one means of building up the "waste places" in Connecticut, Beecher suggested an effective system for the instruction of children and young people in the doctrines and duties of religion. His remarks may have been influential in bringing about the establishment of Sunday schools and Bible classes.

It would seem proper, where the season will permit, that the children of the congregation (who ought all of them, as far as possible, to attend public worship) be catechised by a committee of the church, in the interval of public worship; and that stated catechetical examinations of all the children of the congregation, be attended by the pastor and a committee of the church, at least semi-annually, and if practicable, quarterly.

It is also unspeakably important, that a system of religious instruction be provided, to succeed the shorter catechism, adapted to the age and altered feelings of young people. In most cases the whole system of religious instruction, by the church and by parents, also, ceases with the period of childhood.[61]

It is not surprising that Sunday schools, designed to provide the catechetical instruction which the public schools were neglecting, appeared in various parts of Connecticut in 1816.

Two years later the union between church and state was severed, and more completely than ever before religious instruction was ruled out of the schools. At about this time occurred a significant change in the Act for the Educating and Governing of Children which appeared for the first time in the 1821 revision of the laws. Previously, parents

61. *Ibid.*, p. 19. The General Association in 1808 issued an address, *The Importance of United Endeavours to Revive Gospel Discipline*, in which parents were urged to spend at least an hour every Sabbath with their children "in prayer, catechising and familiar instruction in the doctrines and duties of religion." Stewart, *History of Religious Education in Connecticut*, pp. 300–301.

and others who had the care of children were required to have them instructed in the English language, and to provide for their knowing the laws against capital offenses. The law had stipulated, "And if unable to do so much, then at least [to cause the children] to learn some short orthodox Catechism without Book, so as to be able to answer to the Questions that shall be propounded to them out of such Catechism, by their Parents, Masters, or Ministers, when they shall call them to an Account of what they shall have learned of that kind." All mention of the catechism was omitted from the 1821 law which provided merely "that all parents, and those who have the care of children, shall bring them up in some honest and lawful calling or employment; and shall teach and instruct them, or cause them to be taught and instructed, to read and write, and cypher as far as the first four rules of arithmetic."[62] Probably developments such as this helped to account for the great increase in the number of Sunday schools after 1818.

62. *Acts and Laws, Revision of 1796,* p. 60; *Public Statute Laws, Revision of 1821,* p. 107.

VI

DESIGN FOR REFORM

DURING the Second Great Awakening attention was given to the subject of moral reform in various parts of the United States. In Connecticut, probably the most active reform center in the country, Congregational ministers were the leaders. Alarmed by what they considered a lamentable decline in morals, they made vigorous efforts to restore the ascetic code of Puritanism. They directed their crusade especially against Sabbath-breaking, swearing, and intemperance.

As early as 1789 a group of influential men in Litchfield, undoubtedly acquainted with the pamphlet, *An Inquiry into the Effects of Ardent Spirits on the Human Body,* which Dr. Benjamin Rush of Philadelphia had published in 1785, pledged themselves to carry on their business enterprises without "ardent spirits," and to supply their employees with nothing but beer and cider. Their purpose was "to reform a practice which leads so many to poverty, distress and ruin." Their voluntary association was short-lived.[1]

One of the earliest societies for moral reform was the Moral Society of Yale College, a secret organization formed in 1797.[2] Students desiring to become members were required to give affirmative replies to the following questions:

1. John A. Krout, *The Origins of Prohibition,* p. 68; Dorchester, *Christianity in the United States,* pp. 354–355; White, *History of . . . Litchfield,* p. 156.

2. The MS. Journal of this society is in the Yale Library. Evidently some organization preceded the Moral Society of Yale College, for, as has been previously indicated, on April 15, 1796, a Yale student wrote to Thomas Robbins, "I have broken myself of the vulgar habit of swearing & the still more pernicious one of gambling. I expect at the next meeting of the Moralists I shall propose myself as a Candidate to enter." H. Belden to T. Robbins, Robbins Papers.

Will you endeavour to regulate your conduct by the rules of morality contained in the Bible?

Will you endeavour by all prudent measures to suppress vice and promote the interests of morality in this Seminary?

Will you, as long as you continue a member of this Society, wholly refrain from every kind of profane language?

Will you never be guilty of playing any game in which property is concerned; and will you, also, refrain entirely from playing cards, whilst you continue a member of this Society?

Not until a later date was a similar answer required to a fifth question, "Will you as long as you continue a member of this society abstain from the intemperate use of spirituous liquors?"[3]

The Moral Society held monthly meetings over a period of years, with a program usually consisting of a disputation on some such subject as: "Ought infidels to be excluded from holding public offices?" (1797), "Whether Theatres are beneficial?" (1801), "Ought a Christian to bear arms?" (1801), "Is it a duty of the American churches to send the Gospel to the Heathen in the east?" (1818), "Is dancing an innocent amusement?" (1822), "Ought the Indians at the Foreign Mission school to be any further restricted in reference to marriage than the students of Yale College?" (1825), "Is it expedient to form a national society for the suppression of intemperance?" (1826). Occasionally orations on similar subjects were delivered.

Since a close supervision over the morals of members was maintained, at more than one meeting students confessed to breaches of the society's regulations and sought pardon for their offenses. In 1803 a member was expelled

---

3. Apparently this was required after 1823. Henry B. Wright, James B. Reynolds, and Samuel H. Fisher, editors, *Two Centuries of Christian Activity at Yale*, p. 58 note.

"for profane swearing, for taking a copy of the constitution and refusing to give it up and for revealing the secrets of the society." Intoxication caused the suspension of two members in 1808.

On several occasions the society exhibited its interest in the general moral situation in the college. On August 11, 1801, members were reminded of their duty to inspect the morals not only of those who belonged to the society but also of the other undergraduates. When a member reported four months later that profanity and vice were prevalent among the students, a committee was appointed "to inform a number of the most vicious of the impropriety & danger of their conduct & that unless they desisted their conduct would be made known to the authority of [the] college." Shortly afterward it reported that the offenders had been warned and "that those with whom they conversed behaved with propriety and promised reformation." Again in 1804 a special committee was appointed "to inspect the morals of the College, and report to the Society."

The society had twenty-three members in 1797 but only fourteen the following year. In 1802, probably as a result of the revival of that year, the membership rose to seventy-six, a total never exceeded in the years that followed, the number of members being thirty-six in 1803, fifty-five a decade later, forty-nine in 1820, and twenty-nine in 1826. In 1828 the society became the Moral and Theological Society.

During the early years of the nineteenth century the use of "ardent spirits" in Connecticut was widespread.[4] Not only was tavern-frequenting common but drinking was by no means confined to these public places. A social visit invariably called forth strong drink. "In all families, rich or poor," wrote Samuel G. Goodrich, "it [rum] was offered to male visitors as an essential point of hospitality.

---

4. Throughout this period the reformers were concerned only with the use of "ardent" or distilled spirits, such as whiskey, rum, and brandy. Cider, beer, and the lighter wines were not considered harmful.

. . . Women—I beg pardon—ladies, took their schnapps, then called 'Hopkins' Elixir,' which was the most delicious and seductive means of getting tipsy that has been invented."[5] Employers distributed a regular supply of liquor to laborers, while barn- and house-raisings, corn-huskings, and elections occasioned much drinking.[6] When a new cotton mill was opened in Pomfret in 1806, "over 2,000 were present and free punch [was] served to all!" Jail keepers had licenses as tavern keepers so that they might dispense spirits to the prisoners.[7] Yale students consumed much spirituous liquor, "that baleful root of all college evil," one student's father called it.[8] At weddings the cups were filled and refilled, while at funerals so customary was drinking that when the practice was discontinued a chorus of protests arose against what was considered an inhospitable reform. "Temperance has done for funerals!" one old veteran is reported to have declared. One critic of the extensive use of distilled spirits has said, "It was too the universal panacea, good in heat and cold, in weariness and painfulness, when sick and when exposed to sickness; the cure of children in all their complaints, the support of the mother nursing her offspring, and of the old man going down to the grave. It helped the lawyer plead, the minister preach, and the physician go his rounds of duty. None could tell its worth, but all were made to feel its curse."[9] This universal indulgence in distilled liquors made intemperance inevitable.

The fact that "ardent spirits" were served at ordinations and church dedications, at pastoral calls and ecclesiastical meetings, reveals the prevailing attitude of Congregational ministers. Included on the bill rendered the

5. Goodrich, *Recollections of a Lifetime*, I, 69.

6. See, among many, *ibid.*, I, 69; Clark, *History of Connecticut*, p. 369; *Contributions to the Ecclesiastical History of Connecticut*, p. 206.

7. Osborn, ed., *History of Connecticut*, IV, 261; V, 415.

8. E. Pearson to Mills Day, March 11, 1812, Yale University Library.

9. E. P. Parker, *History of the Second Church of Christ in Hartford*, p. 86 note; *Contributions to the Ecclesiastical History of Connecticut*, p. 206.

Second Church in Hartford for purchases made to celebrate the ordination of the Reverend Abel Flint in 1791 were charges for wine, cherry rum, brandy, and the "best spirits."[10] The Reverend Nathan Strong of the First Church in Hartford engaged in the distillery business without reproach for several years during the early part of his ministry. When rebuked for this activity Strong with his customary wit and with reference to his Hartford and West Hartford colleagues replied, "O, we are all in one boat in the business. Brother Perkins raises the grain, I distil it, and Brother Flint drinks it."[11] A poem entitled *The Ordination Ball*, written a hundred years after the event, presents an amusing but accurate picture of the festivities connected with the ordination of the Reverend Lucas Hart in Wolcott in 1811.[12] The refreshments consisted of pumpkin pie, election cake, doughnuts, "popped corn,"

> And cider that was surely sweet
>   A year or two ago.
> And truth compels us to relate
>   That other things were there
> Which we could wish had had no place
>   Upon their bill of fare.
>
> .   .   .   .
>
> "Tody" was there in mammoth "boles,"
>   A mystifying elf,
> With one "d" in its written name,
>   But more in the thing itself.
> And "flip" abounded too, and "punch,"
>   And freely flowed for all,
> But let us hope that few partook
>   At the Ordination Ball.

10. Parker, *History of the Second Church*, p. 164.

11. Walker, "The Historical Address," *Commemorative Exercises of the First Church of Christ in Hartford*, pp. 85–86; Walker, *History of the First Church in Hartford*, pp. 343–344 note.

12. J. G. Davenport, *The Ordination Ball*.

Let it be said for the Reverend Mr. Hart that he demurred against the ball and everything connected with it;[13] but many of his ministerial brethren participated in the festivities—and the refreshments.

There were, however, ministers who advocated temperance, and some who were total abstainers. The Reverend Andrew Yates, pastor in East Hartford from 1801 until 1814, opposed the use of intoxicating liquors, although social custom compelled him to serve them at ecclesiastical meetings. On one occasion he is reported to have produced the customary refreshments and then to have said, "Brethren, here is rum, gin, brandy, laudanum,—all poison. Help yourselves!"[14] Under the leadership of Congregational clergymen in Connecticut American temperance reform began in earnest during the early years of the nineteenth century.

What appears to have been the first temperance sermon in the state was preached by the Reverend Ebenezer Porter in 1805.[15] Inspired by an incident which had occurred in his neighborhood, a man overcome by drink having fallen in the snow and having frozen to death, Porter took his text from Isaiah 5.11, and in his opening sentence declared, "This passage of the sacred volume calls our attention to a subject, which is but rarely made the theme of the pulpit." He pointed out the miserable effects of intemperate drinking, and warned the young men in particular. "As you regard your character, your comfort, or your salvation," he counselled, "shun the company, shun the places, where this sin will beset you. The moment you become familiar with it, you are undone. Chained down in iron bondage, your life will become miserable and your name contemptible. Avoid the men that love strong drink. Their feet go down to death: their steps take hold on hell. If you find yourselves inclined to go in this path of evil

13. Soon afterward, it appears, the young pastor preached a sermon against this festivity. Orcutt, *History of . . . Wolcott*, p. 81.
14. Trumbull, ed., *Memorial History of Hartford County*, II, 92–93.
15. E. Porter, *The Fatal Effects of Ardent Spirits* (1805).

men, set the grave on your right hand, and eternity before you. Pause,—and escape the ruin." This sermon was not published until 1811. In 1808 a temperance society was organized in Moreau, New York, the members of which pledged themselves to use "no rum, gin, whisky, wine or any distilled spirits, or compositions of the same, except by advice of a physician, or in case of actual disease." Two years later the Reverend Heman Humphrey of Fairfield preached a series of six sermons against intemperance, and in 1811 the Reverend Roswell Swan of Norwalk and the Reverend Calvin Chapin of Rocky Hill went so far as to advocate total abstinence from all spirituous liquors. The following year the New Haven County East Association declared the prevailing abuse of "ardent spirits" to be a serious and growing evil, and resolved to take measures to lessen this practice.[16] Thus was the way prepared for an important development in the temperance movement in which the Reverend Lyman Beecher played the leading rôle.

Shortly after Beecher began his Litchfield ministry in 1810, a series of incidents ensued which led this reformer to take action. At two successive meetings of the consociation to which he belonged so much liquor was consumed that Beecher, who had preached several temperance sermons during the last years of his brilliant ministry in East Hampton, Long Island, was profoundly stirred.[17] Probably his championship of temperance induced the Litchfield County North Association to vote in 1811 "that the use of wine and all other ardent spirits shall henceforth be excluded from our associational meetings. That the members of the Association will use their influence to discoun-

16. Krout, *Origins of Prohibition*, p. 78; Eversull, *Evolution of an Old New England Church*, p. 102; minutes of the meetings of the New Haven County East Association, Yale University Library, May 27, 1812.

17. Beecher, *Autobiography*, I, 245–246. Both Beecher and Dwight had been roused to take action against duelling by the death of Alexander Hamilton in 1804. They were leaders in the movement which did much to put a stop to duelling in this country.

tenance the use of wine and all ardent spirits in their
families and in their social visits among their people."[18] In
1812 Beecher attended the annual session of the General
Association. A committee, appointed the previous year at
the request of the Presbyterian General Assembly to devise measures for preventing the numerous mischiefs
threatened by the excessive use of spirituous liquors, reported "that, after the most faithful and prayerful inquiry, they were obliged to confess they did not perceive
that any thing could be done." Indignant at this supine-
ness, the Litchfield pastor moved that another committee
be appointed to investigate the matter. While the General
Association was still in session, this committee, of which
Beecher was a member, made a report which must be considered one of the most important landmarks in the early
history of the American temperance movement.[19]

It included several recommendations to churches and
congregations. Ministers were requested to call attention
to the evils of intemperance and to the necessity of united
action for reform. They were also advised to practice what
they preached by dispensing with the use of "ardent
spirits" at their various ecclesiastical meetings. Church
members were admonished to abstain from the use of liquor
in their families, to relinquish the idea that hospitality required the introduction of spirituous liquors at social
visits, and to instruct those under their care at an early
age concerning the harmful effects of intemperance. The
report directed a special appeal to farmers, mechanics,
and manufacturers "to diminish the quantity of ardent
spirits consumed in their several employments, by the sub-
stitution of other palatable and nutritious drinks, and by
giving an additional compensation, if necessary, to laborers who will dispense entirely with the use of ardent
spirits." In addition, pamphlets and tracts were to be dis-

18. *Contributions to the Ecclesiastical History of Connecticut,* p. 314.
19. Beecher, *Autobiography,* I, 247; *Proceedings of the General Association, 1812,* pp. 7–8, 31–33.

tributed, and voluntary associations formed in various parts of the state to assist in law enforcement and to work for the removal of the evil. "Let ministers, and churches, and parents, and magistrates, and physicians, and all the friends of civil and religious order," the report continued, "unite their counsels and their efforts, and make a faithful experiment." The General Association approved the recommendations as well as an address which the committee prepared.

Tangible results were immediately forthcoming. County associations voted to bar "ardent spirits" from their meetings and to coöperate in carrying out the recommendations of the General Association.[20] In October, 1812, delegates from various parts of the state met in New Haven to make plans for the formation of a society for the suppression of vice and the promotion of good morals. To this gathering Beecher preached one of his notable sermons, *A Reformation of Morals Practicable and Indispensable.* He declared that the public conscience by becoming callous had prevented the enforcement of laws against drunkenness, profane swearing, and travelling on the Sabbath. He pleaded for a renewal of the moral influences which had created an eminently desirable state of society. "It is not as if we were called upon to make new laws, and establish usages unknown before," he insisted. "We make no innovation. We embark in no novel experiment. We set up no new standard of morals. We encroach upon no man's liberty. We lord it over no man's conscience. We stand upon the defensive merely. We contend for our altars and our firesides. We rally around the standard which our fathers reared, and our motto is, '*the inheritance which they bequeathed, no man shall take from us.*'" The creation of a committee of inquiry and correspondence was followed by

20. Records of the Tolland County Association, Congregational House, and of the New Haven County West Association, Yale University Library. The action of the Fairfield County East and West Associations is reported in *Contributions to the Ecclesiastical History of Connecticut,* pp. 299–302.

another meeting in May, 1813, at which time the Connecticut Society for the Promotion of Good Morals was established.[21]

Ex-governor Treadwell became president; Tapping Reeve was one of the vice-presidents, while General Jedediah Huntington, Lyman Beecher, and Calvin Chapin were members of the directing committee. The object of the society was "to promote good morals, and to discountenance vice universally: particularly, to discourage profaneness, gross breaches of the Sabbath, idleness, and intemperance; and especially to discourage intemperance." Any person of good moral caliber who would subscribe to the constitution might become a member. Semi-annual meetings of the society were to be held, while auxiliaries were to be organized throughout the state to carry out the program. A reform in morals was contemplated, not by force or compulsion or any extensive legislative action, but by a vigorous campaign based on good examples, education, and the creation of a public opinion favorable to the enforcement of the existing laws.

The reasons for the organization of this society need to be considered. In describing the founding of the Moral Society in his *Autobiography* Beecher indicated that the political motive was dominant. "It was the anticipation of the impending revolution and downfall of the standing order," he wrote, "that impelled me to the efforts I made at the time to avert it, and to prepare for it in all possible ways."[22] Beecher was indeed the arch-politician among the ministers, but his account of the Moral Society is one of the many sections of the *Autobiography* which were written years after the events described had transpired, and which, therefore, must be used with care and discrimination. In one part of his discussion of the Moral Society Beecher was strikingly inaccurate. He declared that it was "a new thing in that day for the clergy and laymen to

---

21. *Conn. Evang. Mag. and Relig. Intel.,* VI, 230–231. This society will henceforth be called the Moral Society.
22. Beecher, *Autobiography,* I, 260.

meet on the same level and co-operate. It was the first time there had ever been such a consultation between them in Connecticut in our day."[23] For the moment he forgot that consociations had brought ministers and laymen into consultative assemblies for more than a century, and that the two groups were already sharing the management of the missionary and Bible societies.

In spite of the fact that some of the state's leading Federalists were among the founders of the Moral Society and that their opponents accused it, along with the missionary and Bible societies, of being a tool in the politicians' hands, the political motive does not appear to have been important. Religious means were used for religious ends by Congregationalists who also were Federalists. While there is evidence to show what the society did for morals, none exists to reveal its political activities. Beecher's contemporary attitude, disclosed in a letter written to Asahel Hooker in July, 1812, indicates that the organizers were not concerned with political gains.[24] He asserted that the state of public morals, especially the frequent violations of the Sabbath and the alarming prevalence of intemperance, demanded some special action. He referred to the possible good effects of a society which would not only awaken the people to the dangerous state of affairs, but would also serve as a rallying point for their efforts, and would foster a careful study of both the existing conditions and the ways of combatting the evil. "Who can tell how great a matter a little fire may kindle?" he asked.

Beecher's previous experiences with similar voluntary associations probably led him to advocate a moral society for Connecticut. As an undergraduate he had been a member of the Moral Society of Yale College; indeed, he was one of the first who was obliged to plead for forgiveness inasmuch as he had been involved in an incident concerning cups broken by a stone thrown at a college window.[25] During his first pastorate in East Hampton, Long

23. *Ibid.*, I, 259. 24. *Ibid.*, I, 253–254.
25. Journal of the Moral Society of Yale College.

Island, he preached a sermon in which he mentioned four recently established moral societies, and declared that such associations did much good "by turning . . . attention to the rising generation, to schools and private families, and by circulating moral and religious tracts, and by appointing in each school, small premiums, the rewards of good behaviour and laudable progress." Following this discourse the people of East Hampton organized a moral society.[26]

Connecticut was the country's most important center in the reform movement for a decade and a half after 1813, and Beecher and other Congregational ministers and laymen were not only responsible for the formation of the Connecticut Society for the Promotion of Good Morals in that year but also directed its subsequent activities. The widespread desire for improvement in morals was undoubtedly connected with the religious awakening. "May it not be," Beecher had queried hopefully in 1812 when advocating a moral society, "a part of that great and new system of things by which God is preparing to bless the world and fill it with His glory?"[27]

The aims of the society reveal the influence of the new spirit, for the crusade was against intemperance, Sabbathbreaking, and profane swearing. As has been indicated, in the early years of the nineteenth century many religious people came to consider intemperance one of the greatest evils of the time. Timothy Dwight summed up the current arguments in striking fashion. "Our health, our reputation, our safety, our reason, our usefulness, our lives, our souls, our families and our friends," he asserted, "in solemn and affecting union urge, entreat, and persuade us to abstain. God commands; Christ solicits; the spirit of grace influences us to abstain. . . . The Law with a terrible voice thunders in our ears that dreadful denunciation, 'Drunkards shall not inherit the kingdom of God.' "[28]

26. L. Beecher, *The Practicability of Suppressing Vice, by Means of Societies instituted for that Purpose* (1803), pp. 10, 13–14, 25.

27. Beecher, *Autobiography*, I, 254.

28. Quoted in *Relig. Intel.*, IV, 303–304.

The Sabbath occupied a special place in the ideology of Connecticut Congregationalism. It was the Lord's Day, and as such was to be remembered and kept holy; hence any violation was considered an offense against God and was a serious matter to people who cherished the Calvinistic conception of the sovereignty of God. In 1794 Timothy Dwight made some pungent remarks on the subject. "The Sabbath by regularly assembling the congregation for public worship," he said, "arranges with regularity the whole business of the week, and gives birth in a higher degree, than a slight observer would imagine, to neatness, sociability, softness of manners, and universal decorum. By bringing a congregation together on so interesting an occasion, it makes them know, respect, and regard each other. From the moral and religious instructions, the cogent motives to duty, and the encitements to decent, amiable, and useful conduct, which it furnishes, it establishes, perhaps more than any single thing, good order, good morals and happiness public and private. It makes good men; and good men must be good citizens."[29] In 1814 the Reverend Calvin Chapin alluded to another of the benefits to be derived from the Sabbath. "Who has not seen," he asked his listeners, "that more business will be accomplished by the same person, in a year, and, ordinarily, more health enjoyed, where the Sabbath is established as the *stated* period of requisite rest, than if the rest be taken irregularly?" Later in the same sermon Chapin asserted that "wholesome morals, with rational liberty, will not long prevail where the general profanation of the Sabbath becomes fashionable."[30]

Profane swearing, like the violation of the Sabbath, was proscribed in the Old Testament Decalogue, and therefore was frowned upon by people who felt that life should be lived in accord with Biblical dictates. Blasphemy revealed

29. Quoted in Henry Barnard, "History of the Legislation of Connecticut respecting Common Schools, down to 1838," *Annual Report of the Superintendent of Common Schools in Connecticut, 1853,* pp. 100–101.

30. Calvin Chapin, *A Sermon delivered before the Connecticut Society for the Promotion of Good Morals* (1814), pp. 26, 28.

an attitude toward God which threatened the very foundations of the social order. Lyman Beecher deplored the effects of this pernicious habit which "breaks down the moral government of God over men, . . . emancipates them from the restraint of the divine sanctions, and lets them loose upon society to obey, as they may be tempted, the impulse of passion and a depraved inclination."[31]

Immediately after its organization in 1813 the Connecticut Moral Society began to function. Since the extant material dealing with its career is extremely fragmentary, only a brief account of its activities can be given. Auxiliaries were set up in various parts of the state as rapidly as possible, and quiet but intensive efforts were made to secure members. At the time of the first semi-annual meeting in October, 1813, nearly thirty branches had been formed. The following May twenty-three auxiliaries reported, while there were several others from which nothing was received. It was estimated that more than two thousand people had become members.[32] No other figures have been discovered which show the number of auxiliaries and members, but a study of available material seems to indicate an increase during the year 1814–1815, and a decline thereafter. Copies of several sermons delivered at the semi-annual meetings of the society have been preserved, the last one extant showing that Noah Porter preached in October, 1816. The Guilford auxiliary held a meeting in March, 1817.[33] On May 6, 1818, Thomas Robbins referred for the last time to the East Windsor Moral Society. After attending a meeting at which so few persons were present "that the address was not delivered," his final comment was, "Our Moral Society languishes."[34] Indeed, with this record the state society, too, seems to have disappeared.

While it lasted, the Moral Society had some effects, the

31. L. Beecher, *A Sermon delivered . . . on the evening subsequent to the formation of the Connecticut Society for the Promotion of Good Morals* (1813), p. 13.

32. *Panoplist*, X, 17–20; *Conn. Evang. Mag. and Relig. Intel.*, VII, 301–313.

33. *Connecticut Journal*, June 3, 1817.

34. Robbins, *Diary*, I, 740–741.

most significant being the changed attitude of many Congregational ministers and church members toward the liquor question.[35] Those who took a leading part in the campaign against intemperance were henceforth committed to the cause. As has been indicated, "ardent spirits" were banished from ministerial meetings and church functions in many places, never to be restored. Less frequently was the pastoral call the occasion for serving spirituous liquors. An increasingly large number of ministers abstained completely, numerous sermons were preached against intemperance, and the religious publications became crusaders for the cause of temperance. The new position of many churches and clergymen is clearly shown in the minutes of the General Association.

Contemporaries saw other effects. In 1814 a committee of the General Association reported that the informing officers and magistrates, supported by public sentiment, had checked the grosser violations of the Sabbath by a more faithful execution of the laws. The New Haven County East Association noted some success in suppressing "immoralities." "Greater attention to the Sabbath is paid than formerly," was the story from Middlesex County, while the Litchfield County South Association told of improvement "in many places."[36] The Reverend Joseph Harvey testified to the effects of the Moral Society and its auxiliaries in 1815:

Intemperance, that Goliath of the present day, has (we may hope) received a mortal wound. The Sabbath is beginning to be rescued from general profanation. The Magistrate awakes

35. The records of the General Association and of the county and half-county associations reveal this new attitude. The reform, however, was by no means universal. The Reverend Leonard Bacon of New Haven, for instance, recalled, forty years later, that at his installation in 1825 "there was an ample supply not only of wine but also of more perilous stuff," and that when he attended the first meeting of his district association, "the sideboard of good father Swift, at whose house we met, was decorated with decanters containing distilled spirits, and of more than one kind." Bacon added that in a little while "the tyrannical fashion had lost its power." Leonard Bacon, *Four Commemorative Discourses,* p. 32.
36. *Proceedings of the General Association, 1814,* pp. 10–16.

to his duty; the sword of justice no longer sleeps in its scabbard. That which is as a grain of mustard seed in its beginning, waxes great and becomes a tree. The friends of order and religion are rallying to their post, and they find by joyful experience, that with the blessing of heaven, *one may chase an hundred, and an hundred can put ten thousand to flight.*[37]

"The influence of Associations formed for the purpose has evidently been favorable to the interests of morality," the minutes of the New Haven County West Association for 1816 recorded. In Pomfret the laws were enforced more strictly and there was less drinking. A leading citizen of this town who did not drink at public dinners always left money on the table so that his abstinence might not be attributed to niggardliness.[38]

In her charming chapter on Connecticut customs in Osborn's *History of Connecticut*, Mrs. Mary H. Mitchell observes that about 1815 a change occurred in the attitude toward dancing, that it was frowned upon instead of being considered part of a child's education. This the writer attributes to the revivals or to the development of a new culture era.[39] Perhaps the interest in moral reform was a contributing factor. And one wonders whether Thomas Robbins by two entries in his *Diary* unwittingly testified to the success of the reformers. On December 14, 1810, he noted, "A dancing school is set up here which gives us much anxiety." On January 15, 1816, he again referred to the establishment of a dancing school, but this time remarked, "I think it will not excite much attention."[40]

In an outline prepared for a lecture on temperance in the early 1820's Robbins noted that as a result of the Moral Society's activities "taverning diminished & perhaps habitual drunkards. Many temperate people drank

37. Harvey, *A Sermon, preached before the Foreign Mission Society of Litchfield County* (1815), p. 16.
38. Larned, *History of Windham County*, II, 447.
39. Osborn, ed., *History of Connecticut*, V, 298.
40. Robbins, *Diary*, I, 459, 656.

less & not a few left off entirely." Perhaps the work of the society was responsible for the fact that when news of the Peace of Ghent reached New Haven on a Sabbath morning the people were prevented, though with difficulty, "from publicly breaking the Sabbath by the ringing of bells & the firing of cannon." Certainly the English traveller, Hodgson, in 1823 found that the observance of the Sabbath in Connecticut where he had to "tarry on the Sabbath" differed from that in New York where he could travel as he would. The Reverend Noah Porter discussed the benefits derived from these vigorous and organized attempts at moral reform in a sermon preached before the Moral Society in 1816. He spoke of the "check which was given to licentiousness in time of war; of that decent observation of the Sabbath which is now generally apparent; and of that impression of the importance of executing the laws which is extensively made on the public mind."[41]

While the enthusiasm for moral reform was running high, efforts were made to eliminate Sabbath mails. As early as 1811 Ebenezer Porter and Lyman Beecher addressed a paper to Governor Treadwell in which they remonstrated against a law passed the previous year, authorizing the transmission and opening of mail on the Sabbath. On a copy which he kept, Porter wrote, "Written in 1811. The first movement of its kind in the United States."[42] After its organization the Moral Society aided the General Association in securing signatures to a petition to Congress in which Sabbath mails were opposed on the grounds that "the transportation and opening of the Mail on the Sabbath Day is inconsistent with the proper observance of that Sacred Day, injurious to the morals of the nation, and provokes the judgments of the Ruler of nations." The petition was circulated among the people of

41. Robbins Papers (Miscellaneous, Box II); C. Denison to D. Daggett, Feb. 15, 1815, Daggett Papers; *Relig. Intel.*, VIII, 279; N. Porter, *A Sermon delivered at the Meeting of the Connecticut Society for the Promotion of Good Morals* (1816), pp. 17–18.

42. Lyman Matthews, *Memoir of the Life and Character of Ebenezer Porter*, pp. 329–330.

the state, and was finally presented with others to Congress in 1817. There the proposal was rejected, for reasons which the postmaster general advanced. "The contents of the mail," he said, "are not confined to public despatches [sic], nor to subjects of private business or pleasure. The same mail which transports such matters, conveys supplies to those in want, consolation to the afflicted, and, to the pious, evangelical correspondence; and thus, performing works of charity, it may be regarded as doing good on the Sabbath day." During the same year, however, a committee of Congress reported that while it was necessary to transport mail on the Sabbath, it was not obligatory to keep the offices open for the delivery of letters.[43]

How is the disappearance of the Connecticut Moral Society and its auxiliaries to be explained? Certainly the work for which the societies had been established had not been completed. An 1817 address to the churches and congregations made this clear. "It is a painful conviction," these groups were informed, "which, from various evidences, has forced itself upon us, that the sin of intemperance, for a season checked in its progress, is now again gaining ground; and that the use of profane language, and the profanation of the Sabbath, though less flagrant and extensive than formerly, are still lamentably prevalent."[44] Probably the main reason for the disintegration of the Moral Society was the fact that the zealous leaders found themselves in the situation of which Timothy Dwight is reported to have warned them when the campaign was beginning.[45] They were too far in advance of public opinion. Under any circumstances the task of maintaining vol-

43. *Conn. Evang. Mag. and Relig. Intel.*, VIII, 270; *Proceedings of the General Association, 1815*, p. 9; *ibid., 1816*, pp. 10–11; Davis, *The Half Century*, pp. 184–185.

44. *Proceedings of the General Association, 1817*, p. 16. In the outline for a temperance sermon in the 1820's, referred to above, T. Robbins wrote, "Yet, from the cheapness of ardent spirits, it became an article of more common use, & the quantity consumed increased."

45. Beecher, *Autobiography*, I, 251.

untary associations could not be easy. When they ran ahead of public opinion, the difficulties were so tremendous as to warrant the abandoning of formal efforts by the leaders. Interest may have waned, too, because people had so many things to do following the conclusion of the War of 1812. The sponsors and supporters of the movement were disappointed at their failure to achieve greater success. Beecher was undoubtedly thinking of his experiences with the Moral Society when he wrote in 1826, "Voluntary associations to support the magistrate in the execution of the law are useful, but, after all, are ineffectual; for though in a single town or state they may effect a temporary reformation, it requires an effort to make them universal, and to keep up their energy, which never has been and never will be made."[46]

During the years which followed the collapse of the Moral Society, interest in the questions of intemperance and Sabbath-breaking was continued by ecclesiastical associations and other groups, but practically no organized activity resulted.[47] An exception was the meeting held by the heads of families in Hartford in August, 1823, "to consider the alarming prevalence of intemperance and its concomitants," as a result of which a Hartford Society for the Suppression of Intemperance seems to have been formed. Thomas Robbins preached before this society in May, 1825.[48]

It was in this year and the next that a new phase of the reform movement began. Lyman Beecher and Calvin Chapin, who had played leading rôles in the earlier period, once more launched attacks on intemperance. No longer were they content to advocate mere temperance; this idea was shelved on the grounds that temperate drinking too

---

46. Beecher, *Works*, I, 391–392.

47. See, for examples of this interest, the records of the Tolland County Association and the New Haven County East and West Associations; *Relig. Intel.*, VIII, 128; *Proceedings of the General Association, 1820*, pp. 6–7; *ibid., 1824*, p. 6; *Contributions to the Ecclesiastical History of Connecticut*, p. 310.

48. *Relig. Intel.*, VIII, 173; Robbins, *Diary*, I, 1003.

frequently led to excesses. The new principle on which the battle was to be waged was total abstinence. Once again Congregational ministers placed Connecticut in the vanguard of American reform efforts.

Beecher's "Six Sermons on Intemperance," preached in Litchfield shortly before he was called to Boston in 1826, are well known.[49] In these discourses he reviewed the entire subject of intemperance. He showed how the habit developed and pointed out the harmful effects which resulted. His attack was sweeping. "But who are found so uniformly in the ranks of irreligion as the intemperate?" he inquired. "Who like these violate the Sabbath, and set their mouth against the heavens,—neglecting the education of their families, and corrupting their morals? Almost the entire amount of national ignorance and crime is the offspring of intemperance. Throughout the land, the intemperate are hewing down the pillars and undermining the foundations of our national edifice." In three of the six sermons he discussed the remedy. Temperance had not produced the desired results in the past and would not in the future. Therefore, Beecher asserted, the only remedy was the "banishment of ardent spirits from the list of lawful articles of commerce, by a correct and efficient public sentiment; such as has turned slavery out of half of our land, and will yet expel it from the world." He advocated a campaign to spread information regarding the evils of intemperance; he urged the organization of associations to superintend the great objects; he believed that agricultural, commercial, and manufacturing establishments could make greater efforts to exclude spirituous liquors as auxiliaries to labor. The churches, he felt, could render great assistance. Only after such a campaign could legislation be passed against the distillation and importation of "ardent spirits" and against improper methods of selling them. "Republics," Beecher shrewdly observed, "must be prepared by moral sentiment for efficient legislation."

At practically the same time Calvin Chapin delivered a

49. Beecher, *Works,* I, 347–425.

similar attack. His medium of expression he found in the columns of the newly established *Connecticut Observer*, where thirty-three articles, each with the heading "The Infallible Antidote," appeared in as many weeks in 1826.[50] Succinctly and clearly Chapin described what he considered the inadequacy of the doctrine of temperance. On one occasion he even lamented the fact that Dr. Rush's essay, which supported this position, had ever been published. "Harm lies in ambush," Chapin declared, "when even the smallest portion of ardent spirits are swallowed." For him entire abstinence was the only certain preventative of intemperance.

Between them Beecher and Chapin captured the attention of people whose interest in the subject had never completely disappeared. In 1826 the General Association's committee which prepared the report on the state of religion in Connecticut mourned the increasing intemperance, and then made a significant statement to the effect "that there will be yet greater lamentation, until there is a union of ministers and churches, to abstain utterly from the common use of ardent spirits: and till their efforts for the extermination of the evil are directed more immediately to its cause." The next step was taken in Massachusetts, where the campaign against intemperance had closely paralleled that in Connecticut. At a convention held in Boston on February 13, 1826, the American Society for the Promotion of Temperance was formed.[51]

Connecticut was somewhat slow in organizing, perhaps because Beecher left the state early in 1826, perhaps because many people recalled the Moral Society's experience. Interest was evidenced, however, in the new principle of total abstinence and in Massachusetts' action. On September 9, 1826, the editor of the *Religious Intelligencer* praised the Boston society, urged the churches to organize against intemperance, and recommended that "each indi-

50. The first of these articles appeared on January 16, the last on August 21.
51. Krout, *Origins of Prohibition*, pp. 108–111.

vidual enter into an agreement not to keep in his house, never to use himself, and never to offer to his friends, any spirituous liquor of any kind." With the spirit of crusaders various groups entered the campaign. On February 10, 1827, the *Religious Intelligencer* reported a meeting of Yale students at which resolutions were unanimously adopted to do everything possible to suppress intemperance. Two weeks later this paper carried the news that the Medical Association of New Haven, alarmed by the number of deaths due directly or indirectly to excessive drinking, had expressed deep concern regarding the use of spirituous liquors. In March one read that the members of the Mechanics' Society in New Haven had voted to ban "ardent spirits" from their respective establishments and to refuse employment to men who drank to excess.

The Congregational church was a staunch ally. It contributed not only through the pioneers, Beecher and Chapin, but also through its stand for total abstinence. The General Association in 1828 recommended the formation of temperance societies and proposed for them articles of agreement which concluded with the statement, "that we will abstain from the use of distilled spirits except as a medicine in case of bodily infirmity; that we will not allow the use of them in our families nor provide them for the entertainment of our friends; nor for persons in our employment; and that in all suitable ways we will discountenance the use of them in the community." The fourth Wednesday in January, 1829, was set aside for fasting, humiliation, and prayer because of the prevalence of intemperance in the country.

As early as September, 1827, a Young Men's Temperance Society was formed in Hartford which at the end of its first year reported that the sale of spirituous liquors by large dealers had decreased by half. During 1828, with ministers and church members playing leading rôles in the campaign, total-abstinence societies sprang up all over the state. Thirty-three such organizations were reported for Connecticut at the close of the year. The Middlesex

County Temperance Association, instituted in September, 1828, had ten auxiliaries which held monthly meetings. A representative of this association, enthused by the unanimous vote of the town officers of Lyme to abstain from spirituous liquors, reported to the American Temperance Society that the time appeared to him "to be at no great distance, when, with the blessing of God resting on the great movements now making in favour of Temperance, strong drink will be viewed by all as unfit for common use as a beverage, and will be regarded only as a medicine; to be prescribed, if at all, by physicians."[52]

In May, 1829, the Connecticut Temperance Society was organized, and its progress within a year testified to the popularity of the movement. Each of the eight counties had a branch society with auxiliaries, a total of one hundred seventy-two in May, 1830, with a membership of over twenty-two thousand. The wave of enthusiasm and achievement had reached a new high point. Many voices seconded the sentiment expressed in Mount Riga in Salisbury at a Fourth of July celebration, "The next cask of spirit that arrives on Mount Riga, may it share the fate of the tea in the port of Boston."[53] At this time attention was also directed toward the reform of confirmed drunkards, and the plans of the Medical Society to establish an Asylum for the Intemperate were viewed with interest. The drive for total abstinence on the basis of improved physical fitness, increased mental alertness, and great economic benefits, reinforced by appeals to the humanity, patriotism, and religion of the people, produced amazing results in a brief period.

Nor was the problem of intemperance the only one taken up at this time. Attention was again accorded Sabbath-breaking. In 1826 the General Association reiterated the opinion that "the Sabbath is essential to the permanency

52. *Second Annual Report of the Executive Committee of the American Society for the Promotion of Temperance* (1829), pp. 13–15.
53. *First Annual Report of the Executive Committee of the Connecticut Temperance Society* (1830), pp. 8–9, 17.

of all other religious institutions; and is identified with the
existence of the Christian Religion." In view of increasing
violations of the Sabbath ministers and church members
were urged to be especially careful not to offend along this
line, while it was recommended to them that they "guard
the sanctity of the Sabbath by the faithful exercise of
christian discipline; and that they discountenance the
profanation of this sacred day, by patronizing such travelling establishments, and such men, in the different occupa-
tions of life as respect the Sabbath." All ministers were requested to preach on this subject before the first of September.

At a meeting in New York City attended by a large
delegation from Connecticut the General Union for Promoting the Observance of the Christian Sabbath was
formed in May, 1828. In June of that year the General
Association approved the proposed plan of action and
urged the churches to establish auxiliaries. At least three
such societies were soon in existence.[54]

As a part of the renewed endeavors to keep the Sabbath
day holy, the question of the mail was again considered. A
federal law, passed in 1825, aroused much opposition because it required all post offices receiving mail on Sunday
to keep open during the entire day. As was the case a decade earlier, Connecticut furnished many signers to one of
several petitions to Congress; as before, the petitions had
no effect. This time they brought forth a report from
Richard M. Johnson, then senator from Kentucky, in
which he defended the government's position. Of Johnson's effort it was said, "Satan never accomplished a
greater temporary victory over the Sabbath, through any
agency, in any country, than was accomplished by this report, if we except the abolition of the Sabbath in France,
during the reign of infidelity." Friends of the Sabbath

---

54. The *Address of the General Union for Promoting the Observance
of the Christian Sabbath* (1828), pp. 3–4; *Second Report of the General
Union for Promoting the Observance of the Christian Sabbath* (1830),
p. 5; *Proceedings of the General Association, 1828,* p. 9.

found consolation in the hostile feelings roused by this memorandum. "Associations were formed, and conventions held, and means used to promote a better observance of the Lord's day." And the number of Sabbath mails was decreased.[55]

In the 1820's the moral reformers entered still another field by questioning for the first time the propriety of conducting lotteries. Lotteries had long been common in Connecticut as means of raising money to construct bridges and public buildings, to repair roads, to establish manufactories, and even to build churches. Very few voices, if any, were raised against the practice in the early years of the nineteenth century, and the legislature was accustomed to grant most petitions for lotteries without discussion. In 1809 and 1810 several requests were turned down because of financial conditions in the state, but nothing was said about the morals of the matter.

About 1826, however, a different sentiment seems to have appeared. In May of that year the New Haven County West Association proposed for discussion at its next meeting, "Is it the duty of ministers & churches to do anything for the discouragement & suppression of lotteries: & if any thing what?"[56] The editor of the *Religious Intelligencer* on November 11, 1826, was loud in his condemnation, stating that "the practice of lottery gambling has assumed an alarming aspect in this state. . . . Lotteries, we shall maintain, are gambling institutions and like them promote immorality, poverty, idleness, discontent and misery." The following year the legislature rejected almost unanimously the petition of the Military Academy at Middletown to raise $20,000 by a lottery, on the grounds that this practice was "highly injurious to the morals and best interests of the community." In 1828 the legislature stiffened the law regarding lotteries by increasing the penalties to be imposed on those who had to do with

55. Davis, *The Half Century*, pp. 185–186.
56. Records of the New Haven County West Association.

unauthorized lotteries. In 1830 more detailed restrictions were voted.[57]

With the legislation in regard to lotteries the story of this phase of Connecticut's Second Great Awakening may be closed. The organized reform movement was well under way.

57. *Relig. Intel.*, XII, 10; *The Public Statute Laws of the State of Connecticut, 1822–1835,* pp. 206–207, 296–300.

VII

THE AGE OF BENEVOLENCE

THE American humanitarian movement began in the early years of the nineteenth century. For the first time society as a whole was aroused to improve the lot of the poor, the physically handicapped, and the oppressed. Several factors combined to cause this new development.

The United States undoubtedly borrowed from England and France where humanitarianism was the product in large part of the eighteenth-century Enlightenment, the emergent Industrial Revolution, and the rise of evangelical Protestantism, especially among the Methodists. During the Enlightenment the individual as such began to count for more, and the doctrine of the perfectibility of man was widely accepted. The Industrial Revolution, in England, on the one hand created conditions so deplorable as to make reform imperative and on the other fostered the increase and accumulation of wealth which made possible the diversion of a part for the care of the poor and the unfortunate. Methodism was largely the religion of the lower classes and roused interest in their welfare.

In accounting for American humanitarianism, consideration must be accorded the situation in the United States as well as the European influences. The wealth of the country was increasing during the early 1800's, and the United States had an evangelical Protestantism of its own during the Second Great Awakening. In Connecticut, where the people had more money as a result of increased agricultural output, profitable commercial ventures, and nascent manufacturing, and where awakened Congregationalists were the leaders, the humanitarian spirit evidenced itself in many ways.

Attention was first directed to the poor for whose care

the state made inadequate provision. As early as December, 1791, the citizens of Hartford were called on to form a society which should "give relief to honest, industrious and frugal people, especially mechanics and other laborers who may be suddenly reduced to want." A year later such a society was founded, members subscribing not less than a dollar annually. Widows, children, the aged, and laboring people impoverished by sickness or unavoidable misfortune were to be the objects of its care.[1] Very little has been discovered about the career of this pioneer charitable society except that it was incorporated in 1809 and that six years later a committee of which Abel Flint and Nathan Strong were members appealed for more subscribers and reported the education of numerous children in addition to the relief of families and individuals.[2]

With the relief of the poor in Hartford, especially the female poor, as its object, the Hartford Female Beneficent Society was established in 1809 by the women of the First and Second Churches. Part of its funds were to be used to place girls under capable persons who would instruct them "in reading, sewing, and good housewifery, and impress them with moral and religious principles." Membership dues were one dollar a year, with a $15 life membership, while clothing and other suitable articles were solicited.[3] Within a year the society, with a Board of Managers consisting entirely of women, not only had ten girls under its care but was also assisting numerous poor families. It obtained a charter of incorporation in 1813.[4] When Thomas Robbins was invited to preach the annual sermon in 1815, he asked for information regarding the society's activities. From the secretary he learned that it had aided sixty-

1. *Connecticut Courant*, Dec. 12, 1791; Oct. 1, 1792; Jan. 28, 1793.
2. *American Mercury*, Oct. 25, 1815. According to Trumbull, the historian of Hartford County, this society existed when he wrote, *ca.* 1886. Trumbull, ed., *Memorial History of Hartford County*, I, 537.
3. "Constitution of the Hartford Female Beneficent Society," printed with Nathan Strong, *A Discourse delivered by the desire of the Hartford Beneficent Society* (1809).
4. *Resolves and Private Laws of the State of Connecticut, 1789-1836*, I, 328-330.

eight families during the past year, thirty-six being those of widows; that it was caring for eight children; and that "the Managers have lately voted to confine their charities to the poor in sickness, and to the establishment of an asylum for poor Female children."[5] In 1824 a correspondent to the *Connecticut Courant* testified to the accomplishments of the Hartford ladies by asserting that an extension of their project would quickly reduce the number of those "who fill our prisons and poor houses." The Beneficent Society in 1830 sponsored an elaborate fair in the new Hartford market which lasted for three days and produced a profit of about $600. Activity on behalf of young girls drew attention to young boys, and after some delay an orphan asylum for boys was established in 1833.[6]

In 1811 New Haven had three recently organized female charitable societies which aimed on the one hand to relieve want and suffering and on the other to remove or prevent vice and ignorance. For the first purpose they provided clothes and bedding particularly for women and children; for the second they set up several schools for the instruction of poor female children. Timothy Dwight, who was particularly interested in the school intended for young Negro girls, wrote, "I know of no charitable institutions, in which beneficence has more wisely, or usefully, extended its happy efficacy with the same means; or in which its good offices have been more skilfully directed."[7] When Lyman Beecher preached in 1816 at the request of two of the societies, a large audience listened to his sermon and then contributed generously for charitable purposes.[8] In 1819 the ladies of the Female Charitable Society of

5. Jerusha Watson to T. Robbins, Aug. 29, 1815, Robbins Papers.

6. *Connecticut Courant,* Nov. 23, 1824; Mason F. Cogswell to daughter, Mrs. Mary Weld, April 14, 1830, Cogswell Papers, Yale University Library; Edward W. Capen, *The Historical Development of the Poor Law of Connecticut,* pp. 162–163. In 1865 the Hartford Female Beneficent Society was united with the Hartford Orphan Asylum. Parker, *History of the Second Church of Christ in Hartford,* p. 210 note.

7. Dwight, *Statistical Account of the City of New-Haven* (1811), pp. 77–78; Dwight, *The Charitable Blessed* (1810), pp. 16–23.

8. *Connecticut Courant,* July 2, 1816.

New Haven examined the children of the school supported by their patronage. It seems reasonable to believe that this organization was the predecessor of the New Haven Female Society for the Relief of Orphans, Half Orphans, and Destitute Children, formed in 1833, which set up an orphanage.[9]

Similar societies appeared in other parts of the state. A Female Charitable Society was organized in Middletown in 1809, "whose special design is to provide for the education of the children of the poor, and to furnish clothing to the destitute." When it was incorporated in 1818, it possessed $1,100 in bank stock.[10] A Female Cent Society, so named because the dues were a cent a week, was founded in New London in 1810 to help indigent persons in and near the town. Later this was incorporated as the Lewis Female Cent Society after it had received a bequest of $500 from Mrs. Harriet Lewis. The Trumbull Benevolent Society sent a small donation to New Haven to assist the project of educating poor children. In 1811 the ladies of Greenwich formed a society for instructing and clothing the poor, while Goshen had a similar society in 1816. A Widows' Society was organized in Hartford County in 1825 to distribute necessaries to widows and their families.[11] These organizations, and others like them, made small but substantial contributions to the support of Connecticut's poor.

Humanitarian interest during the early nineteenth century turned not only to those lacking in material things but also to the physically handicapped. Among these were the deaf and dumb. The unfortunate affliction of the young daughter of a distinguished Hartford physician, Dr. Mason F. Cogswell, initiated the movement.

9. *Connecticut Journal*, Nov. 30, 1819; Edward E. Atwater, ed., *History of the City of New Haven*, p. 677.

10. Field, *Statistical Account of the County of Middlesex* (1819), p. 58.

11. Caulkins, *History of New London*, p. 663; *Connecticut Journal*, March 23, 1819; *Relig. Intel.*, I, 318; II, 208; Trumbull, ed., *Memorial History of Hartford County*, I, 539.

When his daughter, stricken at the age of two, was five years old, Dr. Cogswell became interested in the possibility of establishing a school for her and others similarly afflicted. He seems to have written first in 1811 to the General Association, in his own name and that of Sylvester Gilbert, an attorney of Hebron who had five deaf and dumb children. After expressing his hopes for some kind of school, he asked that the number of deaf mutes in the state be ascertained. The following June the total was reported as seventy-four.[12] Cogswell then discussed the project with friends for more than two years, during which period he found an enthusiastic supporter in young Thomas H. Gallaudet, a graduate of Yale College and the Andover Theological Seminary who was not yet settled in the ministry. Gallaudet spent several evenings with Alice Cogswell and showed such skill with her that the father decided that Gallaudet should direct the undertaking. In 1814 Cogswell's friends in New Haven, Timothy Dwight, Jeremiah Day, and Benjamin Silliman, advised against delay, and late that year Cogswell wrote Day that he was determined to establish the school as soon as possible.[13]

Accordingly, a meeting was held in Cogswell's house on April 13, 1815, at which Ward Woodbridge, Daniel Wadsworth, Henry Hudson, Nathaniel Terry, John Caldwell, Daniel Buck, the Reverend Nathan Strong, the Reverend Thomas Gallaudet, all of Hartford, and Joseph Battell of Norfolk were present.[14] Fully cognizant of the fact that two obstacles stood in their way—that the methods of instructing the deaf and dumb had to be learned and that money had to be raised—this group decided to launch the enterprise.

The first difficulty was solved by the decision to send Gallaudet, who had accepted the superintendency of the proposed institution, to Europe.[15] Gallaudet went first to

12. *Proceedings of the General Association, 1811,* p. 11; *ibid., 1812,* p. 28.

13. M. F. Cogswell to J. Day, Nov. 15, 1814, Day Papers.

14. Trumbull, ed., *Memorial History of Hartford County,* I, 425.

15. Gallaudet's experiences in Europe are described in Edward M. Gallaudet, *Life of Thomas Hopkins Gallaudet.*

London where a well-known school existed. Here he encountered unexpected trouble, for the methods of instructing the deaf and dumb were considered the monopoly of a certain Braidwood family who had no intention of letting them become public property. Gallaudet's requests for instruction were met with such conditions as to make his acceptance impossible. Discouraged he turned to an institution in Edinburgh, where once again the Braidwood monopoly blocked him. The director of the Edinburgh school had been trained in London and had posted a large bond which would be forfeited if he acceded to the American's request.

While in London Gallaudet had met the Abbé Sicard, who had long been in charge of a Paris school for deaf mutes. Almost in despair the agent of the Hartford group went to Paris to interview the Abbé who received him cordially and allowed him to observe and question as much as he desired. This he did for several months, and when the time came for him to leave France, the Abbé permitted Laurent Clerc, one of his most skilled instructors, to accompany Gallaudet to the United States. One interesting stipulation was made, that no attempt should be made to proselytize Clerc from his Catholic faith.

In the meantime the group at home had been busy trying to raise money. From New Haven came a discouraging report in 1816. "By many," Simeon Baldwin wrote Cogswell, "the object was not understood & when explained the prospect of advantage seemed to them remote, which with a want of sympathy, & the embarrassments of the times was an excuse." The writer feared that no more than $200 would be contributed.[16] Later in the same year Cogswell received a temporary setback when the two houses of the legislature could not agree on the amount of money to be granted to the proposed institution. "Thus all our hopes from the Legislature, *for the present*, are blasted," he wrote.[17]

16. S. Baldwin to M. F. Cogswell, May 14, 1816, Cogswell Papers. Unless otherwise indicated these papers are in the Yale University Library.
17. M. F. Cogswell to wife, Oct. 30, 1816, Cogswell Papers.

The return of Gallaudet with Clerc in August, 1816, provided a great impetus to the undertaking. The fear that a rival institution would be set up was quickly dispelled. At Albany Clerc displayed himself to advantage, Gallaudet preached well, and $1,882 was collected. Clerc demonstrated teaching methods to the Connecticut legislature and answered questions.[18] Wherever he appeared, large audiences attended, and there was general amazement at the accomplishments of this man who had been a deaf mute almost from birth. On January 25, 1817, the *Religious Intelligencer* announced a gift of $500 from the New Jersey philanthropist, Elias Boudinot, as well as receipts of $6,000 from Boston and Salem and $3,000 from Hartford. The Connecticut legislature granted $5,000. Finally, on April 15, 1817, the Connecticut Asylum for the Education and Instruction of the Deaf and Dumb, the first of its kind in the United States, opened. It was estimated that the elementary instruction would take from three to six years. A charge of $200 a year was made, which covered lodging, board, washing, care, fuel, stationery, candles, and tuition. For the present, it was stated, the Asylum could receive no charity students from places which had made no contributions.[19]

Only seven students attended at first, but by the end of the first year thirty were registered. Each succeeding year the enrollment increased until in 1821 there were sixty-two in the institution while thirty had been discharged. The 1823 report showed that a total of 110 pupils had been in the school; in May, 1829, 143 of the afflicted were being instructed.[20]

As announced before its opening, the Asylum was not on a charity basis, not because of a Yankee desire to make money even out of charity as a recent writer has sug-

18. *Relig. Intel.*, I, 283–287, 345–347; M. F. Cogswell to wife, Nov. 10 and 17, 1816, Cogswell Papers.

19. *Relig. Intel.*, I, 700–701.

20. *Ibid.*, VI, 302; Davis, *The Half Century*, pp. 108–109; *Seventh Report of the Directors of the American Asylum* (1823), p. 3.

gested,[21] but because of insufficient funds. Of the one hundred ten students who attended the school up to May, 1823, forty-four paid their own expenses, while sixty-six were supported by the charity of their townsmen or by the contributions of their state governments. Some grants were also made from available funds of the Asylum. In 1821 after the enrollment had increased considerably and the school had moved to its new buildings, the annual charge was lowered to $150, but at both the old and the new price all students were instructed below cost, a fact which the directors were anxious to have generally known. The enterprise involved the outlay of large sums of money, disbursements of $23,808 being noted in the eighth annual report (1824) and expenditures of nearly $21,000 for the year 1827–1828.[22]

The funds which supported the Asylum were derived from a variety of sources. As early as 1819 Massachusetts made arrangements to send its deaf and dumb to Hartford, the legislature voting an annual grant to the Connecticut institution. Since New Hampshire, Maine, and Vermont followed Massachusetts' example, it was quite fitting that the Connecticut Asylum should have had its name changed to the American Asylum in 1819. Not until 1830, at which time a grant of $2,500 a year for three years was voted, did the Connecticut legislature add to its first appropriation. Contributions were also received from the churches of the state, more than $2,500 being credited to this source in 1819. What proved to be the largest gift to the American Asylum during its early years was a grant made in 1819 of twenty-three thousand acres of Alabama land by the United States Congress.[23] The estimated value of this tract was $50,000, and the total received, more than $33,000 during the year 1821–1822, nearly $7,000

21. Morse, *A Neglected Period of Connecticut's History*, p. 176.
22. American Asylum, *7th Rept.* (1823), p. 4; *5th Rept.* (1821), p. 5; *Relig. Intel.*, IX, 89; American Asylum, *12th Rept.* (1828), p. 26.
23. *Ibid.*, pp. 14–15; *Proceedings of the General Association, 1830*, p. 18; *Connecticut Journal*, March 16, 1819.

the next year, and $15,000 in 1823–1824, exceeded this amount.

This Hartford establishment was of great interest to all visitors to the city. Soon after its founding President Monroe during his New England tour inspected the school and witnessed the work of the students.[24] One English traveller pronounced the American Asylum the most interesting object in Hartford and described the methods of instruction in his journal.[25] In addition, the Connecticut school had a profound influence on similar institutions subsequently set up in other parts of the country. Clerc spent a winter in Philadelphia to aid the Pennsylvania institution. Kentucky and Ohio each sent a representative to Hartford to learn the methods used there, while the man who became principal of the asylum in Canajoharie, New York, was an instructor in the American Asylum for five years.[26] Gallaudet and Clerc trained many of the teachers who carried on the instruction of the deaf and dumb in the United States during the first half of the nineteenth century.

That this humanitarian enterprise was closely connected with Connecticut Congregationalism is clear. Dr. Mason F. Cogswell, the son of the Reverend James Cogswell of Canterbury and later of Scotland Parish in Windham, was reared in the home of a Congregational minister. Gallaudet was an ordained minister when he accepted the principalship of the proposed institution, while the men who encouraged Cogswell were for the most part members of Connecticut's dominant church. The General Association rejoiced in the establishment of the Asylum and recommended it as deserving their patronage to the Christian public who in turn gave it financial support.[27] From the beginning, too, Cogswell was concerned because his daughter and other deaf mutes were completely ignorant about

24. *Connecticut Courant*, July 1, 1817.
25. *Relig. Intel.*, VII, 405–407.　　26. *Ibid.*, IX, 71.
27. *Proceedings of the General Association, 1818*, p. 5.

religion, and he wanted a school in large part to remedy this deficiency.

As a result, much attention was given to spiritual instruction at the Asylum. Evidence for this is found in the annual reports and in the newspaper accounts of the public exhibitions which occurred from time to time. Students showed their proficiency by their ability to answer questions. Not only did the many inquiries concerning religious matters indicate the public's interest in this aspect of instruction, but the replies also gave abundant assurance that the young deaf mutes understood basic religious doctrines. Religious exercises were held in the chapel each morning and evening. The task of transmitting the abstractions of religion to untutored minds by means of signs, facial expressions, and writing proved difficult, but progress was made in this as in every other phase of the Asylum's work. Thus were the foundations laid for an institution which has had a long and honorable career.

The deaf and dumb were not the only unfortunates whose infirmities received attention, for during this period began, in addition, the institutional care of the insane. At its 1812 session the Connecticut Medical Society first discussed the question, but no action was taken.[28] Three years later Dr. Cogswell, then much absorbed in his proposed school for deaf mutes, and Dr. Nathan Strong, Jr., also of Hartford, on behalf of the medical organization, requested the General Association to determine the number in the state affected in any degree with "lunacy." Such a census was not easy, and incomplete returns in 1816 showed a total of but 146 whereas the best informed observers were convinced that the number was much larger.[29] With this the matter was dropped for five years.

28. "Report of the Committee on the Progress of the Retreat," *Annual Meeting of the Society for the Relief of the Insane* (1823), p. 11.
29. *Proceedings of the General Association, 1815,* pp. 7–8; *ibid., 1816,* p. 11.

In 1821, after at least four asylums for the insane had been established elsewhere in the United States, Connecticut people again displayed interest in the subject. Roused by the cases in their district and perhaps by the success of the American Asylum, the doctors of Hartford County instructed their delegates to the state convention to bring up the question. Following the presentation and approval of a plan of action, it was agreed that to ascertain the number of mentally deranged persons in Connecticut should be the first step. A thorough inquiry showed at least a thousand such sufferers, whereupon the promoters of the enterprise sought to raise the necessary funds for buildings and operating expenses. It was decided to solicit contributions by liberally compensated agents, and by May, 1822, the surprisingly large total of $12,000 had been subscribed.[30]

A petition to the legislature was next in order, as the result of which an act of incorporation, a grant of $5,000, and a brief authorizing annual contributions in the churches for five years were all obtained. Contributions totalled $20,000 by October, 1822, not including the Assembly's grant. There were both large and small givers. Joseph Battell of Norfolk, for instance, contributed $200 for land and buildings and $300 to the permanent fund.[31] While about thirty-five persons qualified by gifts of $100 or more as directors of the Society for the Relief of the Insane which was organized in 1822, on the other hand the sums coming from farmers were generally $5 or $10— sometimes as much as $20.[32] Some funds were received from other New England states, although not so large a proportion as in the case of the American Asylum, for the institution for the insane was primarily a state enterprise. The substantial financial backing indicated such wide-

30. "Report of the Committee on the Progress of the Retreat," pp. 11–14.

31. J. Battell to T. Robbins, Jan. 28, 1822, Robbins Papers. Battell was Robbins' brother-in-law.

32. "Report of the Committee on the Progress of the Retreat," p. 14; Dr. G. Sumner to T. Robbins, Jan. 19, 1822, Robbins Papers.

spread popular approval that the society in December,
1822, voted to locate the Retreat—more felicitously named
than the American Asylum—in Hartford, fixed a site for
it, and authorized the construction of buildings to cost no
more than $12,000.[33]

Among the most zealous workers on behalf of the Retreat was the Reverend Thomas Robbins. The author of a
plan for raising money in Connecticut's smaller towns, he
attended numerous committee meetings and wrote effective addresses to the public. With Roger M. Sherman he
appeared before the state senate in May, 1822, and spoke
in favor of a petition asking for support of the project.[34]
It is not surprising, therefore, that the East Windsor
pastor was invited to deliver the address at the dedication
of the Retreat on April 1, 1824. As his subject for the occasion he chose "The design and tendency of Christianity
to diminish the miseries and increase the happiness of mankind." After assuring his listeners that "the liberality of
this town, for public charities, will not be unnoticed or un-
rewarded on high," he alluded to the fact that from the
eminence on which he stood, "we view the Asylum for the
Deaf and Dumb, the first institution of the kind in this
country, and the Retreat for the Insane, two of the distinguished ornaments of our State, and contemplate the im-
mense amount of human suffering they may be made in-
strumental of relieving." "These," he continued, "are the
triumphs of the religion of the Prince of Peace."[35]

The president of the society which sponsored the Retreat was Nathaniel Terry of Hartford, the superintendent of the institution Dr. Eli Todd, a physician of the
same town. Dr. Cogswell labored long and successfully for
this enterprise from the time it was projected until his

33. "Report of the Committee on the Progress of the Retreat," pp.
15–16.
34. Dr. G. Sumner to T. Robbins, Jan. 19, 1822, Robbins Papers; Robbins, *Diary*, I, 879, 882, 884, 892, 908, 936.
35. Robbins, *An Address delivered at the Dedication of the Retreat
for the Insane* (1824), p. 16.

death in 1830. Mrs. Lydia Huntley Sigourney was secretary of the ladies' society which furnished the buildings.[36] Accommodations for fifty patients were at first available. Like the American Asylum the Retreat was not on a charity basis but was intended for those who could pay for treatments. Once again the reason was inadequate funds. Any person subscribing $200 could name one indigent patient, while any town, corporate body, or group of individuals paying $250 enjoyed the same privilege. From the beginning, however, it was hoped that patients could be treated gratuitously, and in 1830, when the quarters were enlarged to house ninety patients, the existing rules were modified so that the benefits of the Retreat could be extended to indigent sufferers at a reduced rate.[37]

Dr. Todd and his associates inaugurated at the Retreat a plan of treatment which marked a significant advance over methods used elsewhere. The practice of non-restraint was adopted to make the patient realize, if such a thing were possible, that he had not come to a madhouse but to a pleasant, peaceful place where he could have every opportunity to regain his health. Bolts and keys were replaced by an adequate number of attendants who were to walk with the patients, join them in their exercise, amuse and divert them, and persuade them, if possible, to participate in the work which was a part of each day's program. A portion of the instructions to attendants read as follows:

The attendants must be continually alive, and on the watch; must study the various humours of the patients, be ready to gratify their little wants, when not unreasonable, never to make sport of their complaints or absurdities, but treat them with undeviating kindness & even respect; & thus convince the unfortunate sufferers that they are surrounded by friends.[38]

36. *Connecticut Courant*, April 6, 1824.

37. *Annual Meeting of the Society for the Relief of the Insane* (1823), p. 6; Capen, *Historical Development of the Poor Law of Connecticut*, pp. 157–158.

38. MS. directions for attendants, April 27, 1825, Cogswell Papers, Conn. Hist. Soc. See also Trumbull, ed., *Memorial History of Hartford County*, I, 527–528.

Such methods were expensive, but they pleased those whose liberality had made the Retreat possible. The act of incorporation required that the Retreat should have six physicians or visitors, two of whom at least should visit the institution each month. It was their duty, the act continued, "to invite an equal number of females to accompany them. They shall enquire into the medical and moral concerns of the institution, suggest improvements and designate abuses."[39]

Another phase of the early humanitarian movement was the establishment in New Haven of the state's first public hospital. The New Haven Medical Society approved this project at its 1826 meeting and declared that "the hospital shall be a charitable institution, and no physician or surgeon shall receive any compensation for his services." The same year the legislature chartered the institution under the name of the General Hospital Society of Connecticut, and in 1828 granted it $5,000. One more appeal was made to the people of the state who responded handsomely. A contribution of $100 gave the donor, whether a town, an individual, or a group of individuals, the privilege of having an indigent person cared for at no expense for six weeks during the year. In 1831 a petition for a second $5,000 was made to the legislature which turned down the request at the time but later approved it. In 1832 the hospital building was completed and the hospital opened.[40]

During this period Americans gave attention for the first time to prison reform. Inevitably, once humanitarian efforts turned in this direction, Connecticut would be affected, for the state prison was one of the worst. Located in the town of East Granby it bore the ominous name of Newgate and more than lived up to the fears roused by this appellation. An abandoned copper mine had been con-

39. *Resolves and Private Laws, 1789–1836*, I, 342–343.
40. Capen, *Historical Development of the Poor Law of Connecticut*, p. 143; Atwater, ed., *History of the City of New Haven*, pp. 281, 675; John W. Barber, *Connecticut Historical Collections*, pp. 148–149.

verted into a prison, where prisoners for some years were lodged below the ground at night. All types of men were crowded together, and sanitary conditions were unspeakable. New buildings were constructed shortly after 1800, and the cavern was used only for temporary punishment. Nevertheless, conditions at Newgate continued to be deplorable.[41]

As early as 1799 Governor Trumbull in a speech to the legislature recommended that measures be taken for the better regulation of the prison. He particularly condemned the practice of putting hardened criminals with first offenders, and urged the use of the solitary cell, privation of the usual diet, and the absolute prohibition of "ardent spirits," as effective means of controlling the most dangerous types of prisoners.[42] No action was taken. A decade later Lieutenant Governor Treadwell told the legislature that no religious or moral teaching was given the prisoners except for a few sermons which neighboring ministers, on their own initiative, had recently preached. The distribution of Bibles and tracts, Treadwell contended, together with occasional preaching would cause much improvement in conditions.[43]

Not until 1814, when the question of religious instruction at Newgate Prison was raised as the result of agitation led by the Hartford County North Consociation, was action forthcoming.[44] Thomas Robbins, as a member of the consociation's committee, labored strenuously for this cause. The memorial which he wrote to the legislature requesting an appropriation for permanent instruction at the prison ex-Governor Treadwell presented to the lower house. A grant was made for a chapel, and on the occasion of its dedication in May, 1815, Robbins preached and re-

41. Adams, *New England in the Republic,* p. 370; Barber, *Connecticut Historical Collections,* pp. 95–96.

42. *Connecticut Courant,* May 13, 1799.

43. MS. speech delivered at the opening of the General Assembly, Oct., 1809, Treadwell Papers, Conn. Hist. Soc.

44. Records of the Hartford County North Consociation, Congregational House, Oct., 1814.

corded that the fifty-two prisoners seemed "much gratified with the prospect of stated religious ordinances." Bibles and tracts were soon supplied, and the legislature provided year-by-year support for a chaplain at Newgate but refused to make a permanent grant.[45] Ebenezer Clark was ordained in the combined rôle of pastor of the East Granby Church and chaplain at the prison.[46] When the new Democratic overseers of the prison dismissed Clark in 1819, Robbins, always a staunch Federalist, called it "a most wanton abuse of power," and the following year he appeared before the legislature on behalf of both the chaplaincy and Clark. The legislature continued the grant but would not reappoint the man; a year later no money was appropriated to supply Newgate with preaching.[47]

About this time serious consideration was being accorded the question of prison reform in various parts of the world. The *Panoplist* in 1807 printed an article about John Howard, whose name was already known to many, and the appearance in London in 1813 of the *Memoirs of the Public and Private Life of John Howard the Philanthropist* by James Baldwin Brown turned general attention to the man and his work. In 1818 the English Society for the Improvement of Prison Discipline and the Reformation of Juvenile Offenders was organized.[48]

In the United States prison reform began shortly after 1820. The practice of permitting free intercourse among the prisoners had been harshly criticized on the grounds that it made the prisons practically schools of vice. Accordingly, experiments emphasizing solitary confinement were made in New York and Pennsylvania, the most effective scheme being the one adopted in the Auburn, New York, Penitentiary in 1824. Under the Auburn system

45. Robbins, *Diary,* I, 605, 606, 607, 626–627, 646.
46. Centennial Discourse delivered by the Reverend C. Chamberlain of East Granby in 1876, Yale University Library.
47. Robbins, *Diary,* I, 787, 820.
48. *Relig. Intel.,* VIII, 628–631; *Report of the Committee of the Society for the Improvement of Prison Discipline, and for the Reformation of Juvenile Offenders* (1818).

prisoners in the same trade worked together during the day and met in chapel for religious services but were not allowed to talk with one another. At night they were placed in single cells. To coördinate the efforts being made to improve conditions, a Prison Discipline Society was formed in Boston in 1825.[49]

Connecticut needed not only prison reform but a new institution as well. The legislature, inaugurating in 1825 an inquiry into the question of removing the prison from East Granby, appointed a committee which strongly favored such action. After vigorously denouncing the conditions in which the 117 prisoners at Newgate were found, the committee declared, "We feel assured that no Legislator—that no man—can, after visiting this *pit*, ascend from it and say, that this, either in a physical or moral point of view, is a fit and proper place for the confinement and lodging of his fellow men." There was, too, an economic reason for advocating the removal of the prison from East Granby. In a new location nearer the markets the employment of the convicts at brick-making especially would enable the institution to run at a profit. Wethersfield was recommended as the most promising site for the new prison.[50]

As a result, early in 1828 a new state prison, where the Auburn system was introduced, was opened at Wethersfield. For the first eighteen months officials reported little sickness, no deaths, and no escapes. In an economic sense, too, the new plant came up to expectations, for whereas the Newgate Prison had cost the state annually an average of $8,400 during its last ten years, a year at Wethersfield saw a profit of more than $3,000.[51] Religious instruction was given much attention. Bibles and tracts were dis-

49. Davis, *The Half Century*, pp. 171–172.
50. *Report of the Committee appointed by the Legislature of Connecticut, to Inspect the Condition of New-Gate Prison* (1826), pp. 9, 11, 18.
51. *Fourth Annual Report of the Board of Managers of the Prison Discipline Society* (1829), pp. 19–23.

tributed among the prisoners, services were held each morning and evening, and on the Sabbath there was preaching and a Sunday school. In the 1829 report of the directors and warden it was pointed out that every possible effort was made "to instruct and reclaim these men, and to restore them to society, at the expiration of their sentences, as sound and safe men." Of the Connecticut institution the Prison Discipline Society reported in 1830 that "as an example of neatness, order, quiet industry, mild and wholesome discipline, faithful instruction, economy, and productive labor, it stands, at least, on the level with the Prison at Auburn."[52]

In the summer of 1829 the Connecticut Auxiliary Prison Discipline Society was organized in Hartford. Like the parent society this auxiliary, as its founders intended, had a significant moral influence. The Connecticut governor in his 1829 message to the legislature emphasized the need for revising the criminal code, extending the improved system of prison discipline to workhouses for the benefit of the poor confined there, and taking steps to reform juvenile delinquents.[53] The friends of prison reform could feel that substantial progress had been made.

The attitude of Connecticut people toward Negroes and slavery during this period of humanitarian beginnings is of interest. As early as 1773 Samuel Hopkins and Ezra Stiles, both ministers in Newport, Rhode Island, but natives of Connecticut, conceived the idea of sending two or three Negroes as pioneer missionaries to Africa. The outbreak of the Revolution, the decline of the slave trade, and the death of one of the Negro missionaries put an end to this enterprise. Before the Revolution, too, the Reverend Levi Hart of Preston preached one of the earliest sermons against the slave trade and slaveholding, and the colonial

52. *Report of the Directors and Warden of the Connecticut State Prison* (1829), p. 4; Prison Discipline Soc., *5th Rept.* (1830), p. 338.
53. Prison Discipline Soc., *4th Rept.* (1829), pp. 22–23.

legislature passed a law freeing all slaves thereafter brought into the colony.[54]

After the war Connecticut provided for the gradual emancipation of slaves held within the state borders.[55] In 1790 the Connecticut Anti-Slavery Society, an organization which seems to have had a brief and not very active existence, was founded with Ezra Stiles, then president of Yale, as its presiding officer. For four or five years an annual meeting was held at which a sermon or an oration was delivered. The Connecticut society was one of nine which in 1791 presented a petition against slavery to Congress. At a convention of delegates from abolition societies held in Philadelphia in 1794 Uriah Tracy represented the Connecticut society, while the following year, in addition to Tracy, Jonathan Edwards the younger and Zephaniah Swift were present. In 1796 no Connecticut delegates appeared,[56] and nothing more has been discovered about this early attempt at abolition.

For the next two decades very little consideration seems to have been accorded the Negro question. Two schools for Negro children were set up in New Haven about 1810, one for girls and the other for boys. Timothy Dwight's comment was that "these institutions furnish the first rational hope of a reformation among the people."[57] There was no public discussion when in 1814 the legislature disfranchised Negroes by voting that "no person shall be admitted a freeman in any town of this state, unless, in addition to the qualifications already required by law, he shall be a free white male person." This racial distinction was

54. Early L. Fox, *The American Colonization Society, 1817–1840,* pp. 39–40; *The Literary Diary of Ezra Stiles,* III, 327 note; Trumbull, ed., *Memorial History of Hartford County,* II, 192 note; J. Franklin Jameson, *The American Revolution Considered as a Social Movement* (Princeton, 1926), p. 36.

55. *Ibid.,* p. 37.

56. Clark, *History of Connecticut,* pp. 375–376; *The Literary Diary of Ezra Stiles,* III, 400, 431, 437, 494.

57. Dwight, *Statistical Account of the City of New-Haven* (1811), p. 58.

continued after a debate in the 1818 constitutional convention, and not until 1876 was the word "white" removed.[58]

The American Colonization Society dispelled the general indifference to the condition of the African race.[59] Founded in Washington in 1817, this organization was concerned with transporting to Africa and colonizing there all Negroes who in one way or another received their freedom in this country. Samuel J. Mills, Jr., became deeply interested in this project; indeed, he died in 1818 on a return trip from Africa where he had conducted inquiries for the society.

When an agent of the Colonization Society appeared in Connecticut in 1819, he addressed a large audience in New Haven, and as a result of his efforts an auxiliary was formed with Simeon Baldwin as president and with David Daggett and President Jeremiah Day of Yale among the vice-presidents. The editor of the *Religious Intelligencer* took advantage of this opportunity to appeal to the benevolence of the people. "The people of New-England," he wrote, "have probably looked at the situation of our brethren at the South with a feeling of indifference, or with other feelings, that are not justifiable. Being exempt from the curse of slavery themselves, they have doubtless felt that those who continue the practice must suffer the consequences: but this will not remedy the evil; it is a National sin, and calls for National judgments."[60] What this auxiliary did has not been discovered; probably it raised small sums of money which were sent to the parent society. There was little enthusiasm for the movement because of the general impression that it was backed by southern slaveholders who desired to keep free Negroes away from their slaves.

58. J. T. Adams, "Disfranchisement of Negroes in New England," *American Historical Review*, XXX (1925), 545.

59. The early history of this enterprise is told in Fox, *The American Colonization Society, 1817–1840*.

60. *Relig. Intel.*, IV, 320, 336, 384.

Nevertheless, the Colonization Society continued to seek support in Connecticut. In September, 1822, an agent spoke before a meeting in New Haven at which a committee of five was appointed to deliberate on the expediency of forming a state auxiliary. They reported that they were not much interested if the society had as its sole object the colonization of free Negroes, and continued, "It is only from the belief which the committee very cordially entertain, that the active members of the American Colonization Society are perfectly disposed to frame their measures with reference to the *entire* suppression of the slave trade, and to a gradual and prudent, but complete emancipation of those now held in slavery, that we can regard the Society as having any claim upon the sympathy or assistance of the people of New-England."[61]

The years 1824 and 1825 brought some new developments. After expressing in the former year its approval of the activities of the Colonization Society and urging ministers to do all in their power to aid it, the General Association in 1825 recommended an annual contribution for the society on the Fourth of July or on the Sabbath immediately preceding or following.[62] As a consequence, it became customary in some places to hold a religious service on Independence Day at which a sermon on the work of the society was preached and a collection taken. In 1824 the African United Ecclesiastical Society of New Haven was established "for improving the morals, promoting the piety, and increasing the religious knowledge of that part of the population." The old Methodist meeting house was purchased for $600, of which $500 was paid by the citizens of the town and the Negroes. The remainder was still owed in 1827 when the Connecticut Auxiliary Colonization Society was finally formed. This institution collected but $170 during its second year, a testimonial to the fact that Connecticut interest in people of color had as yet

61. *Ibid.*, VII, 256, 268–269.
62. *Proceedings of the General Association, 1824*, p. 7; *ibid.*, *1825*, p. 7.

reached no high point.[63] In 1826, however, five young men, one of whom was Leonard Bacon, the recently installed minister of New Haven's First Congregational Church, met in Bacon's study and formed an Antislavery Association and an African Improvement Society. The aim of these societies was to stir up interest in Negroes both in Connecticut and in the theological seminaries of the country.[64]

Another group which received attention were the Jews. The London Society for Promoting Christianity among the Jews was organized in 1808, but the United States was slow in following the English example, the American Society for Meliorating the Condition of the Jews not appearing until 1822. Since it was originally planned to provide a refuge in the United States to which converted Jews might come to escape persecution, a farm was purchased. At the end of its first year the society had a bal-

63. *Relig. Intel.*, XI, 780, 826; *Second Annual Report of the Managers of the Colonization Society of the State of Connecticut* (1829), p. 12.
64. Richard A. Warner, *New Haven Negroes* (New Haven, 1940), p. 46.
   In his *The Antislavery Impulse, 1830–1844* (New York, 1933), Professor Gilbert H. Barnes indicates that the revivals of 1830 and 1831 in New York and in the area north of the Ohio River prepared the ground for Theodore Dwight Weld and his associates. Professor Barnes does not mention the fact, however, that Weld, born in 1803 as the son of a Congregational minister, was reared in the religious atmosphere of Connecticut. Indeed, both in his sketch of Weld in the *Dictionary of American Biography* and in his Introduction to the *Letters of Theodore Dwight Weld, Angeline Grimké Weld, and Sarah Grimké, 1822–1844* (2 vols., New York, 1934), which he edited in collaboration with Professor Dwight L. Dumond, Barnes writes that Weld's family moved to western New York during his childhood and that there the future antislavery leader "passed an active, vigorous youth." As a matter of fact, Weld's father, the Reverend Ludovicus Weld, was pastor of the Congregational church in Hampton, Connecticut, from 1792 until 1824, and as such preached the Election Sermon in 1821. See Larned, *History of Windham County*, II, 242, 521; *Contributions to the Ecclesiastical History of Connecticut*, p. 403; L. Weld, *A Sermon delivered before the Legislature of the State of Connecticut at the Anniversary Election* (1821). That Mrs. Weld's letter of September 28, 1822, to her son was undoubtedly written from Hampton, rather than "[Fabius, N. Y.]," is borne out by the references to "W—m," which is undoubtedly Windham, and to "Killingby" which is Killingly, Connecticut. *Letters of Theodore Dwight Weld, etc.*, I, 3–4.

ance of over $4,000 after all expenses were paid. Great help was rendered by 150 auxiliaries, some of which were established in Connecticut where the Reverend C. F. Frey, a converted Jew and an agent of the American Society, preached several sermons.[65] Among those who formed auxiliaries in 1822 were New Haven, Hartford, and Litchfield ladies. About fifty New Haven ladies became members immediately, and collected between $30 and $40; two years later the receipts were nearly $100. Mrs. Lydia Huntley Sigourney, interested in many charities, was secretary of the Hartford branch. Within four years of its founding the American Society abandoned the idea of colonizing Jews in this country and turned its efforts and those of its auxiliaries to the project of sending missionaries to Jews throughout the world.[66]

The peace movement had its beginnings during the early years of the nineteenth century. Professor Curti has indicated that this was more than the result of war-weariness, that it was connected with the humanitarianism originated by eighteenth-century idealists.[67] It was also furthered by the religious awakening. The New York Peace Society, "probably the first one that was ever formed in the world for that specific purpose," was organized in August, 1815, as a result of the labors of David Low Dodge, a Connecticut merchant who was living in New York City. Four months later the Massachusetts Peace Society was founded. Both the Reverend Noah Worcester of Brighton, Massachusetts, the prime mover in this instance, and Dodge took the position that war was inconsistent with the Christian religion, but they differed in that Worcester believed that all war was contrary to Christianity while Dodge justified defensive war.[68] That the success of this

65. *Connecticut Courant*, Jan. 14, 1817; Davis, *The Half Century*, p. 338; *Relig. Intel.*, VII, 124–125; VIII, 119.

66. *Ibid.*, VI, 752, 784; VIII, 752; X, 796–797; *Connecticut Courant*, April 6, 1824; *American Eagle*, April 14, 1823.

67. Merle E. Curti, *The American Peace Crusade, 1815–1860*, p. 19.

68. *Ibid.*, pp. 6–8, 9, 19, 67.

movement depended in large part on people with religious convictions is shown by the circular letter sent out by the Massachusetts society in 1816. It was addressed to the various associations, presbyteries, assemblies, and meetings of ministers in the United States. The writers called attention to the fact that they were dealing with a subject of great importance to Christianity, and after striking their keynote in the statement that "the crimes and desolations of war have long been a subject of deep regret and lamentation to reflecting Christians," continued in this vein throughout the letter.[69]

A branch of the Massachusetts Peace Society which was formed in East Haddam in December, 1818, had upwards of sixty members at its first annual meeting.[70] By far the most zealous worker for the peace movement in Connecticut was the Reverend Samuel J. May, Unitarian minister in Brooklyn and the only one of his denomination in the state, who from the time he entered his pastorate in 1822 labored against war. Aided by his Congregational colleagues, May succeeded in organizing in 1826 the Windham County Peace Society, the dues of which were fifty cents a year while a contribution of five dollars secured a life membership. Thomas Hubbard, a doctor in Pomfret, was elected president. "The funds of this Society," the constitution declared, "shall be exclusively employed to diffuse information on the uselessness, miseries and criminality of War; and to cultivate the spirit of Peace." Once again religion was brought squarely into the foreground of the movement, for in a pamphlet the society declared that it was "to the influences of Christianity we must chiefly look, for the abolition of this scourge of our race."[71]

When the Hartford Peace Society, with 102 members, was formed in February, 1828, as an auxiliary of the pro-

69. *A Circular Letter from the Massachusetts Peace Society* (1816).

70. *Connecticut Courant,* Jan. 18, 1820.

71. Larned, *History of Windham County,* II, 475–477; *Peace Society of Windham County, Its Institutions, Sentiments and Purposes* (1827), pp. 4–6, 19.

posed American Peace Society, several of its trustees, who represented the entire county, were Congregational ministers.[72] As a capstone to the activities in the state, the next step was the establishment in 1831 of the Connecticut Peace Society. This federation of several local societies remained independent of the national organization and became for a few years, according to Professor Curti, "by all odds the most important local association during the period."[73]

Of factory legislation there was practically none in Connecticut during the first three decades of the century, an act of 1813 preventing the period from being a complete blank. The legislature then voted that proprietors of manufacturing establishments had duties toward children in their employ, and that they must see to it that these children received an elementary education and adequate moral training and that they attended public worship.[74] J. T. Adams has observed that the law was vaguely drawn and that it "probably was merely to placate a certain amount of public hostility to the factory system as a whole."[75] It seems more reasonable, however, to interpret this act not as a palliative designed by factory-owners to protect themselves but as the product of the humanitarian spirit of the time. Support for this position is found in the close resemblance between the 1813 law and a clause in the act by which the Humphreysville Manufacturing Company was incorporated in 1810. David Humphreys, the owner and a well-known philanthropist and humanitarian, was responsible for the provision which read: "It shall be the duty of the president and directors of said corporation to provide an instructor, for at least three months in each year, for the purpose of teaching the children employed in the manufactory, to read and write, and also the first four

72. Curti, *American Peace Crusade*, p. 33.
73. *Ibid.*, p. 47.
74. *Public Statute Laws, 1808–1820*, pp. 117–118.
75. Adams, *New England in the Republic*, p. 313.

rules of arithmetic, and in religion, morals, and manners, as is by law directed to be taught in other schools."[76] No more was done along this line because the Industrial Revolution had made only slight headway in agricultural Connecticut.

Two other societies need but to be mentioned, the American Society for Promoting the Civilization and General Improvement of Indian Tribes within the United States organized in Washington in 1822, and the Society for the Improvement of Common Schools formed in Hartford in 1827. The General Association approved the former, and some assistance was given it in Connecticut. The latter grew out of attacks launched against Connecticut's school system. Schools were languishing, it was felt, because people had become so dependent on the School Fund that they were averse to making any exertions to support these institutions. Thomas Robbins and Thomas Gallaudet were among the leaders in the movement for school reform.[77]

This is the story of humanitarian endeavors in Connecticut during the first three decades of the nineteenth century. Puritanism showed a side too little recognized in its vigorous assumption of the rôle of the Good Samaritan.

76. Fuller, *An Introduction to the History of Connecticut as a Manufacturing State,* p. 14.
77. *Relig. Intel.,* VI, 650; *Proceedings of the General Association, 1822,* p. 15; Barnard, "History of the Legislation of Connecticut respecting Common Schools, down to 1838," *Annual Report of the Superintendent of Common Schools in Connecticut, 1853,* p. 154.

VIII

THE RELIGIOUS MINORITIES

CONNECTICUT'S Second Great Awakening was not exclusively a Congregational phenomenon. Episcopalians, Baptists, and Methodists, the religious minorities, also experienced a religious renewal during the closing years of the eighteenth and the first quarter of the nineteenth century and developed the same sort of interests as their Congregational neighbors. While they may have influenced in minor ways the activities of the dominant denomination described in previous chapters, in general they were the followers and not the leaders.

It will not be amiss to repeat statements previously made about the status of the dissenting groups when the Awakening began. The Baptists who had established their first society in 1705 reported sixty churches, forty ministers, and about 3,500 members in 1795, while the Episcopalians, organized in Connecticut since 1707, had their own bishop and twenty ministers in about forty churches. There were no Methodists in the state until 1789, and in 1796 they numbered only 1,200 with very few ministers. As a result of various acts passed during the eighteenth century, the dissenters had practically complete toleration. After October, 1791, a non-Congregationalist had only to sign his own certificate attesting regular attendance at meetings and support of his church and to deposit it with the clerk of the nearest Congregational society in order to escape financial obligations to the dominant church.[1]

A few remarks about the struggle which resulted in the Connecticut constitution of 1818 will suffice.[2] The Baptists, who took the lead among the dissenters in the 1790's, protested against the 1793 legislation which would have

1. Greene, *Development of Religious Liberty in Connecticut*, p. 376.
2. See Purcell, *Connecticut in Transition*, for the detailed account.

placed the proceeds from the sale of western lands in ecclesiastical hands inasmuch as this would have meant primarily Congregational control. They won their case in 1795. The 1802 petition calling for voluntary support of the ministry emanated from the Baptists, as did those of succeeding years. Methodists and Baptists voted for Republicans in elections beginning with 1800.

The Episcopalians were relatively late in joining their fellow dissenters. Although they found many of the actions of the dominant Standing Order irritating, especially the Federalist refusal to incorporate as a college the Episcopal academy located at Cheshire, they disliked the attack on an establishment and could not stomach a political alliance with Baptists, Methodists, and Republicans. Not until the legislature in 1814 disposed of the Phoenix Bank bonus in such a way as to discriminate against them did the churchmen join the others in a Toleration Party. The new political allies won a partial victory in 1816 and a complete triumph in 1817. When this was repeated a year later, a constitutional convention was held as the result of which a new constitution was substituted for the 1662 charter as the state's basic law. So far as the churches were concerned, voluntary support of religion replaced compulsory support.

But what about the Episcopalians, Baptists, and Methodists and the Awakening? Historians of the three denominations all refer to a decline in religion in the years following the Revolution, and available contemporary evidence tells the same story. Furthermore, the revulsion against the excesses of the French Revolution and the fears for revealed religion threatened by deism and rationalism which were common among Congregationalists in the last decade of the eighteenth century appeared also in dissenting circles. E. E. Beardsley, the historian of the Episcopal church in Connecticut, has written that by 1792 the internal dissension in the church was checked and that the battle was then of a different kind. "A body of speculators in morals, religion, and politics arose," he asserts, "and threatened to entail mischief upon the rising generation. The school of French philosophers was just looked into, and in some places received with evident favor."[3] One prominent Episcopalian layman, recalling his youth, reported, "My own memory runs back to a dividing point of time, when I could see something of the *old world and new.* Infidel opinions came in like a flood. Mr. Paine's 'Age of Reason,' the works of Voltaire, and other deistical books, were broadcast, and young men suddenly became, as they thought, wiser than their fathers; and even men in high places among us here were suspected of infidel opinions."[4] When the Episcopal ministers in Connecticut read the Bishop of Landaff's reply to Paine's *Age of Reason,* which he called *Apology for the Bible,* they were so roused that they wrote a letter to the bishop in 1796 in which they said, "Happy are we to find that your excellent defence has in a good degree strengthened the faithful, confirmed the doubtful, roused the indifferent, and silenced the gainsayer. And we have reason to believe that it will, by the blessing of God, be a means of checking that spirit of infidelity among us which has produced such horrid scenes in a powerful nation of Europe."[5]

A Baptist historian of the time called it a "very wintry season" for religion throughout the country.[6] Another in speaking of this period referred to "infidelity, keenly scented on the track of war, like the jackall [*sic*], on the battle-field, [which] cared not whose cause is just, or who triumphs, so it can find victims to gorge a carrion, craving appetite," and mentioned the Waterford minister who arrayed himself against the swelling tide of skepticism, "which came from the camp, or had been brought from France." "The gibes of the open unbeliever," the historian of the Waterford church continued, "and the ribald songs of the freethinker made both pastor and people their un-

3. Eben E. Beardsley, *The History of the Episcopal Church in Connecticut,* I, 432.
4. Quoted in *ibid.,* I, 432–433.   5. Quoted in *ibid.,* II, 14.
6. Quoted in W. W. Sweet, *Methodism in American History,* p. 135.

blushing butt of ridicule, as we are told by men who remembered the shameless songs, and coarse jests of a large class in this vicinity, at the close of the war."[7] The following extract from a letter sent out by the Stonington Baptist Association in 1798 reveals the contemporary attitude:

[The] melancholy and truly alarming situation of the United States, has not failed to excite our lamentation. But while we lament the prospect of war; The variety of political sentiments: The destruction of our fellow citizens in the city and country by epidemical diseases—above all, The cause of these calamities, The prevalence of infidelity and immorality. We rejoice that many of our brethren of different denominations have united in a concert of prayer, and meet at stated seasons, to offer up their fervant [sic] supplications, that God would avert his judgments; prevent the spread of error and iniquity—and pour out his spirit in plentiful effusions on our guilty land.[8]

Like the Episcopalians and Baptists—and the Congregationalists—the Methodists lamented the prevailing irreligion and spiritual deadness. It is to be expected that Bishop Asbury would comment unfavorably on religious conditions in Connecticut, and yet his *Journal* note of June 4, 1791, when he first visited the state, cannot be omitted. "There may have been a praying ministry and people here," he wrote, "but I fear they are spiritually dead, and am persuaded that family and private prayer is very little practiced. Could these people be brought to constant, fervent prayer, the Lord would come down and work wonders among them." A Methodist historian, describing general conditions in the country in 1803, queried, "Had those principles of infidelity with which the minds of many of the leading men of our nation had been infected, and which, at one time, were descending with

7. "History of the 1st Baptist Church, Waterford," *Historical Sketch of the New London Baptist Association, 1817–1850*, p. 22.
8. *Minutes of the Stonington Baptist Association, 1798*, p. 5.

fearful rapidity to the lower ranks of society, been permitted to operate unchecked, . . . is there not reason to apprehend that . . . [they] must have washed our civil and religious institutions into the whirlpool of destruction?"[9]

Of greatest significance was the action taken by the various annual conferences of the Methodist Church in 1795. Alarmed by the enthusiasm with which Americans were receiving the writings of Tom Paine and by what they considered a dangerous increase in indifference to religion accompanied by an abounding immorality, the Methodist clergy recommended a general fast and issued an address in which they bewailed "our manifold sins and iniquities—our growing idolatry, which is covetousness and the prevailing love of the world . . . the profanation of the name of the Lord—the contempt of the Sabbath . . . disobedience to parents, various debaucheries, drunkenness and such like."[10]

With the Congregationalists and their fellow denominationalists outside the state, the dissenters met the threat to religion by becoming militant defenders of the faith and of supernatural religion. Ministers and church members bestirred themselves to bring new life into their churches in Connecticut. As a result there were revivals among the Baptists and Methodists and a new religious spirit among the Episcopalians whose doctrines and practices did not include revivals.

Apparently relying on the statements of Judge Church of Litchfield, the Episcopalian layman who recalled that in the 1790's infidelity was widespread and the works of Paine, Voltaire, and other deist writers eagerly read, Beardsley asserts that "the Church, with her Liturgy and Order . . . spurned the teachings of infidel casuistry; and her clergy finding access to the works of the best English Divines, learned to feed their flocks with food that nour-

9. Nathan Bangs, *A History of the Methodist Episcopal Church*, II, 146.
10. *Ibid.*, II, 21–22.

ished their souls and kept them from wandering into the
dry pastures of doubt and speculation."[11] In 1800 there
were sixty-two Episcopalian parishes in the state but only
seventeen preachers and about 1,500 communicants. The
number of clergymen had increased to twenty-six in 1809,
forty-four in 1822, and fifty-four in 1826, and the number of communicants to 3,400 in 1818 and to 4,000 in
1825. During the same period only twelve churches were
added, to make a total of seventy-four in 1817.[12]

Large increases over the previous year were reported in
1811, and there were unusually heavy gains in 1816 and
1821, years when great revivals occurred in the Congregational churches. In connection with the 1816 developments the historian of Connecticut Episcopalianism writes
that extensive examination of the Episcopalian doctrines
and standards was stimulated by the teachings of the ministers of the Standing Order in regard to the nature of
conversion and of regeneration, with the result that in-
quirers relinquished their old religious connections and
joined the Episcopalian communion.[13]

Bishop Brownell's address at the annual convention of
the Diocese of Connecticut in 1821 is of special interest.
After reporting that during the preceding year he had
confirmed 836 people in thirty-four churches, he referred
to "the excitement with regard to religion, which seems to
prevail through the greater part of the State." "The present," he went on, "is certainly a period when people in
general are more disposed than usual to attend to the concerns of religion. . . . The excitement which has been
raised in the community, has led people to give more heed
to those ordinary influences of the Holy Spirit, and to
those ordinary means of grace which are at all times dis-
pensed in such measure as to enable all who will coöperate
with them, to work out their salvation through the merits

11. Beardsley, *Episcopal Church in Conn.*, I, 433.
12. Osborn, ed., *History of Connecticut*, III, 360–361; Beardsley, *Episcopal Church in Conn.*, II, 56; *Churchman's Magazine*, II (1822), 158.
13. Beardsley, *Episcopal Church in Conn.*, II, 70, 129–130, 139; *Churchman's Magazine*, VIII (1811), 200.

of the Redeemer."[14] Four years later, as has been indicated, there were four thousand communicants of the Episcopalian church in Connecticut.

The Baptists and Methodists were strong revivalists. Indeed, Baptist records tell a revival story not unlike that of the Congregationalists, although, of course, on a smaller scale. Revivals, not unknown in the churches of this denomination before 1795, appeared more frequently in the closing years of the eighteenth and the first three decades of the nineteenth century. In 1797 the Hartford Baptist Association announced to the associations with which it corresponded, "We are happy to inform you that unity and peace, to a good degree, still abound in our churches. From some of them we are saluted with the joyful tidings that Christ has lately been riding in triumph among them upon the chariot of his Word, favoring his people with a more than ordinary degree of divine influence; causing them to shake off their spirit of sloth, and vigorously to exert themselves for the promotion of religion. Sinners who had long had their eyes closed in the sleep of carnal security have been, numbers of them, awakened, and with deep concern inquired what they should do to be saved, and many who but a little before were ringleaders in vice, are now become the trophies of invincible grace, and shining examples of piety."[15] The following year the Stonington Baptist Association announced revivals among Baptists and Congregationalists in a number of towns, especially in Mansfield, Ashford, and Hampton, and recommended to the churches associated with it "that they unite with our brethren of different denominations in supplicating the throne of grace, the first Tuesday in January, April, July, and October, at two o'clock, P.M. for the outpouring of the Divine Spirit."[16]

14. Beardsley, *Episcopal Church in Conn.*, II, 243–245.
15. "A Brief History of the Hartford Baptist Association," *Minutes of the Hartford Baptist Association, 1889*, p. 14.
16. *Minutes of the Stonington Baptist Association, 1798*, p. 4.

From incomplete returns it can be stated that there was a revival in at least one church each year between 1797 and 1831, with high points in 1798–1801, 1808–1809, 1812–1814, 1816, 1818–1819, 1820–1821, and 1824–1825.[17] The association which in 1805 reported a state of warfare between the forces of religion and irreligion, "the open infidel" and the "saints of God," a decade later rejoiced in the numerous revivals and declared, "Zion's borders are enlarging—Converts are multiplying—additions making unto the Church of such as shall be saved. Oh Brethren! How firm the foundation of our hope! . . . How consoling the thought, that notwithstanding the enemy sometimes comes in like a flood, the spirit of the Lord does and will lift up a standard against him."[18] Early in 1826 the *Christian Secretary* commented on the numerous reports of revivals, pointing out that "on whatever side we turn our eyes, we see the light shining in darkness."[19] The 59 churches and 4,600 members of 1800 increased to 61 churches and 5,100 members in 1810, to 73 churches and 7,500 members in 1820, and to 83 churches and 9,200 members in 1830.[20]

Baptist revivals in Connecticut closely resembled those of the Congregationalists in the way they began and were conducted. The Hartford revival of 1798–1800 was described in the following manner:

The Lord seems to have stepped out of the usual path of ordinances, to effect this work more immediately in the displays of his Almighty power, and outpouring of his Spirit; probably to show that the work is his own. It is not attended with

17. This is based on a study of the *Christian Secretary*, the *Religious Intelligencer*, and the pamphlet histories of the Baptist churches and associations contained in the archives of the Connecticut Baptist Convention.

18. *Minutes of the Stonington Baptist Association, 1805*, p. 7; *ibid., 1815*, pp. 7–8.

19. *Christian Secretary*, March 27, 1826.

20. Henry S. Burrage, *A History of the Baptists in New England*, p. 235.

noise and confusion, but with solemnity and reverence. No fire; no rushing wind; no earthquake; but a still small voice goes before this wonderful work, no doubt, to hide pride from man. The ministers are stirred up to uncommon diligence and labor, so that they have scarcely time to prepare for public exercises.[21]

This awakening appeared in both the Baptist and the Congregational churches and the Congregationalist minister, Nathan Strong, is reported to have said to the Baptist pastor, Stephen Nelson, "The work evidently is begun with you, and I honor the grace of God in you."[22] Informing, indeed, is the following general statement regarding Baptist revivals:

There were then no protracted meetings; no special efforts to secure a revival, otherwise than as they were called forth under the special enkindlings of the Holy Spirit in the bosoms of christians. . . . Revivals then usually originated in this way: christians would be quickened in an unusual degree, under the preaching of the gospel; a few, at first, would begin to realize deeply their obligations to God, and be burdened in spirit, for the salvation of sinners; and would pour out their souls, in warm and thrilling exhortations, following up the preaching of their pastor, with earnest appeals to the impenitent. Immediately succeeding this state of feeling in the church, a general seriousness would be observed, especially in the youthful part of the community. The usual gayeties attendant upon this period of life, would be laid aside; the house of prayer would become the place of resort; and then the downcast look, the falling tear, the half suppressed sigh, would plainly indicate the presence of the Holy Spirit; and from such a period, the work would gradually move on with

21. Robert Turnbull, *Memorials of the First Baptist Church, Hartford,* pp. 15–16.

22. *Ibid.,* pp. 12–13. In writing about the revival in Colebrook in 1815, the Congregational minister, Chauncey Lee, said that it began in the Baptist society before it did in his own, and that 115 persons had been added to that church. *Relig. Intel.,* I, 205.

increasing power, till as many as were ordained to eternal life believed."[23]

A distinct difference in the pattern of revivals is found among the Methodists. Very poor throughout the period under consideration, this dissenting group had only a few church buildings and almost all societies were supplied by itinerating ministers who rode their circuits in the approved manner. Indeed, in 1822 only New Haven, New London, and Middletown had stationed ministers, with Hartford hoping to be added to the list in the near future.[24] The financial arrangements made for the travelling ministers in New England reveal the humble status of the Methodists. They were given no salary but rather an allowance which in 1800 was increased from $64 a year to $80, with an equal amount for the preacher's wife as well as $16 for each child below seven years and $24 for each between seven and fourteen. In 1816 the allowance was raised to $100 per annum, and the stewards of the church were to estimate the amount necessary to furnish fuel, rent, and table expenses for the preachers. In 1813, and again in 1816, when economic conditions were very bad, the following action was taken: "Resolved, that in future the preachers and ministers of the New England Conference will receive no money or other means of support, directly or indirectly, by taxation or legal assessment."[25] Local ministers should also be mentioned, men in the various societies of the state who derived their support from their own industry and who preached on the Sabbaths when the minister on circuit was not scheduled to appear. After four years of service a local minister was eligible for deacon's orders, and after four years as a deacon, he could become an elder. A deacon could perform baptism

23. Albert G. Palmer, *A Discourse delivered at the One Hundredth Anniversary of the Organization of the First Baptist Church in North Stonington, 1843*, pp. 47–48.

24. *Methodist Magazine*, V (1822), 35.

25. James Mudge, *History of the New England Conference of the Methodist Episcopal Church, 1796–1910*, pp. 70–72.

and marriage and assisted the elder in administering the Lord's Supper.[26]

Although Methodist revivals in Connecticut differed from those of the Congregationalists and were similar to those of their own denomination in other parts of the country, and although Congregationalists commented unfavorably on the singing, haranguing, clapping of hands, hallooing, shouting, shaking, and falling at Methodist meetings,[27] nevertheless it appears that strenuous efforts were made to keep them as subdued and orderly as possible. Of the 1826 Methodist awakening in New Haven the minister observed, almost exultantly, "We have no wild fire, no extravagance, no strange hollowing, jumping, or screaming. Now and then we have heard a strong and bitter cry for mercy from heart-broken mourners, and a hearty shout of glory from those whom God had graciously delivered into the liberty of his dear son, with a responding amen from the people of God. I think I may say, with the utmost propriety, that the work is solid, rational, and Scriptural."[28]

Some revivals appeared in individual Methodist societies, especially when other denominations were experiencing religious stirs, but the introduction into Connecticut of the camp meeting, that religious phenomenon which originated among the Presbyterians on the American frontier and was then adopted by other groups, especially the Methodists, represented an innovation. The first recorded gathering of this sort was at Haddam in 1802, when the ministers of the Middletown circuit assembled with a number of people, many of whom had come by boat to the meeting place with the ministers. "A stand was erected in the center of a level piece of ground," one Methodist writer has recorded, "and seats were provided for about one hundred persons. There were no tents or trees.

---

26. *Meth. Mag.*, V (1822), 35–36.
27. See, for instance, letter from S. T. Hosmer to D. Daggett, Oct. 29, 1803, Daggett Papers.
28. *Meth. Mag.*, IX (1826), 276.

Meetings at night or when it rained, as it did, were held in near-by houses or barns, or on the vessel. The meetings continued for three days, and thirty or forty were supposed to be converted amid great demonstrations and fallings into catalepsy. All Middletown was moved when the vessel returned, also the villages that were passed on the river."[29]

Records of a number of camp meetings during succeeding years have survived. The first camp meeting in Windham County was held in 1808. Great crowds attended, and there was much excitement. A Congregational minister, Daniel Dow of Thompson, spoke on this occasion when "hundreds of Methodists were preaching, praying, exhorting, singing and shouting after their peculiar fashion," and boldly expressed his disapproval of the whole procedure.[30] For a memorable meeting in Hebron in 1809 the Reverend Elijah Hedding was responsible. "Many came fifty or sixty miles, provisioned for the week. During one of the evening sermons so great was the power manifested that not less than five hundred lay prostrate and helpless on the ground."[31] An 1821 camp meeting in East Hartford was called "one of the greatest and best meetings of the kind that we have ever witnessed in this section of our country. There were nearly one thousand members present, and on the Sabbath, about eight thousand people. The meeting was conducted with a good deal of order, and religious decorum; but above all, was attended with great displays of the awakening, converting, and sanctifying power of God."[32]

A remarkable camp meeting, held at Compo, Fairfield County, in August, 1825, was described at length in the *Methodist Magazine*.[33] It was a four-day meeting, extended for three more days because of the wind and rain. The encampment stretched for three-quarters of a mile

29. Mudge, *New England Conference of the M.E. Church*, p. 385.
30. Larned, *History of Windham County*, II, 442, 445.
31. Mudge, *New England Conference of the M. E. Church*, p. 386.
32. *Meth. Mag.*, V (1822), 116.   33. *Ibid.*, VIII (1825), 436–440.

through a beautiful grove of oaks and cedars. There were many tents, some of which accommodated several hundred people, while the general gathering was held in a natural amphitheater, in which a congregation of ten thousand, it was reported, could be assembled. This was filled on several days of the meeting. Four times a day the people were summoned to hear preaching, after which they gathered in smaller groups for prayer. "Many found the blessing of perfect love," declared the New York minister who described the meeting, "and testified that the blood of Jesus Christ cleanses from all sin.—Others were exhorted to seek it, nor did they seek in vain. Some were impressed to tell their experiences. . . . It would be impossible to relate the exercises of individuals, and not at all easy to compute the number of those who experienced a change of heart;—but we believe the effects of this meeting will be seen after many days." The New Yorker then wrote in conclusion, "I had never before been in New England; but from my childhood I had heard of the orderly conduct of its inhabitants, and their great respect for divine worship. I anticipated much, and all my anticipations were more than realized." Perhaps it should be added that the high sheriff of Fairfield County with two of his deputies was in attendance, and according to the contemporary account, "though he had but little to do as a civil officer, yet his presence, in the dignified manner in which he deported himself, no doubt contributed to awe the volatile into a respectful submission to the order of the meeting."

Data on Methodist growth in Connecticut is difficult to secure, but in 1818 there were fifty-three churches, while a membership of five thousand was reported in 1821.[34] Writing in that year, the Reverend H. Bangs of New Haven referred to the constant emigration from Connecticut to the West and South and concluded, "The progress of Methodism is truly astonishing, when we consider the means employed, and instruments engaged in it, and the

34. Osborn, ed., *History of Connecticut,* III, 376; *Meth. Mag.,* V (1822), 35.

many difficulties and much opposition through which they had to pass."[35] In 1831, a year when in a single issue of *Zion's Herald* five Connecticut camp meetings were either reported or announced, the Reverend Wilbur Fisk, in his inaugural address as president of the newly established Wesleyan University in Middletown, declared, "The religious enterprises of the Christian church, give another striking feature to the character of the present age. . . . This kingdom is gaining strength, and enlarging its operations; and wherever it goes, it spreads the harmonizing influences of its own spirit."[36]

Since the religious developments among Connecticut Episcopalians, Baptists, and Methodists, which have been considered, parallel so closely those among the Congregationalists, it is not surprising to find that the dissenters also participated in the missionary movement. Naturally, because of their relatively small numbers and vastly inferior financial means, they operated on a much less extensive scale than did the Congregationalists. Furthermore, very little support could be given to activities outside Connecticut by groups which found it difficult to supply the churches within the state.

As in the early phases of the struggle for the disestablishment of religion, the Baptists led the way in the missionary venture. When in 1792 the state legislature authorized the first collection for missionary purposes and invited every religious society to contribute to the support of missionaries to be sent out under the auspices of the General Association, the Baptists in the state approved the missionary enterprise as "a laudable and benevolent design," but objected to this particular request. The General Association, they said, represented but one denomination and would not appoint missionaries in a manner which they would consider fair and impartial. They wanted it clearly understood, moreover, that they "do not recog-

35. *Ibid.*, X (1827), 266.
36. Mudge, *New England Conference of the M. E. Church*, p. 388; *Methodist Magazine and Quarterly Review*, II (1831), 422–423.

nize the right of the General Assembly to control them as a religious body, but only as members of civil society." The Baptists in the New London Association appointed a special committee to solicit funds, and voted that "such funds, so raised, should be placed at the disposal of any Baptist Missionary Society that might be formed; and to promote this good object, the Church stood pledged to co-operate with any sister Church or Churches, or with any individual brethren who might be disposed to unite in carrying out this worthy object." Fourteen dollars was raised at this time.[37]

The Massachusetts Baptist Missionary Society was formed in Boston in 1802 and in the following year began to publish the *Massachusetts Baptist Missionary Magazine*, the earliest Baptist publication in this country.[38] Connecticut Baptists continued to do a little missionary work on an unorganized basis until 1811 at which time they set up the Connecticut Baptist Missionary Society, "to supply destitute Churches and Societies, and to extend the knowledge of salvation as far as possible." Twelve missionaries, all settled ministers, were appointed to labor for a few weeks each in various parts of the state.[39]

Very shortly after this, foreign missions attracted the attention of the Baptists. Indeed, the Baptist Board of Foreign Missions, established in 1814, was the second foreign-missionary society in the United States. In August, 1814, the Connecticut Society Auxiliary to the Baptist Board of Foreign Missions was organized at a meeting attended by Luther Rice, pioneer Baptist organizer for missions.[40] All persons who subscribed to the constitution and contributed one dollar or more annually were members of this auxiliary. Much support came, as it did for the do-

37. "History of the 1st Baptist Church, Waterford," *Historical Sketch of the New London Baptist Association, 1817–1850*, pp. 23–24.

38. Burrage, *History of the Baptists in New England*, pp. 138–139.

39. "Historical Sketch of the Missionary Work of the Connecticut Baptist Convention," *Forty-Third Annual Meeting of the Connecticut Baptist Convention, 1866*, pp. 43–44.

40. *Ibid.*, p. 44.

mestic missionary group, from the female mite societies which sprang up throughout the state. Money was remitted irregularly to the Baptist Board, $300 in August, 1815, the same amount in November, 1817, and apparently smaller sums at other times. A vote of February, 1817, shows that the auxiliary had begun to foster domestic missionary work, and to avoid unnecessary duplication of effort the society founded in 1811 transferred its funds to the larger organization which in 1820 took the name of the Connecticut Baptist Missionary Society. Unincorporated and supported by annual and life memberships and by the mite societies, this combined organization supported domestic missions and coöperated with the Baptist Board of Foreign Missions until October, 1823. Then the Connecticut Baptist Convention was formed, the feeling being that "the business of missions may be better conducted by a convention of churches than by a society of individuals."[41]

It is impossible to state how much these Baptist societies collected and expended from 1811 to 1823. In November, 1819, the treasurer reported that during the previous year $969.93 had been received, $420.70 spent for work in Connecticut, and apparently $200 sent to the Board of Foreign Missions. The following year credits of $701.23 and expenditures of $346.50 were reported, while in 1822 the corresponding figures were $990 and $330.05. Sixteen different missionaries were employed in Connecticut after 1817, all of them for a few weeks a year with the exception of the Reverend William Bentley who served practically full time after 1820. In 1822 the Board of Trustees voted "that the money in the Treasury, contributed for Indian reform, be sent to the Baptist Society among the Oneida Indians, called 'The Hamilton Baptist Missionary Society.' "[42]

41. *Ibid.*, pp. 45–46; Philip S. Evans, *History of the Connecticut Baptist State Convention, 1823–1907*, pp. 12–16; William H. Potter, "Early Missionary Movements in Connecticut," *Fiftieth Annual Meeting of the Connecticut Baptist Convention, 1873*, pp. 141–152.

42. *Ibid.*, pp. 141–152.

Formed by delegates from thirty Baptist churches, the Connecticut Baptist Convention aimed "to assist the destitute Baptist Churches in this State and vicinity, in supporting the regular ministry of the Gospel; and whatever else may tend to promote the edification of the Churches in holiness, and to spread the influence of evangelical religion." Contributions were to be made at the monthly meetings of the churches, and the records show continued support from female mite and primary societies. By February, 1824, three men were in the employ of the Convention, six dollars a week and expenses having been voted to them. Annually, the Fourth of July was to be a day on which funds were to be solicited for the support of missions to the Indians. In June, 1824, the compensation for state missionaries was reduced to five dollars a week and expenses, and it was reported that $769.44 had been received and $491.54 expended.

In 1825, the Reverend Henry Stanwood became the agent of the Convention at a salary of $400 a year; he was succeeded by the Reverend Seth Ewer in 1827. The Reverend William Bentley continued as general itinerant, while several other ministers were assigned to missionary work for short periods. A brief summary of the early work of the Convention is found in the 1829 minutes. "This body has been in existence nearly six years," it was stated, "and has expended for foreign and state missions over $6,000. A number of state missionaries have been annually in their employment, churches have been constituted, and revivals of religion promoted, feeble churches strengthened, and we have reason to believe that many souls will through a long eternity bless God that they were permitted to hear the Gospel preached by those servants of the Lord Jesus Christ."[43]

43. W. H. Potter, "Rise and Early Progress of the Connecticut Baptist Convention," *Fiftieth Annual Meeting of the Connecticut Baptist Convention, 1873*, pp. 153–160; Evans, *History of the Connecticut Baptist State Convention*, pp. 16–28; *Christian Secretary*, June 22, 1824; *Proceedings of the Connecticut Baptist Convention, 1837*, p. 3.

John Mason Peck, a native of Connecticut and a distinguished Baptist home missionary in the employ of the Massachusetts Baptist Missionary Society, attended the 1826 meeting of the Convention and described conditions in Indiana, Illinois, and Missouri. He raised money for western missions both at the Convention and in other Connecticut meetings. In 1832 the Convention became an auxiliary of the American Baptist Home Missionary Society formed in that year, the Convention agreeing to devote itself to work in Connecticut and to appropriate something to the national society.[44]

Both in Connecticut and elsewhere in the United States, the Episcopalians and Methodists were less active than the Baptists in supporting missionary endeavors. In 1798 the Connecticut Episcopalians voted that the money collected in accordance with the acts of the legislature to send missionaries to the new settlements should be turned over to the Episcopal academy recently established in Cheshire.[45] A decade later a voluntary Society for the Promotion of Christian Knowledge was formed, but efforts to organize a missionary society shortly afterward produced no results.[46] In 1814, however, a Diocesan Missionary Society was created, "which looked both to the supply of vacant parishes and the aid of young men in their education for the Christian ministry." This society did practically nothing to accomplish its object and went out of existence in 1817 when the state convention established the Protestant Episcopal Society for the Promotion of Christian Knowledge, the purpose of which was to supply missionaries for the vacant parishes of the diocese and to distribute Bibles, copies of the Book of Common Prayer, and religious tracts. In 1819 this society reported receipts of about $900 and the employment of three itinerant missionaries who had made tours of observation into the most destitute

44. *Christian Secretary,* June 26, July 3, Sept. 11, 1826; *Proceedings of the Connecticut Baptist Convention, 1832,* p. 6; ibid., *1833,* p. 8.
45. Beardsley, *Episcopal Church in Conn.,* II, 11.
46. *Ibid.,* II, 151.

sections of the state. The directors wrote, "Though the Society is in its infancy, though its receipts have been small, and though its operations have not yet been perfectly systematized, yet it cannot be doubted that its effects have already proved beneficial to the interests of the Church and the cause of religion."[47]

In the September, 1821, issue of the *Churchman's Magazine* a writer who emphasized the need for ministers in both the old and the new settlements lamented the fact that the Episcopalians were deliberating while other denominations with strong financial support were working and had plenty of missionaries. "Their missionaries," he wrote, "cross the ocean—traverse every section of the United States, and penetrate the savage tribes of the West." The same issue of this Episcopalian periodical contained an extract from a letter written by an emigrant to Ohio to an Episcopal clergyman in Connecticut. The settler described the strenuous efforts to save the church in the West. A missionary society had been organized which had appointed an agent "to go from Maine to Georgia, both to entreat for means to maintain faithful labourers, and arouse the zeal of the young and pious among the Clergy, to come over into *our Macedonia and help us.*"

At the October, 1820, meeting of the General Convention the Domestic and Foreign Missionary Society of the Protestant Episcopal Church, in the United States of America, was established. The Connecticut Society for Promoting Christian Knowledge continued to function, the treasurer reporting in June, 1822, that $307.63 was still in his hands.[48] In August of that year, a correspondent to the *Churchman's Magazine* after urging greater support of the Society for Promoting Christian Knowledge asserted, "We are even behind our brethren in some of the neighbouring states; and far, very far behind the sects around us, in missionary zeal." Two missionaries were employed in Connecticut during the latter part of

47. *Ibid.,* II, 96, 151–152, 187.
48. *Ibid.,* II, 251–252; *Churchman's Magazine,* II (1822), 26, 215.

1822, and auxiliary societies were formed in many parishes, the Young Churchman's Missionary Society and the Young Ladies' Church Missionary Society in New Haven having more than sixty members each.[49] "It is greatly to be regretted," it was stated in the *Churchman's Magazine* in August, 1826, "that the Society should not be furnished with more ample means of doing good, when the opportunities are so abundant, and the calls for their assistance are so numerous and pressing." Certainly the missionary endeavors of the Episcopalians were very limited in scope.

In writing about the Methodists Professor Sweet accounts for the slowness of this denomination in forming formal missionary societies in two ways. In the first place the church was young and had limited financial resources, and in the second place Methodism as a whole was a missionary venture "with no line of demarcation between missions and evangelism." Methodist itinerants were missionaries wherever they went, in Connecticut or on the frontier, and they early paid much attention to Negroes and became interested in Indians.[50] When J. F. Schermerhorn commented in 1813 on the rapid growth of Methodism, he attributed it to the complete system of missions, "which is by far the best for domestic missions ever yet adopted. They send their laborers into every corner of the country; if they hear of any particular attention to religion in a place, they double the number of laborers in those circuits, and place their best men there, and endeavor, generally, to adapt the character of their preachers, to the character of the people among whom they are to labor."[51]

In 1819, however, the Missionary and Bible Society of the Methodist Episcopal Church was formed which supported missionaries among the Indians and in the old as well as the new settlements, two being maintained within the bounds of the New England Conference in 1823.[52]

49. *Ibid.,* II (1822), 232, 287–288.
50. Sweet, *Methodism in American History,* p. 187.
51. Schermerhorn and Mills, *A Correct View, etc.,* p. 41.
52. *Meth. Mag.,* VI (1823), 277.

That this society's funds were limited is shown by the fact that its receipts, which were as low as $823 in 1820, totalled only $2,547 in 1822 and $4,964 in 1826, and that the total received in its first five years was but $14,-716.24½ for the entire country, of which $11,011.40¾ was expended.[53] Connecticut support of Methodist missionary activities was expressed in the formation of three auxiliary societies—one each on the Goshen, Burlington, and Stratford circuits—which made small contributions to the national society.[54] Twenty-one missionaries were employed in 1825–1826, ten among the Indians, the rest in "places in the white settlements which could not be conveniently provided for in the regular way;—and our brethren in the South Carolina conference are directing their attention to the slave population of that part of our common country." The managers of the society in the report for 1826 paid a tribute to all those in Europe and in America who were participating in the missionary venture and extended the right hand of fellowship to other societies. "The world is large enough," they concluded, "and alas! the moral desolation is sufficiently widespread, to engage all hearts and all hands to cultivate its wilds, and to build up the waste places of Zion."[55] Not until 1832 did the Methodists send out their first foreign missionary, M. B. Cox being dispatched to Liberia where he died four months after his arrival.[56]

Connecticut Episcopalians, Baptists, and Methodists organized or supported Bible societies, tract societies, education societies, and Sunday schools. The Society for the Promotion of Christian Knowledge formed by Connecticut Episcopalians in 1808 aimed to publish and distribute at reduced prices the Bible and other religious works, while the Episcopalian Bible and Common Prayer Book Society, established a year later in New York City, referred

53. Charles C. Goss, *Statistical History of the First Century of American Methodism,* p. 76; *Meth. Mag.,* VII (1824), 278–280.
54. *Ibid.,* VI (1823), 120.   55. *Ibid.,* IX (1826), 269–272.
56. Mudge, *New England Conference of the M. E. Church,* p. 302; Sweet, *Methodism in American History,* pp. 202–203.

to the need for religious publications in a new country where it was essential that religious and moral principles should keep pace with the growth of population and wealth.[57] In 1816 a Bible and Common Prayer Book Society of the diocese of Connecticut appeared which soon urged the General Convention of the Episcopal Church to establish an edition of the Old and New Testaments without note or comment in view of the fact that in the Bibles recently issued by the Connecticut Bible Society Acts 6.3 was translated in such a way as to pervert the apostolic ordination.[58] Upon its organization in 1817 the Connecticut Protestant Episcopal Society for the Promotion of Christian Knowledge took over the distribution of Bibles, and in its third report announced that calls for Bibles and Prayer Books, as well as for tracts and missionary labors, were very numerous and that the society had been able to supply the needs only partially.[59]

Baptist and Methodist relations with the American Bible Society, established in 1816, may be described very briefly. The missionary activities of what the Methodists called the Missionary and Bible Society of the Methodist Episcopal Church in America have already been considered. A second object of this society was "to supply the destitute with Bibles gratuitously, and to afford a cheap supply to those who may have the means of purchasing." When this national organization decided shortly after its founding to devote itself solely to missionary work, it left the Bible distribution to the American Bible Society.[60]

The Baptists, on the other hand, began by coöperating with the national Bible society for two decades, a number of auxiliaries being formed by Connecticut Baptists. When the American Bible Society refused, however, to assist in

57. Beardsley, *Episcopal Church in Conn.*, II, 73; *Conn. Evang. Mag. and Relig. Intel.*, III, 27–30.

58. *Connecticut Courant*, Dec. 3, 1816; Beardsley, *Episcopal Church in Conn.*, II, 145.

59. *Churchman's Magazine*, I (1821), 234.

60. *Meth. Mag.*, II (1819), 278; Bangs, *History of the Methodist Episcopal Church*, III, 83, 93, 150–151.

publishing translations of the Bible in foreign languages which satisfied the Baptists on the rendition of the word "baptize," a break occurred in 1836, and the Baptists organized the American and Foreign Bible Society. Later that year the newly formed Connecticut Baptist Bible Society became an auxiliary.[61]

Tracts were of interest to all the dissenting groups; indeed, John Wesley is credited with having organized the first tract society in 1782 to circulate them among the poor.[62] It is quite likely that the Methodist Book Concern, set up in Philadelphia in 1789 and moved to New York fifteen years later, published tracts, but not until 1817 was the Tract Society of the Methodist Episcopal Church formed. In 1824 this society reported the printing of 15,100 tracts during the previous year but regretted that since auxiliaries had furnished no help, all financial support had been derived from the sale of tracts and members' contributions. When the American Tract Society was established in 1825, some Methodists coöperated, but the Methodist tract society continued its independent existence.[63]

Connecticut Episcopalians organized a Society for the Promotion of Christian Knowledge in 1808 and the Protestant Episcopal Society for the Promotion of Christian Knowledge in 1817, both of which aimed, among other things, to distribute religious tracts. It seems reasonable to suppose that Connecticut Baptists depended to some extent on the Congregationalists until their own national tract society was formed in 1824. Then auxiliaries to this Baptist General Tract Society were set up in the state, membership dues being only twelve and a half cents a year. The Connecticut Baptist Convention and the district

61. "A Brief History of the Ashford Baptist Association," *Minutes of the Ashford Baptist Association, 1844*, pp. 18–19; Evans, *History of the Connecticut Baptist State Convention,* p. 41; *Proceedings of the Connecticut Baptist Convention, 1836*, pp. 43–46.
62. Goss, *Statistical History*, p. 119.
63. Bangs, *History of the Methodist Episcopal Church*, III, 55; *Meth. Mag.*, VII (1824), 437; IX (1826), 141–144.

associations supported the tract-society movement, and 1827 was called "the year of tracts and tract societies." Immediately after the Connecticut branch of the Baptist General Tract Society was organized in 1830, about twenty-five societies became auxiliaries, and the Convention recommended it to the patronage of the churches of the state.[64] The editor of the Baptist *Christian Secretary* in 1826 applauded the denominational coöperation in Bible and tract societies. To those unbelievers who pointed to divisions among professing Christians, he wrote, it could now be announced that this stumbling block had been removed to such an extent that it could no longer be used against the Church of Christ. Coöperation among Bible societies had opened the way to coöperation among tract societies. He pointed out that when the president of the American Tract Society took office he requested that all sectarian views be excluded from tracts published by the society, and that nothing be taught except the doctrines of the Gospel on which all Christians were agreed. What was to be sought was "*common ground*" on which the individual strength of the Church of Christ, may be exerted for the upbuilding of his kingdom, and the demolition of the kingdom of darkness and death."[65]

Only the Episcopalians and the Baptists in Connecticut had sufficient funds to support education societies, and the latter group was much more active than the former. The Connecticut Baptist Education Society was organized in 1818, its object being "to assist young men who are called of God to preach the Gospel, in acquiring such mental discipline and culture as shall render them more useful in the Kingdom of Christ." Prejudices against an educated

---

64. *Christian Secretary*, Sept. 21, 1824; Sept. 26, 1825; Aug. 2, 1828; Potter, "Rise and Early Progress of the Connecticut Baptist Convention," *Fiftieth Annual Meeting of the Connecticut Baptist Convention, 1873*, p. 159; *Minutes of the New London Baptist Association, 1827*, p. 5; Burrage, *History of the Baptists in New England*, p. 240; *Proceedings of the Connecticut Baptist Convention, 1830*, p. 12.

65. *Christian Secretary*, Sept. 4, 1826.

ministry, based to some extent on the fear that intellectualism would interfere with the operation of the Holy Spirit, had disappeared. Incorporated in 1820, the Baptist society consisted of all persons who paid a dollar or more annually to the treasury and of delegates from auxiliaries. Constantly in need of funds, it collected small sums each year which it used to support young men at the Baptist Theological Seminary located in Hamilton, New York. Larger sums were subscribed in years when agents of the seminary or of the society worked in the state, and in 1826 the permanent fund totalled $1,520.[66]

Not until 1827 did Connecticut Episcopalians set up an education society. In their first report the directors of the Church Scholarship Society, as it was called, said that the need for an education society, based on principles somewhat different from those then in vogue, had long been felt, and that the Scholarship Society had received substantial support. In order to eliminate unworthy motives in the choice of a profession, recipients of aid were not required to pledge themselves to be ministers although it was hoped that many would choose that calling. "The cause of this society, then," the report continued, "is the common cause of learning and religion, and it will be successful in proportion as men of real worth and talents shall be aided to surmount the difficulties of poverty and to occupy useful stations in the learned professions." All assistance was in the form of loans to be repaid without interest within three years after leaving college and was restricted to students at Washington College in Hartford.[67]

The opening of this Episcopal college in 1824 and of the Methodist Wesleyan University in Middletown in 1831 was not unconnected with the religious awakening, and the

66. "Historical Sketch of the Connecticut Baptist Education Society," *Ninety-Sixth Annual Session of the Connecticut Baptist Convention, 1919*, p. 146; "The Seventy-Fifth Meeting of the Connecticut Baptist Education Society," *Seventy-First Annual Meeting of the Connecticut Baptist Convention, 1894*, pp. 102–103; *Relig. Intel.*, VII, 558; *Christian Secretary*, May 18, June 22, 1824; March 27, May 22, 1826.
67. Beardsley, *Episcopal Church in Conn.*, II, 266–269.

setting up of the Connecticut Literary Institution in Suffield in 1833 by the Baptists was a direct outgrowth of the education-society movement. The Episcopalians had long desired a collegiate institution which would be to them as Yale was to the Congregationalists. When Cheshire Academy began to operate in 1796, "to be a nursery to that church, and to prepare young men for her Ministry," Episcopalians hoped that this institution would soon become their college. From 1802 on there was much discussion of the subject, and in 1804 and 1810 unsuccessful attempts were made to secure a charter from the legislature. Episcopalians bitterly resented the Federalist-Congregationalist opposition to their project. When in 1820 the General Theological Seminary, established in New York City in 1817, was moved to New Haven, they were satisfied; but within a year, as the result of a munificent bequest from a New York benefactor, the seminary which had made an auspicious beginning in Connecticut returned to that city. Renewed efforts to establish a college finally achieved success when in May, 1823, Washington College (now Trinity College) was chartered. Somewhat over a year later it opened its doors to students. Cheshire Academy continued to operate, but the loss of funds in a bank failure, the death of its principal, and the establishment of the Hartford college caused it to languish, and for a time after 1826 it was closed.[68]

With Brown University and the theological seminary in Hamilton, New York, near at hand, the Baptists had adequate collegiate facilities, but in 1833 they set up their own school in Suffield, the Connecticut Literary Institution (now Suffield School), "for the purpose of affording additional advantages to worthy young men called of God to the ministry." A sum of $10,000 was raised, half from the inhabitants of Suffield and the rest from churches and

68. *Ibid.*, I, 435–436; II, 3, 26, 66–68, 222–227, 246–250, 263; *Churchman's Magazine*, III (1806), 440; I (1821), 370–372; Joseph P. Beach, *History of Cheshire, Connecticut, 1694 to 1840* (Cheshire, 1912), pp. 246–248.

individuals in the state.[69] Similarly coming to see the value
of an educated ministry, the Methodists accepted with
thanks the offer of the trustees of the American Literary,
Scientific, and Military Academy, which had been conducted in Middletown since 1825 on the West Point model,
to let them have gratuitously the Academy's buildings and
nearly fifteen acres of land, provided that an endowment
of $40,000 was raised. Wesleyan University was opened
in 1831.[70]

Sunday schools were established in Connecticut by the
dissenting denominations, and while exact dates cannot be
determined, in part because of the difficulty in distinguish-
ing between schools held on Sunday for poor children and
schools wherein religious instruction was the main item, it
would appear that Episcopalian, Baptist, and Methodist
Sunday schools were practically contemporaneous with
those of the Congregationalists. In his address to the Episcopal state convention in 1820, Bishop Brownell referred
to Sunday schools as if they were fairly recent innovations. "I believe," he said, "that they are very generally
established throughout the Diocese; and much praise is
due to the clergy, and others who have promoted them, as
well as to those individuals who have taxed their charity
with the labor of instruction. To withdraw the young from
profane amusements, or a thoughtless indolence on the
Lord's day; to assemble them together for religious worship; to store their minds with the elements of Christian
knowledge; to excite in their hearts devout affections, and
to familiarize them to the pious and evangelical services of
our liturgy, are objects which may well call forth the charities of the friends of religion."[71] According to the same

69. "The Seventy-Fifth Meeting of the Connecticut Baptist Education
Society," *Seventy-First Annual Meeting of the Connecticut Baptist Convention, 1894*, pp. 104–105; *Proceedings of the Connecticut Baptist Convention, 1833*, p. 21.
70. Bernard C. Steiner, *The History of Education in Connecticut*, pp.
258–259; *Meth. Mag. and Quart. Rev.*, II (1831), 419–441; James M.
Buckley, *A History of Methodism in the United States*, I, 459.
71. Beardsley, *Episcopal Church in Conn.*, II, 235–237.

bishop, by 1822 Sunday schools had been established in nearly all the parishes of the diocese. He referred to the fact that elementary education was so universal that it was not necessary to use Sunday for secular education and concluded by saying that, accordingly, Sunday schools could be devoted to religious instruction.[72] Certainly religious instruction was the aim of the class in the Fairfield church which in 1821 learned "the catechism, twenty-two Collects, twenty Epistles, twenty Gospels, fifty-seven Hymns, seventeen Psalms, Jones' catechism, eleven chapters in Rayner's catechism, the thirty-nine Articles of Religion, thirty-six chapters in the Bible, and thirty-six answers to questions from Dr. Barrow's Collection."[73] In 1826 the General Protestant Episcopal Sunday School Union was formed in Philadelphia.[74]

A Methodist Sunday school is reported in Windham County in 1814, and in 1818 in Hartford four schools were operating in the two Congregational, the Episcopal, and the Baptist churches, all under the patronage of a union society.[75] In 1824 the Connecticut Sunday School Union was established, an organization which embraced schools in three denominations, the Congregationalists, the Methodists, and the Baptists.[76] When in the same year the American Sunday School Union was formed, the Baptists in particular among the dissenters coöperated with it. Very shortly thereafter the trend was toward denominational unions, the Sunday School Union of the Methodist Episcopal Church being organized in 1827, and the Connecticut Baptist Sabbath School Society in 1830.[77]

It remains only to say a few words about the relation between the dissenters and the moral reform and humani-

72. *Churchman's Magazine*, II (1822), 200–201.
73. *Ibid.*, I (1821), 220.   74. *Ibid.*, V (1827), 315.
75. Larned, *History of Windham County*, II, 441; Walker, *History of the First Church in Hartford*, p. 374.
76. J. M. Morse, *The Rise of Liberalism in Connecticut* (New Haven, 1933), p. 26.
77. Bangs, *History of the Methodist Episcopal Church*, III, 337; Burrage, *History of the Baptists in New England*, p. 261.

tarian developments. John Wesley had been a pioneer in inveighing against intemperance, his rule prohibiting "drunkenness, buying or selling spirituous liquors, or drinking them, except in cases of extreme necessity."[78] Although the American Methodist Church formally adopted Wesley's precepts in 1784, a dozen years later a relaxation of discipline was effected by a vote which enabled Methodists to sell liquor, provided that no disorder followed. Increased consumption of liquor by preachers and church members resulted.[79] So far did American Methodists retreat from Wesley's stand that at the 1812 General Conference a motion was defeated which provided that any stationed or local preacher who sold spirituous liquor would forfeit his position. The following statement, however, appeared in the pastoral letter:

It is with regret that we have seen the use of ardent spirits, dram-drinking, and so forth, so common among the Methodists. We have endeavored to suppress the practice by our example, but it is necessary that we add precept to example; and we really think it not consistent with the character of a Christian to be immersed in the practice of distilling or retailing an article so destructive to the morals of society, and we do most earnestly recommend the Annual Conferences and our people to join with us in making a firm and constant stand against an evil which has ruined thousands both in time and eternity.[80]

In 1816 the motion defeated four years earlier was passed.[81]

Shortly after the Congregationalist-led drive for total abstinence began in Connecticut, the New England Methodist Conference in 1827 expressed its deep satisfaction at witnessing the efforts being made to suppress the use of "ardent spirits" and urged the assembled ministers to en-

78. Dorchester, *Christianity in the United States,* p. 352.
79. Sweet, *Methodism in American History,* pp. 136, 171; Buckley, *History of Methodism,* I, 349–350.
80. *Ibid.,* I, 410.   81. *Ibid.,* I, 427.

force the rules regarding the use of spirituous liquors.[82] The following year, on motion of the Reverend Wilbur Fisk who became Wesleyan University's first president, the General Conference passed a moderate resolution urging Methodists "to do all they prudently can, both by precept and example, to suppress intemperance throughout the land." The Conference also declared it important "that we neither drink ourselves (except medicinally) nor give it to visitors or workmen."[83]

The historian of Connecticut Episcopalianism makes no mention of the temperance movement. May it not be assumed that the Episcopalians were divided, as they were elsewhere, and took no action?[84] The Reverend Harry Croswell, rector of the Episcopal church in New Haven, was no friend of total abstinence. On December 13, 1829, he preached a sermon on "intolerance and bigotry, from Romans xiv, 4, 'who art thou that judgest another's servant,' &c.," having in mind the Congregationalists who had "entered into a combination to denounce and proscribe every man, woman, and child, who will not subscribe to the total abstinence system."[85]

Connecticut Baptists, however, through their several associations passed resolutions in 1826 and 1827 against the use of "ardent spirits," especially at associational meetings. Even stronger resolves were voted by the New Haven Association in 1828, the Ashford Association in 1830, and the New London Association in 1832.[86] "Ardent

82. Mudge, *New England Conference of the M. E. Church,* p. 298.
83. Buckley, *History of Methodism,* I, 451.
84. William W. Manross, *The Episcopal Church in the United States, 1800–1840* (New York, 1938), p. 227.
85. F. B. Dexter, "The Reverend Harry Croswell and His Diary," *Papers of the New Haven Colony Historical Society,* IX, 62.
86. Asa C. Bronson, "Historical Discourse preached at the Centennial Anniversary of the New Haven Baptist Association, Oct., 1875," *Fifty-Second Annual Meeting of the Connecticut Baptist Convention,* p. 114; "A Brief History of the Hartford Baptist Association," *Minutes of the Hartford Baptist Association, 1889,* p. 18; "A Brief History of the Ashford Baptist Association," *Minutes of the Ashford Baptist Association, 1844,* p. 17; *Minutes of the New London Association, 1827,* p. 5; *ibid., 1832,* p. 3.

spirits" are useless, the committee on temperance of the Connecticut Baptist Convention reported in 1830. "Touch not, taste not, handle not," was the motto suggested by the committee which offered the following resolution:

Resolved, That we do greatly rejoice in the success of the cause of Temperance, and that we do most earnestly recommend to the members of all Baptist churches, not barely to refrain from being rum-drinkers, but that we solemnly entreat them not to keep or encourage the sale of intoxicating liquors. We deem the taverns and shops, &c., keeping for sale this destroying poison, the very root and fountain head of this evil.[87]

Not until 1833, however, does a formal resolution on the subject appear in the minutes of the Convention. Then it was voted,

As it has been incontrovertibly proved that alcohol is never necessary, except as a medicine—that every temperate drinker is in danger of becoming a drunkard—that no drunkard can inherit eternal life—and that even a small quantity of ardent spirits so deadens the moral sensibilities, and stupefies the conscience of the unconverted, when under their operation, that the preaching of the gospel has no effect therefore, Resolved, That we recommend to all the members of the Baptist churches in this state, that they wholly abstain from the use and vending of ardent spirits.[88]

Practically everybody in Connecticut was interested in the establishment of the Asylum for the Deaf and Dumb in 1817 and the Hartford Retreat in 1825. Evidence is plentiful to show Episcopalian and Baptist support in particular of the project for caring for the insane.[89] The editors of the Episcopalian *Churchman's Magazine* praised the efforts being made for these unfortunates, and

---

87. *Proceedings of the Connecticut Baptist Convention, 1830*, p. 16.
88. *Ibid., 1833*, p. 7.
89. See files of *Churchman's Magazine* and *Christian Secretary*.

shortly after the Retreat was opened the editors of the
Baptist *Christian Secretary* commented very favorably on
the wholesome and practical sentiments which had led to
coöperation in behalf of such a worthy cause.[90]

John Wesley had been a leader in England's eighteenth-
century struggle against slavery and the slave trade. In
his last letter, written on February 24, 1791, and addressed to Wilberforce, then in Parliament engrossed in
efforts to abolish the slave trade, Wesley said in part, "O,
be not weary in well-doing! Go on, in the name of God
and in the power of His might, till even American slavery
(the vilest that ever saw the sun) shall vanish before it."[91]
On several occasions after 1779 the General Conference of
the American Methodist Episcopal Church expressed its
feelings strongly on the subject of slavery. In 1780 it was
called "contrary to the laws of God, man, and nature, the
dictates of conscience and pure religion"; in 1784, "contrary to the Golden Rule of God and the inalienable rights
of mankind"; in 1796 a "great evil"; in 1816 an evil past
remedy. In the latter year the General Conference voted to
bar from official positions in the Methodist church all
slaveholders living in states whose laws permitted the
manumission of slaves. Concessions had to be made to
Southerners in 1804 and 1808.[92]

Connecticut Methodists, as well as Baptists, took no action until they began to evince interest in the work of the
American Colonization Society. In 1823 the editors of the
Methodist Magazine praised the society and asserted that
it deserved the sympathies "of every well-wisher to the
civilization, and christianization of the depressed descendants of Africa."[93] The editors of the *Christian Secretary*
in July, 1824, wished the society success as one which
should enlist the attention of philanthropists and Chris-

90. *Churchman's Magazine*, I (1821), 187; *Christian Secretary*, June
13, 1825.
91. Sweet, *Methodism in American History*, p. 230.
92. Mudge, *New England Conference of the M. E. Church*, pp. 277–
278; Buckley, *History of Methodism*, I, 427; II, 1.
93. *Meth. Mag.*, VI (1823), 463.

tians.[94] Included in the committee of correspondence appointed to keep in touch with the American Colonization Society after its agents visited Connecticut in August, 1824, were representatives of the several church groups, Dr. Mason F. Cogswell, the Reverend Joel Hawes, the Reverend J. H. Lindsey, the Reverend Elijah Cushman, Samuel Tudor, H. L. Ellsworth, and S. H. Huntington.[95] Not until 1835 was the first antislavery resolution offered to the Connecticut Baptist Convention. Then it was referred to a committee, and no more was heard of it.[96]

It is evident that Episcopalians, Baptists, and Methodists were involved in Connecticut's Second Great Awakening along with the Congregationalists. The spirit of the times was well expressed in the first issue of the *Methodist Magazine* in January, 1818. "The few years of the present century which have already passed away," the editors asserted, "have opened the most important and auspicious events, relative to the establishment of the kingdom of Jesus Christ upon earth. The united exertions of thousands of all denominations of Christians to spread the holy scriptures—the unadulterated word of God, savours much of the catholic spirit by which the friends of christianity should be governed, and furnishes a pleasing prospect of the extensive triumph of evangelical truth."

94. *Christian Secretary,* July 6, 1824.
95. *Ibid.,* Aug. 17, 1824.
96. Evans, *History of the Connecticut Baptist State Convention,* p. 37.

IX

NEW WINE IN NEW BOTTLES

THE Reverend Lyman Beecher preached the annual Election Sermon in New Haven on May 3, 1826. His accomplishments and prestige secured for him a large group of interested listeners. It was his valedictory to the state where he had been born and educated and where he had labored effectively in his chosen calling, for after a brilliant pastorate of sixteen years at Litchfield he had accepted a call to a wider field of activity in Boston.

This sermon may also be considered the valedictory of Connecticut's Second Great Awakening.[1] By 1826 there had been nearly three decades of revivals, and all the new developments, which were, in part at least, outgrowths of the religious quickening had appeared. Indeed, the age of exciting beginnings had to a large extent given place to one of organized administration.

It was peculiarly fitting that Beecher should have been the preacher on this occasion, for he had been an outstanding leader in the Awakening. As a revivalist he had achieved success both in his own parish and in other parts of the state. He had taken the lead in organizing the Connecticut Society for the Promotion of Good Morals and in the ensuing campaign to improve moral standards. When his trumpet had been raised to call attention to the "waste places" within the state borders, his blast had led to the formation of the Domestic Missionary Society. Beecher had represented Connecticut in 1816 when the American Bible Society was organized, and he was still an agent of

---

1. The Awakening was not definitely ended. Its various phases were to be extended and refined during the years that followed Beecher's sermon, and 1831 was to be a brilliant revival year. Is it possible—or necessary—to date the end of such a movement?

the Cornwall School. As a parting contribution he had offered the six sermons which helped to inspire a new era in the temperance movement. In his Election Sermon he chose to survey the momentous developments of the period during which he had lived.

The revivals, he declared, had no parallel in the world's history. "Already," he asserted, "the churches look chiefly to them for their members and pastors, and for that power upon public opinion, which retards declension, gives energy to law, and voluntary support to religious institutions." He rejoiced in the work of the missionary societies, and he praised the widespread distribution of Bibles and tracts, as well as the assistance accorded young men by education societies. The state, indeed the nation, was making every possible effort to extend religion at home and abroad. "Philosophers and patriots, statesmen and men of wealth," Beecher continued, "are beginning to feel that it is righteousness only which exalteth a nation, and to give to the work of moral renovation their arguments, the power of their example, and the impulse of their charity. And the people . . . are disposed at length to build again those institutions . . . they had either neglected or trodden down." An era of moral power had been established, an array of moral influence created such as "was never before brought to bear upon the nation." In these developments, Beecher believed, lay the fulfillment of the promise contained in his text from Revelation, "And He that sat upon the throne said Behold, I make all things new."

Such a survey revealed the attitude of one who had lived through the Awakening toward the events in which he had participated. In completing this study it is necessary, from the vantage point of more than a century, to consider some general aspects of the period. It may well be reëmphasized at this juncture that the Awakening was not limited to Connecticut, but appeared, in no two areas in exactly the same form, throughout the country.

Of great importance was the victory of revealed religion over its enemies, indifference and infidelity. The revivals resulted in an increased church membership, this in spite of the complete abandonment of the Half-Way Covenant by the Congregationalists and the enforcement of stricter discipline. Religious meetings now commanded sizable audiences, and interest in the churches, once aroused, was maintained by the many new activities now forming part of their programs. Sermons and writings no longer bristled with attacks on the *philosophes* and Tom Paine as they had earlier. The Fairfield County Bible Society in its second annual report in 1816 struck a triumphant note. "The present," it declared, "has been emphatically called the age of Bibles and Missionaries. The atheism of Voltaire and his associates, is gone down, almost with their dust to the grave. The blasphemies of Paine are remembered only to be abhorred."[2]

One contemporary remarked that "the millennial day appears to have dawned upon this benighted world. Satan is alarmed, and making every possible effort to stop the progress of piety & godliness but his efforts are in vain."[3] Many an address began as did one by the Reverend Joab Brace in 1829.[4] "Let us ascribe glory to God," the Newington minister declared, "for our living in an age of the world, when so much is doing to promote the peace and happiness of man." An abundant confidence had replaced the earlier attitude of fear for the future of Christianity. That this was not limited to Connecticut is indicated by Alexis de Tocqueville's comment on religion in the United States in 1831. "There is no country in the world," the French observer wrote, "where the Christian religion retains a greater influence over the souls of men than in America."[5] It is not to be supposed, however, that indifference was completely abolished or that all people were won to the support of revealed religion. The General Associa-

2. *Relig. Intel.*, I, 331.
3. MS. letter addressed by Thomas Ritter to "My Posterity," Sept. 18, 1824.
4. Joab Brace, *Address delivered before the Peace Society of Hartford County* (1829), p. 3.
5. Tocqueville, *Democracy in America*, I, 388.

tion, indeed, went so far in 1830 as to propose as causes for mourning and humiliation, "the prevalence and boldness of infidelity in many ensnaring forms; . . . the extensive indifference of members of our churches to all the periodical vehicles of religious intelligence; and the consequent ignorance and apathy which prevail in religion to the dangers which threaten to subvert the foundations of many generations." But that there had been an upturn, wrought by the determined efforts of a militant group of religious conservatives, could not be denied.

The forces of supernatural religion did not win their victory without profound changes in the theories and practices as well as in the theology of Connecticut's dominant faith, Congregationalism.[6] For one thing, emotional tendencies, formerly nonexistent, appeared and affected both ministers and churchgoers. Innovations in both the matter and the manner of preaching were apparent. Ministers discovered that they could increase their effectiveness and still maintain their dignity if they softened their methods, dropped some of their austerity, and preached deliberately to the hearts of men. In fact, they were obliged to adopt new methods in order to make their appeals successful. In sermons of a type unlike those which had previously been delivered, they called upon men to repent, reform, and contribute. On the other side of the pulpit the new quality was also evident. The inertness and passivity which had long characterized Congregational congregations lessened, and people warmed up to religious matters —even became excited about them. The revivals and the new enterprises were responsible for the change.

Ministers, compelled to give much attention to the newly created societies and institutions with which they were connected, found their duties greatly increased. In addi-

6. These changes were not the outcome of any deliberate scheme to alter the character of Connecticut Congregationalism. They represented the adjustments which an active group made to keep religion alive. Like many other changes, they are more apparent to a later generation than they were to the innovators themselves.

tion, the closer relation between churches and members and the manifold activities of the Awakening necessitated much ministerial visiting. Pastoral calls, neglected in the latter part of the eighteenth century, were more frequent. During revival periods the number of religious services increased. Evening meetings, opposed earlier because of the fear that they might incite excesses or disorderliness, were instituted at this time, and henceforth, their worth and safety having been demonstrated, were regular parts of the churches' programs.

The Half-Way Covenant, a practice which, it was felt, had made for "half-way" Christians, was definitely eliminated from Connecticut churches. Conversion became the sole test for church membership, and those who presented themselves were carefully scrutinized. Baptism was accorded only to the children of full members or to those who made confessions of faith. Stricter discipline was enforced.

The rôle of the church in society was altered. Previously, churches had been places where people worshipped and through which they obtained salvation. They continued to fulfill these functions, but in addition, almost overnight it seemed, many societies sprang up, the roll of which has been called and their activities enumerated in earlier chapters of this study. Most of these societies were associated with the churches and were fostered by them. As a result of this concern about projects and enterprises hitherto nonexistent, the outlook of churches was broadened and their activities became more numerous.

The creation of what may be called the "activity" church wrought several fundamental changes in orthodox theology. Of great importance was the new implied relationship between man and God. The doctrine of the sovereignty of God was affirmed and reaffirmed in the sermons preached by the leaders of the Awakening, for they clung tenaciously to the basic tenet of Congregationalism. At the same time the doctrine of the ability, responsibility, and freedom of man was stressed. The intellectual climate

of the times demanded it. The manifold activities in which
the people connected with the churches were engaged furthered it. The Congregational clergy recognized it. Timothy Dwight spoke for many of his colleagues when he said,
"In my apprehension, it is never true, that the attempts
of the man concerned, towards the attainment of salvation,
make no difference as to the event. On the contrary it is
clear, that of those, who are saved, few, very few, indeed,
can be found, who have not made such attempts; nor is
there any satisfactory reason to believe that those, who
make them with persevering earnestness and zeal, ultimately fail."[7] The people of the time were not disturbed
by this juxtaposition of the conflicting doctrines of the
ability of man and the sovereignty of God. The Reverend
Samuel Nott, for seventy years pastor of the church in
Franklin, wrote, "My mind for some time, was perplexed,
about divine sovereignty, & free agency, but I became convinced, that both were taught, in the word of God."[8]

No longer were men regarded as mere pawns in the
hands of supernatural forces. Their fellow beings could
do things for them, reform them, make life more endura-
ble, prepare them for the next world, improve their chances
of securing salvation. This emphasized the ability of man
but did not infringe on the sovereignty of God. It simply
made man more important in relation to God.

The effects were twofold; the doctrine of works was
given a new importance in Congregational ideology, and
the doctrine of election passed into the background. People
with many things to do would not carry their efforts to
the desired heights unless they could visualize the reward
to be derived therefrom. Men were reminded that in giving they would be serving both their neighbors and themselves.[9] From this one might deduce that by their works
were men to be known; by their works were they to be

7. Dwight, *Theology,* I, 261. See also Beecher, *Works,* II, 28; Dwight,
The True Means of Establishing Public Happiness (1795), p. 15.
8. MS. autobiography, Congregational House, p. 67.
9. See, for instance, *Connecticut Observer,* March 22, 1825.

helped to enter the kingdom of heaven. In 1795, the very year when Timothy Dwight became president of Yale and New Divinity forces became dominant in the state, Zephaniah Swift wrote in his penetrating study, *A System of the Laws of the State of Connecticut:* "They [mankind] begin to entertain an idea, that religion was not instituted for the purpose of rendering them miserable, but happy, and that the innocent enjoyments of life, are not repugnant to the will of a benevolent God. They believe there is more merit in acting right, than in thinking right; and that the condition of men in a future state, will not be dependent on the speculative opinions, they may have adopted in the present."[10] The editor of the Litchfield *American Eagle* went so far as to query whether the missionary spirit did not lead to the doctrine that "salvation can be purchased with *money,* if that money is expended in *spreading the Gospel.*"[11]

Inevitably, the doctrine of election was affected. It was not formally rejected, but in many circles it became the "forgotten doctrine." Practically nobody preached on the subject, so few indeed that the Reverend Noah Porter, who had occasion in 1829 to berate Lyman Beecher for modifying the Gospel "to appease opposition" and "to render it palatable to men," wrote, "You know as well as I, but, if I am not mistaken, thirty years ago, ten sermons were preached in New England, on *total depravity* and *election* to one that is preached on those subjects now."[12] As if by common consent, the doctrine ceased to be the subject of public discussion or even incidental reference. For this development three reasons may be cited. A revival period during which every possible effort was being made to win souls to God did not seem a fitting time to discourse on the somewhat discouraging doctrine of election. Nor could any good be accomplished by preaching an idea that

10. Zephaniah Swift, *A System of the Laws of the State of Connecticut* (2 vols., Windham, Conn., 1795–1796), I, 145.
11. *American Eagle,* June 23, 1823.
12. Beecher, *Autobiography,* II, 162.

smacked of religious aristocracy to people who were on speaking terms, at least, with political democracy. Finally, the notion that man could by his works help to win salvation ran counter to the conception of salvation by election.

With the development of the "activity" church and the acceptance of such ideas as the ability of man and the doctrine of works, together with neglect of the doctrine of election, Connecticut Congregationalism had strayed far from what had been considered orthodox. That such an evolution had indeed occurred is proved by the fact that an effort was made to check it. This came in the late 1820's and centered in the so-called Taylor-Tyler controversy.[13] The immediate cause of this dissension in the ranks of Connecticut ministers was the celebrated *Concio ad Clerum* sermon, preached in 1828 by the Reverend Nathaniel W. Taylor. Student and theological heir of Timothy Dwight, this member of the Yale Divinity School faculty declared that moral depravity was "man's own act, consisting in the free choice of some object other than God, as his chief good;—or a free preference of the world and of worldly good, to the will and glory of God." He took the position that man was guilty of sin and man alone, that God could not keep him from sinning if he so desired. This made man more of a free agent than had ever been admitted in orthodox circles. It was too much for the conservative elements. Headed by Bennet Tyler, formerly pastor in Southbury, Connecticut, and president of Dartmouth College, and at the time pastor of a church in Portland, Maine, the opposition took the field. The details of this quarrel are of no importance here. One of the results, because of Taylor's connection with the Yale Divinity School, was the founding of a new theological seminary in East Windsor (now the Hartford Theological Seminary) where the conservatives entrenched themselves.

With Taylor's conception of the free agency of man,

13. See discussions of the controversy in Foster, *Genetic History of the New England Theology;* Boardman, *History of New England Theology;* Eversull, *Evolution of an Old New England Church.*

religious thought among Connecticut Congregationalists had come almost a full circle from Jonathan Edwards. Edwards had made a vigorous assault on Arminianism, and now Taylor was expressing what were called Arminian doctrines. Thus had the thinking of a strong wing of Congregationalism, Connecticut Puritanism to give it another name, moved in three-quarters of a century. It must not be forgotten, however, that Edwards had really started this line of thought, for he had not denied the freedom of the will. He himself had given man certain attributes; the neo-Edwardeans had "improved on" Edwards.

The influence of Jonathan Edwards in the Second Great Awakening in Connecticut has already been indicated. It is now necessary to consider further his relationship to Connecticut religious thought. Edwards is a central figure in New England religious thought and intellectual development as a whole. From him one line, which has been brilliantly traced by Professor Perry Miller, leads through the Unitarians to Emerson.[14] But there was another line, leading from Edwards to Timothy Dwight and then to Nathaniel Taylor, along which were the champions of orthodoxy rather than the rebels. Whereas the Unitarians had revolted, the neo-Edwardeans had fought for orthodoxy within the church through revivals, modifying it, liberalizing it, rendering it more acceptable by making it more reasonable.

It has been stated that one line led from Edwards through Unitarianism to Emerson. What about the other line after Dwight and Taylor? Next came Horace Bushnell, Hartford minister, who had studied under Taylor. Bushnell raised questions about one of the most important parts of the Second Great Awakening, revivalism. His doctrine of Christian nurture resulted from his belief that Connecticut Congregationalism was depending too exclusively on revivals, that the reliance on "conversion" had caused church people to neglect rearing children as Chris-

14. Miller, "Jonathan Edwards to Emerson," *New England Quarterly,* XIII (1940), 589–617.

tians. Bushnell contended that "the child is to grow up a Christian, and never know himself as being otherwise."[15]

Bushnell's connection with the other line from Edwards is revealed in his treatise, *Nature and the Supernatural Together Constituting One System of God.* Professor Miller has good reason for writing that with its publication "Calvinism itself was, as it were, transcendentalized."[16] As the Unitarians attacked the transcendentalists, so religious conservatives in Connecticut threatened Bushnell with trial for heresy. But Bushnell was much closer to the orthodox tradition, although another modifier of it, than the Unitarians and the transcendentalists, and so far as Connecticut at least is concerned, there was no breakdown of Calvinism in the manner described by Oliver Wendell Holmes in *The One-Hoss Shay.* From Bushnell stemmed much of the social-gospel movement of the post-Civil War days.

The Second Great Awakening in Connecticut—and throughout the country—assumes historical importance as the period during which organized charity began. Practically every phase of the Awakening except the revivals involved the expenditure of money, whether it was to send missionaries and Bibles to the frontier, or to build an asylum for the insane. People, especially those connected with the churches, were called on to support these numerous enterprises, and societies were organized to supervise the collection and expenditure of the funds. There were national, state, and local societies, the latter type existing in quantity and variety. There were charitable societies, beneficent societies, fragment societies, cent societies, praying societies, sewing societies, "Owyhean" societies, gleaning societies, retrenchment societies. Some gave their contributions to the foreign-mission enterprise, some to young men studying for the ministry, some for the care of widows and orphans. The Charitable Society of Windham County

15. Theodore T. Munger, *Horace Bushnell,* chap. V.
16. Miller, "Jonathan Edwards to Emerson," p. 616.

went so far as to divide its funds among the American and
Connecticut Bible Societies, Foreign Missions, Transla-
tions, Cornwall School, Aborigines, Domestic Missions,
Yale College Education Society, the New England and
Hartford Tract Societies, and the Deaf and Dumb Asy-
lum.[17]

Various methods were employed to raise money. In many
societies membership involved the payment of dues. For
some of the enterprises contributions were received in the
churches at stated times, or at annual, semi-annual, or
monthly meetings collections were taken up, frequently
after a minister invited for the occasion had preached an
appropriate sermon. Sometimes, subscription books were
opened in designated places, and those desiring to give
were asked to write their names. A few societies employed
special agents who presented the cases of their respective
institutions to the public. And of course people were requested to send in contributions whenever they felt so inclined without waiting for any special occasion.

Generous was the response to the numerous appeals during this unprecedented age of benevolence, especially so
for a state which was still predominantly agricultural. To
belong to the societies and to contribute to the religious
cause became popular and fashionable in most communities. Articles appeared in religious publications advocating thrift so that more money would be available for the
purpose. One writer resolved that when anything he bought
cost less than he expected, he would use the amount saved
for charity, and that he would also give a tenth of all
money unexpectedly received in payment of debts "to promote the cause of the Redeemer." Another urged the use
of rye in place of coffee. The money saved was to be applied to benevolences.[18]

Since most of the people of Connecticut were in moderate circumstances, contributions were usually small, but
there appeared for the first time that familiar American

17. *Relig. Intel.*, V, 187.   18. *Ibid.*, IV, 255–256; VI, 190.

figure, the philanthropist. Men with adequate means at their disposal, for one reason or another, religious in the main it would seem, became supporters of the newly established enterprises. Connecticut had no one to equal Elias Boudinot of New Jersey, who distributed gifts lavishly while he was alive and then in his will made large bequests to numerous charities, as much as $5,000 and forty-five hundred acres of land to the A.B.C.F.M., and thirteen thousand acres to the mayor and corporation of Philadelphia to set up a fund to supply the poor of the city with wood.[19] But the state philanthropies had several large benefactors. General Jedediah Huntington, a leading New London merchant, was noted for his munificence, which, it has been asserted "for its profusion, its uniformity, its long continuance; and for the discretion by which it was directed, was, unquestionably, in this state, without an example, and without a parallel." He aided the poor in his vicinity and young men seeking education; he supported weak churches and the endeavors to spread religion at home and abroad.[20]

Among the earliest and most liberal donors to the American Asylum and the Hartford Retreat was Joseph Battell of Norfolk, who contributed to other charities as well. Benjamin Tallmadge of Litchfield in 1814 presented the Missionary Society of Connecticut with $800 and a strip of land in Ohio. His gift would have been larger, he wrote, but he was also helping the Bible society.[21] Reference has already been made to the bequest of Dr. Solomon Everest of Canton, who divided somewhat over $16,000 among the A.B.C.F.M., the Missionary Society of Connecticut, and the General Association. Less known but quite generous was Mrs. Harriet Lewis of New London, who bequeathed $8,500 to the First Ecclesiastical Society of New London, a Cent Society of the town, the Asylum

19. *Ibid.*, VI, 447–448.
20. Abel McEwen, *A Sermon, preached at the Funeral of Gen. Jedediah Huntington* (1818), p. 15.
21. Tallmadge to A. Flint, Oct. 8, 1814, Congregational House.

for the Deaf and Dumb, the Domestic Missionary Society, the Yale College Education Society, and the Missionary Society of Connecticut.[22] There were others who would have to be included in any complete list.[23]

A problem which attracted some attention was concerned with the publication of donations with the names of the donors in magazines and newspapers. In some quarters it was felt that such action was unscriptural, and that these acts should be performed in secret and not before men. On the other hand arguments were advanced in favor of publication. As a scriptural defense it was pointed out that Jesus Christ himself had enjoined Christians to glorify God in public. Furthermore, certain definite gains accrued from the publicity. Those destitute of religion might see in such liberality the effects of Christianity on people and be moved thereby; and others might be incited to do good works. It was essential, moreover, that individuals and societies should know that their contributions had been received. And by publication interesting facts were presented to the many readers of religious news. The arguments of the latter group were overwhelming; and since Scripture could be met with Scripture, the practice of publication continued.[24]

Not only did this Awakening have to do with the beginning of organized charity but it also constituted an important chapter in the history of the rôle of women in society. Since many references to the organization of societies by women have been made, the extent of their influence must be clear. It was indeed an age of "female societies," for in practically every community the ladies raised small sums of money, sewed, and collected clothing. They met regularly, frequently listening to a sermon by their minister, whose their contributions may have made a

22. *Connecticut Courant*, Feb. 16, 1819.
23. Note the men mentioned in Trumbull, ed., *Memorial History of Hartford County*, I, 657–667.
24. *Christian Spectator*, I (1819), 181–183, 569–575; *Relig. Intel.*, X, 266–269.

life member of the A.B.C.F.M. or of the national or state Bible society. They operated schools for poor children, furnished the Retreat for the Insane, and manifested a special interest in the Cornwall School by their gifts of money and wearing apparel. Every one of the new ventures was a source of interest to the ladies.

These endeavors on the part of the fair sex represented an innovation. Up to this time they had not only obeyed the strictures of Paul in regard to silence in the churches, but had taken no part in the activities of these institutions. The religious awakening during the early years of the nineteenth century, however, brought a change. With a new spirit in Christianity and with many new enterprises to be conducted, the women, who probably always constituted a majority of the church members, began to organize and to lend their individual and collective efforts to the tasks at hand.

There were many comments on this development and general approval. As early as 1811 the General Assembly of the Presbyterian Church noted in its minutes the work of pious women and expressed the hope that the spirit which was animating them would spread.[25] This hope was fulfilled, and in surveying the state of religion in the world in 1816 the editor of the *Religious Intelligencer* remarked, "But it is a peculiar honour to our age, that, as a sex, women have discovered, and extensively entered, the path, in which their peculiar glory is to be found. No preceding period has seen them in such numbers, with such unanimity, with such zeal, engaged in the great work of doing good."[26] While ministers praised the ladies' accomplishments and urged them to extend their efforts, female societies called on members of their sex to persevere in activities which, they felt, were in no wise contrary to feminine decorum. Such organizations as the American Bible Society, the Connecticut Bible Society, and the American

25. *Conn. Evang. Mag. and Relig. Intel.*, IV, 268–269.
26. *Relig. Intel.*, I, 210.

Education Society acknowledged gratefully the assistance rendered by women. Most people seemed to agree with the sentiments expressed in the *Religious Intelligencer* in 1822, "One of the most delightful features of the benevolent efforts of the present age, is the active cooperation of the female sex."[27]

The importance of all this is obvious. Emergence upon the public scene was gracefully made through these religious activities in which women might properly engage. Herein, they learned how to organize, how to play rôles other than the traditionally silent and domestic ones; perhaps through their accomplishments they gained a new sense of their importance in the general scheme of things. From these beginnings there was slow but steady progress in succeeding decades.

It will not be inappropriate at this point to call attention to a fact made clear by this study, namely that the humanitarians and reformers of the 1830–1860 generation were to a larger extent than has previously been realized building on foundations laid down from 1800 to 1830. This is illustrated by the preceding paragraphs on women's activities, as well as by the temperance movement, the care of such physically handicapped as the deaf and dumb, and the societies to care for the poor. There was much of the humanitarian and reform spirit, too, in the missionary enterprise, the distribution of Bibles and tracts, and the establishment of education societies and Sunday schools. Influenced by the new religious spirit, these early reformers and humanitarians were motivated by a desire to do their Christian duty.

A striking feature of Connecticut's religious history is also to be explained, in part at least, in terms of the Awakening. This is the fact that Unitarianism made little headway; indeed, as has been indicated, the Unitarians captured only one Congregational church, that in Brooklyn, of which the Reverend Samuel J. May became pastor

27. *Ibid.*, VII, 285.

in 1822. The situation was very different from that in eastern Massachusetts where Unitarianism flourished during the early portion of the nineteenth century. The absence of a large, active center of culture like Boston helped to account for this. In addition, the closely knit church organization which had existed in the more southern of these two New England states since the adoption of the Saybrook Platform in 1708 provided an admirable defense against the unorthodox invader. But it should also be noted that the rise of Unitarianism coincided with the Second Great Awakening. In Connecticut the aroused clergy were struggling against infidelity, revivals were renewing the strength of revealed religion, and people were so busy with the restoration of the old faith that they had no time for the new. True, Massachusetts also had an awakening and still Unitarianism gained ground.[28] In that state, however, in addition to the basic differences already mentioned, Harvard had no one to compare with Timothy Dwight of Yale; in fact, the Massachusetts college was lost to Congregationalism. The clergy, moreover, were less aggressive than their Connecticut brethren, and the revivals less widespread. Furthermore, Massachusetts Congregationalism was less liberalized and reasonable, tending to follow the theology of Nathaniel Emmons, while to the south the more liberal ideas of Dwight and his colleagues prevailed.[29] Connecticut Congregationalism as it developed after 1795 was the more formidable foe of Unitarianism.

Connecticut's literary history was also affected by the religious developments. At this time appeared the first journals devoted to religious matters, among the earliest of which was the *Connecticut Evangelical Magazine* which began its monthly appearances in 1800 and continued through 1815, with a break of six months in 1807 when

28. In studying the Second Great Awakening in Massachusetts much attention would be given to the rise of Unitarianism.

29. Walker, *History of the Congregational Churches in the United States,* pp. 300–303.

there was a reorganization and a slight change in name.[30] During its first five years the average monthly circulation totalled 3,730 copies, while in fifteen years the sum earned by the magazine for the Missionary Society of Connecticut amounted to $11,520.07.[31] Shortly after this journal suspended publication, the *Religious Intelligencer* was established. This innovation, a weekly newspaper containing nothing of secular affairs, was widely read, its subscribers numbering about 4,700 in 1823.[32] Other publications which appeared in the state during the first three decades of the nineteenth century included the *Quarterly Christian Spectator* (1819), founded to combat Unitarianism; the *Connecticut Observer* (1825), established to further the Congregational cause; and three dissenting periodicals. As early as 1804 the Episcopalian *Churchman's Magazine* appeared, the only publication of its kind in the United States. Moved from New Haven to New York City in 1808 it met with misfortunes and was discontinued in 1815. Six years later it was revived under the auspices of Connecticut Episcopalians and was published in Hartford. In 1818 the *Methodist Magazine* was started in New York City, and in 1824 the Baptist *Christian Secretary* in Hartford. In addition, journals of the same type published in other parts of the country were read in Connecticut, the *Panoplist* being the most popular.

The literature of the Awakening also included sermons whose number is legion, tracts, the annual reports of the multitudinous societies, and pamphlets. It was a veritable "age of pamphlets." There was also the poetry of Mrs. Lydia Huntley Sigourney, the "sweet singer of Hartford," who may be considered the poetess of the Awaken-

30. This magazine was published by ministers closely connected with the Missionary Society of Connecticut, to which organization the profits were given. After a temporary suspension in 1807 the publication was known as the *Connecticut Evangelical Magazine and Religious Intelligencer.*
31. Hawes, *Historical Sketches of the First Church in Hartford,* p. 20 note.
32. *Relig. Intel.,* VII, 689.

ing. She was interested in its various phases, and as was
always the case with Mrs. Sigourney, interest was translated into poetry. A few titles from one of her volumes[33]
reveal the influence of the Awakening, for she wrote on
such subjects as, "Death of Rev. Dr. Cornelius," "Funeral
of Dr. Mason F. Cogswell," "Missions to Africa," "Religious Tracts," "Bible-Class in the Connecticut State
Prison," "The Jews," "The Departure of Miss Hannah
More," "Sale of Ardent Spirits by Christians." Mrs. Sigourney was not a great poet; she was important, however,
as a spokesman of her age.

A brief recapitulation of other effects of the Awakening
which have been mentioned in previous chapters is not out
of order. Its influence was important on the frontier to
which missionaries carried the culture of the older settlements, and the foreign missionary activities gave a mighty
impetus to the Christianization of the world. In the United
States religion must be given its due in explaining the development of a national spirit. People in various parts of
the country were concerned about the same projects and
had common interests in religious developments. The movement which led to the formation of national societies was a
cause as well as a result of the greater unity which appeared
among the people of the various states. Furthermore, the
events of the period encouraged a certain amount of interdenominational coöperation in both the state and the nation. The Plan of Union brought the Presbyterians and
Congregationalists close together in missionary activities,
while the Bible and tract societies in particular were limited to no one denomination. Presbyterian, Congregational, Reformed, and Associated Reformed churches
joined in 1826 to form the American Home Missionary
Society. In his *History of the Second Church of Christ in
Hartford*, E. P. Parker commented on the results of the
Awakening. "The consciousness of wider, yea, of world
relations," he wrote, "was quickened in the people. They

33. *Zinzendorff and Other Poems.*

began to realize the fact of their nationality, and the
boundless extent and resources of their country. With the
feeling of independence came the consciousness of power
and responsibility."[34]

During Connecticut's Second Great Awakening great
changes were wrought and new habits formed. A deep and
lasting impress was made on the lives of the people of the
state. Much new wine was poured into many new bottles.

34. Parker, *History of the Second Church in Hartford*, p. 189.

BIBLIOGRAPHICAL NOTE

MANUSCRIPT SOURCES

THE manuscript material used in preparing this study is fairly voluminous. In the Connecticut Congregational House, 37 Garden Street, Hartford, are the complete records of the Missionary Society of Connecticut, including the records of the Board of Trustees and the Committee on Missions, letterbooks which contain copies of the letters sent out by Abel Flint, Samuel Whittelsey, and Horace Hooker, the three secretaries of the society, 1798–1830, hundreds of letters and reports from missionaries, and the remainder of the society's correspondence. Here, too, are the less complete records of the Domestic Missionary Society of Connecticut, and the records of the Connecticut branch of the American Education Society which was formed in 1826. The Congregational House contains also a manuscript autobiography by the Reverend Samuel Nott of Franklin, and the records of several associations and consociations, those of the Fairfield County East and West Associations and Consociations, the Litchfield County North and South Associations and Consociations, the Hartford County North Association and Consociation, the Hartford County South Association, the Tolland County Association and Consociation, the Windham County Association, and the Eastern Association of Windham County. Of value, as well, is the miscellaneous data regarding the Congregational churches of Connecticut, collected by the Reverend William H. Moore, secretary of the Missionary Society of Connecticut, 1864–1899.

The Yale University Library has the David Daggett papers, the Jeremiah Day papers, the Alexander M. Fisher papers, the Jedidiah Morse papers, some of the Mason F. Cogswell papers, a few Timothy Dwight letters, and some miscellaneous items. Here have been deposited the records of the New Haven East and West Associations and Consociations. The Benjamin Silliman diary, the Matthew Dutton diary, Dutton's essay entitled "Reflections on the Life & Character of Doct. Dwight," and the Journal of the Moral Society of Yale College have all been useful. Yale also has the "Diary, 1821–1858," of the Reverend Harry Croswell, rector of Christ Church, New Haven.

The Thomas Robbins papers in the Connecticut Historical Society have been particularly valuable in connection with several phases of the Awakening. The remainder of the Mason F. Cogswell papers, the Lydia Huntley Sigourney papers, and a few John Treadwell items, all in the Connecticut Historical Society, have also been used.

In the Connecticut State Library are the brief records of the New Haven County Bible Society, as well as "Connecticut Archives, Ecclesiastical Affairs, Second Series, 1666–1820," vol. I and Index, photostatic copies.

PUBLISHED SOURCES

Records of Religious Bodies

Indispensable for an understanding of religious developments in Connecticut are the records of the General Association, published as follows: *The Records of the General Association of Connecticut, 1738–1799* (Hartford, 1888); *Acts and Proceedings of the General Association of Connecticut, 1800* (Hartford, 1900); *Extracts from the Minutes of the General Association of Connecticut, 1801–1810* (Hartford, 1801–1810); *Proceedings of the General Association of Connecticut, 1811–1830* (Hartford, 1811–1830). Some use has been made of the following pamphlets in the Connecticut Baptist Convention, 455 Main Street, Hartford: *Proceedings of the Connecticut Baptist Convention, 1830, 1832, 1833, 1836, 1837; Minutes of the New London Baptist Association, 1832, 1837;* and *Minutes of the Stonington Baptist Association, 1798, 1805, 1815.*

Pamphlets

Of inestimable value in telling the story of Connecticut's Second Great Awakening have been hundreds of pamphlets. The Yale University Library has the enormous collection known as the College Pamphlets, the small but very useful Brace Variety, and other miscellaneous pamphlets. Thomas Robbins' collection is in the Connecticut Historical Society, while the Williams College Library has a few volumes which have been designated the Williams Pamphlets. The Congregational House is also rich in this form of literature which was so abundant during the early years of the nineteenth century, and the Connecticut Baptist Convention has pamphlets relating to Baptists.

It would be impossible to list all the pamphlets; a few items will illustrate their value. *A Summary of Christian Doctrine and*

Practice: Designed Especially, for the Use of People in the New Settlements, 1804 (Conn. Hist. Soc.), published under the auspices of the Missionary Society of Connecticut, outlines the then current Congregational theology. *An Address of the General Association of Connecticut to the District Associations on the subject of a Missionary Society,* 1797 (Congregational House), served as a prelude to the organization of the Missionary Society of Connecticut. Revivals are described in Edward D. Griffin, *Letter to William B. Sprague,* 1832 (Williams Pamphlets, v. 36), and Noah Porter, *Memorial of a Revival,* 1821 (Brace Variety, v. 26). John F. Schermerhorn and Samuel J. Mills, *A Correct View of that Part of the United States which lies West of the Allegany [sic] Mountains, with regard to Religion and Morals,* 1814 (Brace Variety, v. 10), is an important publication. The stories of the numerous societies and institutions are told in part in the following pamphlets:

Narratives of Missions . . . of the Missionary Society of Connecticut, 1799–1831 (Brace Variety, v. 15, 23, 24).

Annual Reports of the American Board of Commissioners for Foreign Missions, 1810–1831 (Brace Variety, v. 9, 11, 13, 24, 25; College Pamphlets, v. 1900, 2033; and Yale University Library, general stacks).

Annual Reports of the Directors of the Domestic Missionary Society of Connecticut, 1817–1830 (Congregational House and Brace Variety, v. 11, 12).

Address, Constitution, and Subscription Proposal, of the Connecticut Bible Society, 1809 (Brace Variety, v. 2).

Annual Reports of the Directing Committee of the Connecticut Bible Society, 1810–1831 (Brace Variety, v. 4, 11, 12, 20, 23).

Annual Reports of the Board of Managers of the American Bible Society, 1817–1831 (Yale University Library).

An Account of the Receipts and Disbursements of the Education Society of Connecticut and of the Female Education Society of New Haven, 1816 (College Pamphlets, v. 1900).

An Address of the Charitable Society for the Education of Indigent Pious, Young Men, for the Ministry of the Gospel, [1814] (Williams Pamphlets, v. 26).

Annual Reports of the American Education Society, 1817–1830 (Yale University Library).

Third Annual Report of the Connecticut Sunday School Union, 1827 (Conn. Hist. Soc. Pamphlets, v. 292).

Second Annual Report of the Executive Committee of the

American Society for the Promotion of Temperance, 1829 (Brace Variety, v. 24).

First Annual Report of the Executive Committee of the Connecticut Temperance Society, 1830 (Brace Variety, v. 23).

The Address of the General Union for Promoting the Observance of the Christian Sabbath, 1828 (Brace Variety, v. 17).

Second Report of the General Union for Promoting the Observance of the Christian Sabbath, 1830 (Brace Variety, v. 23).

"Constitution of the Hartford Female Beneficent Society," printed with Nathan Strong, *A Discourse delivered by the desire of the Hartford Beneficent Society,* 1809 (Brace Variety, v. 5).

Annual Reports of the Directors of the American Asylum, 1817–1831 (Connecticut State Library).

"Report of the Committee on the Progress of the Retreat," *Annual Meeting of the Society for the Relief of the Insane,* 1823 (Brace Variety, v. 20).

Thomas Robbins, *An Address delivered at the Dedication of the Retreat for the Insane,* 1824 (Williams Pamphlets, v. 32).

Report of the Committee of the Society for the Improvement of Prison Discipline, and for the Reformation of Juvenile Offenders, 1818 (College Pamphlets, v. 205).

Report of the Committee appointed by the Legislature of Connecticut, to Inspect the Condition of New-Gate Prison, 1826 (Brace Variety, v. 20).

Reports of the Board of Managers of the Prison Discipline Society, 1829–1830 (Brace Variety, v. 24; College Pamphlets, v. 65).

Report of the Directors and Warden of the Connecticut State Prison, 1829 (Brace Variety, v. 23).

Second Annual Report of the Managers of the Colonization Society of the State of Connecticut, 1829 (Brace Variety, v. 23).

Leonard Bacon, *A Plea for Africa* (New Haven, 1825).

A Circular Letter from the Massachusetts Peace Society, 1816 (Conn. Hist. Soc. Pamphlets, v. 252).

Peace Society of Windham County, Its Institutions, Sentiments, and Purposes, 1827 (Conn. Hist. Soc. Pamphlets, v. 252).

Sermons

A vast array of sermons throws much light on the period under consideration. Collections of sermons by two of the leaders in the Awakening are Lyman Beecher, *Works* (3 vols., Boston, 1852–1853), and Timothy Dwight, *Sermons* (2 vols., New Haven,

1828). In Timothy Dwight, *Theology Explained and Defended, in a Series of Sermons, with a Memoir of the Life of the Author* (2d edition, 4 vols., New Haven, 1823), will be found not only the basic ideas of the Yale president but also an excellent statement of the New Divinity theology which prevailed in Connecticut. It took Dwight four years to preach these sermons to the Yale undergraduates, and when he finished, he began at the beginning and preached them again. Very interesting but not particularly useful for this study are the *Election Sermons, 1783–1830* (Yale University Library), preached each May at the state's annual election.

Among the individual sermons which have been consulted, the following have been the most valuable. Some of those listed are found in several pamphlet collections; the location given is that of the copy used by the present author.

Lyman Beecher, *The Practicability of Suppressing Vice by Means of Societies Instituted for that Purpose,* 1803 (Conn. Hist. Soc. Pamphlets, v. 291).

Lyman Beecher, *The Remedy for Duelling,* 1806 (College Pamphlets, v. 115).

Lyman Beecher, *A Reformation of Morals Practicable and Indispensable,* 1812 (College Pamphlets, v. 147).

Lyman Beecher, *A Sermon delivered . . . on the evening subsequent to the formation of the Connecticut Society for the Promotion of Good Morals,* 1813 (College Pamphlets, v. 147).

Lyman Beecher, *A Sermon delivered at Woolcot* [*sic*] *. . . at the Installation of Rev. J. Keyes,* 1814 (Brace Variety, v. 14). This is the sermon usually known as "Building the Waste Places of Connecticut."

Lyman Beecher, *A Sermon, addressed to the Legislature of Connecticut, at New-Haven, on the day of the Anniversary Election,* 1826 (Brace Variety, v. 17).

Joab Brace, *Address delivered before the Peace Society of Hartford County,* 1829 (Hartford, 1829).

Calvin Chapin, *A Sermon delivered before the Connecticut Society for the Promotion of Good Morals,* 1814 (Conn. Hist. Soc. Pamphlets, v. 291).

James Dana, *On the Completion of the Eighteenth Century,* 1801 (College Pamphlets, v. 59).

Timothy Dwight, *The True Means of Establishing Public Happiness,* 1795 (Conn. Hist. Soc. Pamphlets, v. 31).

Timothy Dwight, *The Nature, and Danger, of Infidel Philoso-*

phy, exhibited in two Discourses, 1797 (Conn. Hist. Soc. Pamphlets, v. 31).

Timothy Dwight, *The Duty of Americans, at the Present Crisis,* 1798 (College Pamphlets, v. 1109).

Timothy Dwight, *A Discourse on Some Events of the Last Century,* 1801 (College Pamphlets, v. 59).

Timothy Dwight, *The Folly, Guilt and Mischiefs of Duelling,* 1804 (College Pamphlets, v. 548).

Timothy Dwight, *The Charitable Blessed,* 1810 (Brace Variety, v. 5).

Timothy Dwight, *A Discourse in Two Parts, delivered on the Public Fast,* July, 1812 (Conn. Hist. Soc. Pamphlets, v. 32).

Timothy Dwight, *A Discourse in Two Parts, delivered on the National Fast,* Aug., 1812 (College Pamphlets, v. 544).

Jonathan Edwards, *Sermon preached at the Ordination of the Rev. Dan Bradley,* 1792 (College Pamphlets, v. 90).

John Ely, *A Sermon delivered at the First [Congregational] Church in Danbury,* 1798 (Conn. Hist. Soc. Pamphlets, v. 200).

Eleazar Fitch, *A Sermon, delivered on the Anniversary of the Female Education Society of New Haven,* 1829 (Brace Variety, v. 19).

Abel Flint, *A Charity Sermon, delivered by desire of the Female Beneficent Society,* 1810 (Brace Variety, v. 5).

Abel Flint, *A Sermon, preached at the Anniversary Election,* 1816 (Brace Variety, v. 14).

Joseph Harvey, *A Sermon preached before the Foreign Mission Society of Litchfield County,* 1815 (College Pamphlets, v. 1121).

Heman Humphrey, *Sermon preached at Lenox, Mass., at a Meeting Called for the Purpose of Forming a County Education Society,* 1818 (College Pamphlets, v. 150).

Heman Humphrey, *The Promised Land, a Sermon delivered at the Ordination of the Rev. Messrs. Hiram Bingham and Asa Thurston,* 1819 (College Pamphlets, v. 1906).

Abel McEwen, *A Sermon, preached at the Funeral of Gen. Jedediah Huntington,* 1818 (Williams Pamphlets, v. 30).

Abel McEwen, *Half-Century Sermon* (New London, 1857).

Nathan Perkins, *Two Discourses on the Grounds of the Christian's Hope,* 1800 (Brace Variety, v. 3).

Ebenezer Porter, *The Fatal Effects of Ardent Spirits,* 1805 (Brace Variety, v. 6).

Ebenezer Porter, *A Sermon delivered in Boston, on the Anni-*

versary of the American Education Society, 1820 (Brace Variety, v. 22).

Noah Porter, *A Sermon delivered at the Meeting of the Connecticut Society for the Promotion of Good Morals,* 1816 (Brace Variety, v. 14).

Nathan Strong, *Century Sermon,* 1801 (Conn. Hist. Soc. Pamphlets, v. 63).

Benjamin Trumbull, *A Century Sermon,* 1801 (Conn. Hist. Soc. Pamphlets, v. 63).

Elijah Waterman, *A Century Sermon,* 1801 (Conn. Hist. Soc. Pamphlets, v. 63).

Religious Periodicals

The contemporary religious periodicals have been veritable gold mines. The *Connecticut Evangelical Magazine* began its monthly appearances in 1800, was suspended for six months in 1807, and resumed publication in 1808 as the *Connecticut Evangelical Magazine and Religious Intelligencer.* Its files are particularly useful for studying the revivals. Shortly after this enterprise was given up in 1815, the *Religious Intelligencer* appeared. The weekly issues of this magazine—those from 1816 to 1831 have been examined—abound in material dealing with all phases of the Awakening. The *Connecticut Observer,* which was started in New Haven in 1825, has been of some value, while the *Panoplist,* launched in Boston in 1805 and later known as the *Panoplist and Missionary Magazine,* contains many interesting items. The Reverend Luther Hart's article, "A View of the Religious Declension in New England, and of its Causes, during the Latter Half of the Eighteenth Century," *Quarterly Christian Spectator,* V (1833), has been useful, as has Chauncey A. Goodrich, "Narrative of Revivals of Religion in Yale College," *American Quarterly Register,* X (1838).

Each of the minority denominations had a magazine. The Episcopalian *Churchman's Magazine,* published in New Haven from 1804 to 1808 and in New York City from 1808 to 1815, was revived after a lapse of six years by Connecticut Episcopalians and put out in Hartford. The Baptist *Christian Secretary* was a Connecticut publication, appearing in Hartford in 1824. From 1818 to 1829 the *Methodist Magazine* was published monthly in New York City; after being suspended for a year it became a quarterly in 1830 and was called the *Methodist Magazine and Quarterly Review.*

Secular Newspapers

Secular newspapers have been of service, especially the files of the following in the Yale University Library: *American Eagle* (Litchfield), *American Mercury* (Hartford), *Connecticut Courant* (Hartford), *Connecticut Journal* (New Haven), *Connecticut Mirror* (Hartford).

Autobiographies, Correspondence, Diaries, and Travels

People interested in any phase of Connecticut history should know *The Diary of Thomas Robbins, 1796–1854* (2 vols., Boston, 1886–1887), edited by Increase Tarbox. Lyman Beecher, *Autobiography, Correspondence, etc.* (2 vols., New York, 1864–1865), has been very useful, but should never be used without an awareness of the fact that much of it was written years after the events described took place. Copious information about Connecticut prior to 1795 is contained in *The Literary Diary of Ezra Stiles* (3 vols., New York, 1901). Of some use, too, have been the following: Samuel G. Goodrich, *Recollections of a Lifetime* (2 vols., New York, 1856); *Memoirs of James Morris of South Farms in Litchfield* (New Haven, 1933); and *The Correspondence and Miscellanies of the Hon. John Cotton Smith* (New York, 1847).

From Timothy Dwight, *Travels; in New-England and New-York* (4 vols., New Haven, 1821–1822), the reader gains much knowledge not only about the areas described but also about the writer. An early missionary trip is described in Nathan Perkins, *A Narrative of a Tour through the State of Vermont from April 27 to June 12, 1789* (Woodstock, Vt., 1920).

The books of foreign travellers have been of little value. Perhaps three should be mentioned: John M. Duncan, *Travels through Part of the United States and Canada in 1818 and 1819* (2 vols., New York, 1823); Adam Hodgson, *Letters from North America, written during a Tour in the United States and Canada* (2 vols., London, 1824); Edward A. Kendall, *Travels through the Northern Parts of the United States in the year 1807 and 1808* (3 vols., New York, 1809).

Laws

The following volumes in the Connecticut State Library contain collections of laws which have been useful:

Acts and Laws of the State of Connecticut, in America, 1784–1795 (Hartford, 1795).

Acts and Laws of the State of Connecticut, in America, Revision of 1796 (Hartford, 1796).

Acts and Laws of the State of Connecticut, in America, 1796–1799 (Hartford, 1798, 1799).

Acts and Laws of the State of Connecticut, in America, Edition of 1805 (Hartford, 1805).

The Public Statute Laws of the State of Connecticut, 1808–1820 (Hartford, [1820?]).

The Public Statute Laws of the State of Connecticut, as Revised and Enacted by the General Assembly, in May, 1821 (Hartford, 1821).

Public Statute Laws of the State of Connecticut, 1822–1835 (Hartford, 1822–1835).

Resolves and Public Laws of the State of Connecticut, 1789–1836, vol. I (Hartford, 1837).

General

The religious leaders of Connecticut during the Second Great Awakening owed much to Jonathan Edwards, whose writings and sermons are found in *The Works of President Edwards* (8 vols., Worcester, 1808–1809), or, in abbreviated form, in *Jonathan Edwards, Representative Selections* (New York, 1935), skillfully edited by Clarence H. Faust and Thomas H. Johnson. These same leaders were roused by two deistical publications, Ethan Allen, *Reason the Only Oracle of Man; or a Compendious System of Natural Religion* (Bennington, 1784), and Thomas Paine, *The Age of Reason* (Paris, 1794). They were also alarmed by Abbé Barruel, *Memoirs, Illustrating the History of Jacobinism* (2d edition, London, 1798), and John Robison, *Proofs of a Conspiracy against all the Religions and Governments of Europe, etc.* (4th edition, New York, 1798).

Valuable information about economic and social conditions in Connecticut is contained in Timothy Dwight, *A Statistical Account of the City of New-Haven*, 1811 (College Pamphlets, v. 93); David D. Field, *A Statistical Account of the County of Middlesex* (Middletown, 1819); James Morris, *A Statistical Account of Several Towns in the County of Litchfield* ([New Haven(?), 1815]); and John C. Pease and John M. Niles, *A Gazetteer of the States of Connecticut and Rhode Island* (Hartford, 1819).

Poetry is another type of published source material. Timothy Dwight wrote *The Triumph of Infidelity: a Poem* ([n.p.], 1788); *The Conquest of Canäan* (Hartford, 1785); and *Greenfield Hill*

(New York, 1794). Lydia Huntley Sigourney was the poetess of the Awakening. Of particular interest are her volumes, *Traits of the Aborigines of America* (Cambridge, Mass., 1822), and *Zinzendorff, and Other Poems* (New York, 1835).

SECONDARY WORKS

Connecticut History

The general histories of Connecticut are quite satisfactory, the most complete being Norris G. Osborn, ed., *History of Connecticut* (5 vols., New York, 1925). For this study the most useful sections are those by Simeon E. Baldwin, John C. Goddard, Mary H. (Mrs. Sydney K.) Mitchell, and Stanley Williams. Old histories are Gideon H. Hollister, *The History of Connecticut, from the First Settlement of the Colony to the Adoption of the Present Constitution* (New Haven, 1855), and Benjamin Trumbull, *A Complete History of Connecticut, Civil and Ecclesiastical . . . from the Emigration of the First Planters from England, in 1630, to 1763* (2 vols., Hartford, 1797, and New Haven, 1818), the latter by a minister who wrote at about the time when the Awakening was beginning. More recent works are George L. Clark, *A History of Connecticut, Its People and Institutions* (New York, 1914), and Odell Shepard, *Connecticut Past and Present* (New York, 1939).

Books on New England which contain useful information about Connecticut are James T. Adams, *New England in the Republic, 1776–1850* (Boston, 1926); Mary L. Gambrell, *Ministerial Training in Eighteenth-Century New England* (New York, 1937); Lois K. Mathews, *The Expansion of New England; the Spread of New England Settlements and Institutions to the Mississippi River, 1620–1865* (Boston, 1909); and William A. Robinson, *Jeffersonian Democracy in New England* (New Haven, 1916). In addition there is data on Connecticut economic life in Paul W. Bidwell, *Rural Economy in New England at the Beginning of the Nineteenth Century* (New Haven, 1916), and the same author's *Population Growth in Southern New England, 1810–1860* (reprinted from *Quarterly Publications of the American Statistical Association*, Dec., 1917). Grace P. Fuller, *An Introduction to the History of Connecticut as a Manufacturing State* (Smith College Studies in History, I, no. 1, Oct., 1915), is a good study.

Three books with which all students of Connecticut history

should be familiar are M. Louise Greene, *The Development of Religious Liberty in Connecticut* (Boston, 1905); Jarvis M. Morse, *A Neglected Period of Connecticut's History, 1818–1850* (New Haven, 1933); and Richard J. Purcell, *Connecticut in Transition, 1775–1818* (Washington, 1918). They contain much information about Connecticut and deal with certain aspects of the period considered in this volume. The present writer, however, has been forced to disagree with the conclusions of these three authors at several points.

Education in general is considered in Bernard C. Steiner, *The History of Education in Connecticut* (Washington, 1893), and religious education in particular in George Stewart, *A History of Religious Education in Connecticut to the Middle of the Nineteenth Century* (New Haven, 1924). Henry Barnard, "History of the Legislation of Connecticut respecting Common Schools, down to 1838," *Annual Report of the Superintendent of Common Schools in Connecticut, 1853* (Hartford, 1853), is particularly good on the school legislation of the 1790's. For material on Yale, see two publications by Franklin B. Dexter, *Sketch of Yale University* (New York, 1887), and *Student Life at Yale College under the First President Dwight (1795–1817)* (Worcester, Mass., 1918), as well as Henry B. Wright, James B. Reynolds, and Samuel H. Fisher, editors, *Two Centuries of Christian Activity at Yale* (New York, 1901), and I. Woodbridge Riley, "The Rise of Deism in Yale College," *The American Journal of Theology*, IX (1905).

John W. Barber, *Connecticut Historical Collections* (New Haven, 1836), is well known but has not been of much use. Other miscellaneous items on Connecticut include Edward W. Capen, *The Historical Development of the Poor Law of Connecticut* (New York, 1905); *Litchfield County Centennial Celebration* (Hartford, 1851); *Proceedings of the North and South Consociations of Litchfield County, 1852* (Hartford, 1852); and *Centennial Papers, published by order of the General Conference of the Congregational Churches of Connecticut* (Hartford, 1877).

When Connecticut was celebrating its tercentenary in 1933, a series of pamphlets was published in New Haven under the direction of a Committee on Historical Publications. Attention is called to the following which contain material not easily secured elsewhere: Clive Day, *The Rise of Manufacturing in Connecticut, 1820–1850* (1935); Samuel H. Fisher, *The Litchfield Law School, 1775–1833* (1933); Mrs. Mary H. Mitchell, *The Great*

Awakening and Other Revivals in the Religious Life of Connecticut (1934); and Albert L. Olson, *Agricultural Economy and the Population in Eighteenth Century Connecticut* (1935).

Local Histories

As is frequently the case, county and town histories are numerous but many do not fit local happenings into the general picture. Several, however, are quite satisfactory, including Frances M. Caulkins' two books, *History of Norwich . . . 1660 to 1845* (Norwich, 1845), and *History of New London, Connecticut. From the First Survey of the Coast in 1612, to 1852* (New London, 1852); Ellen D. Larned, *History of Windham County, Connecticut* (2 vols., Worcester, Mass., 1874, 1880); Mrs. Mary H. Mitchell, *History of New Haven County, Connecticut*, vol. I (Chicago, 1930); Edward C. Starr, *A History of Cornwall* (New Haven, 1926); and James H. Trumbull, ed., *The Memorial History of Hartford County, Connecticut, 1633–1884* (2 vols., Boston, 1886). Among the others used are Edward E. Atwater, ed., *History of New Haven to the Present Time* (New York, 1887); William C. Fowler, *History of Durham* (Hartford, 1866); Samuel Orcutt, *History of Torrington* (Albany, 1878); *Torringford: in connection with the Centennial of the Settlement of the First Pastor, Rev. Samuel J. Mills* (Hartford, 1870); and Alain C. White, *The History of the Town of Litchfield, Connecticut, 1720–1920* (Litchfield, 1920).

Church Histories

Much valuable information about Connecticut's Congregational churches and about religious developments in the state is contained in the very useful *Contributions to the Ecclesiastical History of Connecticut* (New Haven, 1861).

In 1876 each of these churches was asked to prepare its history. Many of these were printed in pamphlet form and are in the Congregational House and the Yale University Library. One, which contains an interesting sketch of its Sunday school, is E. E. Lewis, *Historical Sketch of the First Congregational Church in Haddam* (Middletown, 1879).

Connecticut Congregationalism has been fortunate in the historians of its churches. Among the best are Leonard Bacon, *Thirteen Historical Discourses, on the Completion of Two Hundred Years, from the Beginning of the First Church in New Haven* (New Haven, 1839), and *Four Commemorative Discourses* (New

Haven, 1866) ; Alvan Bond, *A Historical Discourse, delivered at the Hundredth Anniversary of the Second Congregational Church, Norwich* (Norwich, 1860) ; Samuel W. S. Dutton, *The History of the North Church in New Haven, 1742–1842* (New Haven, 1842) ; Harry K. Eversull, *The Evolution of an Old New England Church* (New Haven, 1924); George P. Fisher, *A Discourse, Commemorative of the History of the Church of Christ in Yale College, during the First Century of its Existence* (New Haven, 1858); Joel Hawes, *Historical Sketches of the First Church in Hartford* (Hartford, 1836); Edwin P. Parker, *History of the Second Church of Christ in Hartford* (Hartford, 1892) ; George L. Walker, "The Historical Address," *Commemorative Exercises of the First Church of Christ in Hartford . . . 1883* (Hartford, 1883), and *History of the First Church in Hartford, 1633–1883* (Hartford, 1884).

Among those published in the last decade are Wilbur S. Deming, *The Church on the Green. The First·Two Centuries of the First Congregational Church at Washington, Connecticut, 1741–1941* (Hartford, 1941) ; Oscar E. Maurer, *A Puritan Church and Its Relation to Community, State, and Nation* (New Haven, 1938); and Rockwell H. Potter, *Hartford's First Church* (Hartford, 1932).

Minority Churches

Both the Episcopalians and the Baptists in Connecticut have been the subjects of special studies. Eben E. Beardsley, *The History of the Episcopal Church in Connecticut* (2 vols., New York, 1866–1868), is very complete, but Philip S. Evans, *History of the Connecticut Baptist State Convention, 1823–1907* (Hartford, 1909), contains no material on developments prior to 1823 and is sketchy on the 1823–1830 period.

Additional material on the Connecticut Baptists is found in Henry S. Burrage, *A History of the Baptists in New England* (Philadelphia, 1894), and "History of the 1st Baptist Church, Waterford," *Historical Sketch of the New London Baptist Association, 1817–1850* (Boston, 1851). "A Brief History of the Ashford Baptist Association," *Minutes of the Ashford Baptist Association, 1844,* and "History of the Baptist Church at Willimantic," *Minutes of Ashford Baptist Association, 1855,* are useful pamphlets in the Connecticut State Library, which has the records of this association. Among the pamphlets in the Connecticut Baptist Convention the following should be noted: Asa C. Bronson, "Historical Discourse preached at the Centennial Anniversary of the New Haven Baptist Association, Oct., 1875," *Fifty-Second Annual Meeting of the Connecticut Baptist Convention, 1875;* "Historical Sketch of the Missionary Work of the Connecticut Baptist Convention," *Forty-Third Annual Meeting of the Connecticut Baptist Convention, 1866;* "The Seventy-fifth Meeting of the Connecticut Baptist Education Society," *Seventy-First Annual Meeting of the Connecticut Baptist Convention, 1894;* "Historical Sketch of the Connecticut Baptist Education Society," *Ninety-Sixth Annual Session of the Connecticut Baptist Convention, 1919;* "A Brief History of the Hartford Baptist Association," *Minutes of the Hartford Baptist Association, 1889;* Albert G. Palmer, *A Discourse delivered at the One Hundredth Anniversary of the Organization of the First Baptist Church in North Stonington, 1843;* William H. Potter, "Early Missionary Movements in Connecticut" and "Rise and Early Progress of the Connecticut Baptist Convention," *Fiftieth Annual Meeting of the Connecticut Baptist Convention, 1873;* and Robert Turnbull, *Memorials of the First Baptist Church, Hartford, 1857.*

There is less material on the Connecticut Methodists than on the Episcopalians and Baptists, but the following have been useful: Nathan Bangs, *A History of the Methodist Episcopal Church* (4 vols., New York, 1841–1845); James M. Buckley, *A History of Methodism in the United States* (2 vols., New York, 1898); Charles C. Goss, *Statistical History of the First Century of American Methodism* (New York, 1866); James Mudge, *History of the New England Conference of the Methodist Episcopal Church, 1796–1910* (Boston, 1910); and William W. Sweet, *Methodism in American History* (New York, 1933). George C. Baker, *An Introduction to the History of Early New England Methodism, 1789–1839* (Durham, N. C., 1941), appeared when the present writer's manuscript was practically completed.

Religious, Social, and Philanthropic Activities

Various aspects of the missionary movement are treated in a very thorough, recently published study, Colin B. Goodykoontz, *Home Missions on the American Frontier, with particular reference to the American Home Missionary Society* (Caldwell, Idaho, 1939); in a factual account, Oliver W. Elsbree, *The Rise of the Missionary Spirit in America, 1790–1815* (Williamsport, Pa., 1928); and in the standard works, Joseph B. Clark, *Leavening the Nation; the Story of American Home Missions* (New York,

1903), and William E. Strong, *The Story of the American Board, an Account of the First Hundred Years of the American Board of Commissioners for Foreign Missions* (Boston, 1910). Edwin P. Parker, *Historical Discourse in Commemoration of the One Hundredth Anniversary of the Missionary Society of Connecticut* (Hartford, 1898), and *Report of the Directors of the Missionary Society of Connecticut for the Year 1880* (Hartford, 1881), have been very useful. In addition, there is the valuable *Semi-Centennial of the Litchfield County Foreign Mission Society, 1861* (Hartford, 1861).

Ralph H. Gabriel, *Elias Boudinot, Cherokee, & His America* (Norman, Okla., 1941), contains a fine account of the Cornwall School. Merle E. Curti, *The American Peace Crusade, 1815–1860* (Durham, N. C., 1929), and John A. Krout, *The Origins of Prohibition* (New York, 1925), are excellent studies. There are, too, Marianna C. Brown, *Sunday-School Movements in America* (New York, 1901); Henry O. Dwight, *The Centennial History of the American Bible Society* (New York, 1916); and Early L. Fox, *The American Colonization Society, 1817–1840* (Baltimore, 1919).

Biographies

Biographical material is bulky. Sketches of many of the men who were in some way connected with Connecticut's Second Great Awakening appear in the *Dictionary of American Biography* (20 vols., New York, 1928–1936), as well as in Franklin B. Dexter, *Biographical Sketches of the Graduates of Yale College with Annals of the College History* (6 vols., New York, 1885–1912); William B. Sprague, *Annals of the American Pulpit*, vols. I and II (New York, 1857); and the much less extensive Arthur Goodenough, *The Clergy of Litchfield County* (Litchfield, 1909). Jonathan Edwards, Samuel Hopkins, and Leonard Bacon are well treated in Williston Walker, *Ten New England Leaders* (New York, 1901).

There are several biographies of Jonathan Edwards. Alexander V. G. Allen, *Jonathan Edwards* (Boston, 1891), is still good; Ola E. Winslow, *Jonathan Edwards, 1703–1758* (New York, 1940), better on Edwards the man than on Edwards the thinker, was awarded a Pulitzer prize. Clarence H. Faust's introduction to *Jonathan Edwards, Representative Selections* (New York, 1935), which he and Thomas H. Johnson edited, is excellent.

BIBLIOGRAPHICAL NOTE 255

Arthur C. McGiffert, *Jonathan Edwards* (New York, 1932), should be read.

The first full-length biography of Timothy Dwight is by Charles E. Cunningham. Scheduled for publication in the spring of 1942, it has not been used in the preparation of the present work. Previously material on Dwight has been secured from such places as Daniel D. Addison, *The Clergy in American Life and Letters* (New York, 1900); "Memoir of the Life of the Author," in Timothy Dwight, *Theology Explained and Defended, in a Series of Sermons,* vol. I (2d edition, New Haven, 1823); Mark A. de Wolfe Howe, *Classic Shades; Five Leaders of Learning and Their Colleges* (Boston, 1928); Benjamin Silliman, *A Sketch of the Life and Character of President Dwight* (New Haven, 1817); William B. Sprague, "Timothy Dwight," in Jared Sparks, ed., *American Biographies,* Second Series, IV (Boston, 1845); Gardiner Spring, *An Oration . . . in Commemoration . . . of Timothy Dwight* (New York, 1817); and Moses C. Tyler, *Three Men of Letters* (New York, 1895).

Lyman B. Stowe, *Saints, Sinners and Beechers* (New York, 1934), is well done but contains little on Lyman Beecher that is not in the latter's *Autobiography.* Other biographies include Rufus Anderson, *Memoir of Catharine Brown, a Christian Indian of the Cherokee Nation* (Boston, 1825); Leonard Bacon, *Sketch of Rev. David Bacon* (Boston, 1876); Moncure D. Conway, *Thomas Paine* (2 vols., New York, 1892); Edwin W. Dwight, *Memoir of Henry Obookiah* (New Haven, 1818); Bela B. Edwards, *Memoir of the Rev. Elias Cornelius* (Boston, 1833); George P. Fisher, *Life of Benjamin Silliman* (2 vols., New York, 1866); Edward M. Gallaudet, *Life of Thomas Hopkins Gallaudet, Founder of Deaf-Mute Instruction in America* (New York, 1888); Gordon S. Haight, *Mrs. Sigourney, The Sweet Singer of Hartford* (New Haven, 1930); "Memoir of the Reverend Asahel Hooker," *The Adviser; or Vermont Evangelical Magazine,* March–April, 1815 (Brace Variety, v. 13); Edward A. Lawrence, *The Life of Joel Hawes* (Hartford, 1871); Lyman Matthews, *Memoir of the Life and Character of Ebenezer Porter* (Boston, 1837); James K. Morse, *Jedidiah Morse, A Champion of New England Orthodoxy* (New York, 1939); Theodore T. Munger, *Horace Bushnell, Preacher and Theologian* (Boston, 1899); Denison Olmsted, *Memoir of John Treadwell* (Boston, 1843); Edwin P. Parker, *Appreciation of Calvin Chapin* (Providence, 1908); Thomas C. Richards, *Samuel J. Mills, Missionary Pathfinder, Pioneer and Promoter* (Boston, 1906); Gardiner Spring, *Memoirs of the Rev. Samuel J. Mills* (New York, 1820); and Bennet Tyler, *Memoir of the Life and Character of Rev. Asahel Nettleton* (Hartford, 1844).

General

Three books on the Great Awakening appear first in this group, the general work, Joseph Tracy, *The Great Awakening* (Boston, 1842), and the regional studies, Wesley M. Gewehr, *The Great Awakening in Virginia, 1740–1790* (Durham, N. C., 1930), and Charles H. Maxson, *The Great Awakening in the Middle Colonies* (Chicago, 1920).

Frank G. Beardsley, *A History of American Revivals* (3d edition, New York, 1912), and Charles L. Thompson, *Times of Refreshing. A History of American Revivals from 1740 to 1877* (Chicago, 1877), are general works on revivals. Heman Humphrey, *Revival Sketches and Manual* (New York, 1859); William B. Sprague, *Lectures on Revivals of Religion* (Albany, 1832); and Bennet Tyler, *New England Revivals, etc.* (Boston, 1842), are books dealing with the revivals of the Second Great Awakening, written largely from contemporary accounts by men who had first-hand experience with the Awakening. Catherine C. Cleveland, *The Great Revival in the West, 1797–1805* (Chicago, 1916), is a good account of the religious stir on the frontier.

The book just mentioned treats an aspect of the Second Great Awakening in the West. Books dealing to some extent with this Awakening in other parts of the country include David M. Ludlum, *Social Ferment in Vermont, 1791–1850* (New York, 1939), and Neils H. Sonne, *Liberal Kentucky, 1780–1828* (New York, 1939). Gustav A. Koch, *Republican Religion; the American Revolution and the Cult of Reason* (New York, 1933), not only gives a good account of the rise of deism in America, but also has a final chapter entitled "The Triumph of Fidelity."

Capable, indeed, are the men who have written on American religion in general and on Congregationalism in particular. The best general works are Leonard W. Bacon, *A History of American Christianity* (New York, 1897); Daniel Dorchester, *Christianity in the United States* (revised edition, New York, 1895); William W. Sweet, *The Story of Religions in America* (New York, 1930); and Luther Weigle, *American Idealism* (New Haven, 1928). Henry M. Dexter, *The Congregationalism of the*

Last Three Hundred Years, As Seen in its Literature (New York, 1880), and Williston Walker, *A History of the Congregational Churches in the United States* (New York, 1894), are standard as is Williston Walker, *The Creeds and Platforms of Congregationalism* (New York, 1893). For studies of religion, especially Congregationalism, in New England, the following are all valuable: George N. Boardman, *A History of New England Theology* (New York, 1899); Frank H. Foster, *A Genetic History of the New England Theology* (Chicago, 1907); Joseph Haroutunian, *Piety versus Moralism, The Passing of the New England Theology* (New York, 1932); and George L. Walker, *Some Aspects of the Religious Life of New England* (New York, 1897). William W. Sweet, *Religion on the American Frontier,* vol. III, *The Congregationalists. A Collection of Source Materials* (Chicago, 1939), also contains information about religion in New England. Students of American religion should also know Sanford H. Cobb, *The Rise of Religious Liberty in America* (New York, 1902).

American thought is discussed in Vernon L. Parrington, *Main Currents in American Thought* (3 vols., New York, 1927), which never does justice to conservatives; I. Woodbridge Riley, *American Thought, from Puritanism to Pragmatism* (New York, 1915); and Herbert W. Schneider, *The Puritan Mind* (New York, 1930). Perry Miller, "Jonathan Edwards to Emerson," *New England Quarterly,* XIII (Dec., 1940), is a brilliant article.

That developments in Connecticut and elsewhere in the United States during the Second Great Awakening were not unconnected with happenings in Europe is made clear in such books as Mary-Margaret H. Barr, *Voltaire in America, 1744–1800* (Baltimore, 1941); Bernard Faÿ, *The Revolutionary Spirit in France and America* (New York, 1927); Charles D. Hazen, *Contemporary American Opinion of the French Revolution* (Baltimore, 1897); Howard M. Jones, *America and French Culture, 1750–1848* (Chapel Hill, 1927); John H. Overton, *The Evangelical Revival in the Eighteenth Century* (London, 1891); Vernon Stauffer, *New England and the Bavarian Illuminati* (New York, 1918); and Leslie Stephen, *History of English Thought in the Eighteenth Century* (2 vols., New York, 1876).

Interesting developments in Massachusetts which paralleled to some extent those in Connecticut are discussed in Jacob C. Meyer, *Church and State in Massachusetts, from 1740 to 1833* (Cleveland, 1930), and Anson E. Morse, *The Federalist Party in Mas-*

sachusetts to the Year 1800 (Princeton, 1909). General information is contained in Emerson Davis, *The Half Century; or A History of the Changes that have Taken Place, and Events that have Transpired, chiefly in the United States, between 1800 and 1850* (Boston, 1851).

A quaint item is J. G. Davenport, *The Ordination Ball* (Waterbury, 1912). A copy of this poem is in the Congregational House. Oliver Wendell Holmes, *The One-Hoss Shay,* should be read.

INDEX

Activity" church, described, 225
Adams, J. T., on Conn. factory legislation, 186
Adams, John, on France, 2
African United Ecclesiastical Society of New Haven, organized, 182
Alexander I, sponsors Bible society, 114–115
Allen, Ethan, attacks on, 13–14
American and Foreign Bible Society, formed by Baptists, 210
American Asylum for the Deaf and Dumb. See Connecticut Asylum
American Baptist Home Missionary Society, formed, 205
American Bible Society, activities of, 113; relations with Conn. Bible Society, 113–114, 115–117; relations with Baptists and Methodists, 209–210
American Board of Commissioners for Foreign Missions, Conn. importance in, 3; purpose of, 72; founded, 95; first missionaries dispatched, 96; opposition to, 96; activities and finances of, 96–97, 98–99; Conn. interest in, 97–102; missions to Sandwich Islands, 101; establishes Cornwall School, 103
American Colonization Society, activities in Conn., 181–182; Baptist and Methodist interest in, 219–220
American Education Society, relations with Conn. Education Society, 126
American Home Missionary Society, founded, 92–93
American Literary, Scientific, and Military Academy, request for lottery refused, 160; gift to Wesleyan University, 214

American Revolution, effects of, 4, 27
American Society for Meliorating the Condition of the Jews, activities of, 183–184
American Society for Promoting the Civilization and General Improvement of Indian Tribes within the United States, organized, 187
American Society for the Promotion of Temperance, founded, 156
American Sunday School Union, organization of, 132
American Tract Society, work of, 119–120; offers prize, 121; relations with Methodists, 210
Andover Theological Seminary, S. J. Mills, Jr., at, 94–95; attitude of Conn. ministers toward, 123
Arminianism, appearance of, 29; attacks on, 29–31, 34
Asbury, Bishop, on religion in Conn., 191
"Associates of Dr. Bray, The," establishment of, 70
Austin, David, advocates prayer for revivals, 50

Backus, Azel, New Divinity leader, 51; vice-president of Conn. Bible Society, 110
Backus, Charles, teaches candidates for ministry, 123
Backus, Simon, as politician, 57, 59
Bacon, David, mission to Indians, 79–81; in Western Reserve, 81, 82
Bacon, Leonard, on drinking, 150 n; aids Negroes, 183
Badger, Joseph, pioneer missionary, 78; in Western Reserve, 81–82; grant for Indian mission of, 81 n; salary of, 82, 87–88; interest in education, 90

Date

MAR 1 '78

Demco 38-297

Lincoln Christian College